Llewellyn's

# Herbal Almanac

## 2005

© 2004 Llewellyn Worldwide
Editing/Design: Michael Fallon
Interior Art: © Mary Azarian
Cover Design: Lisa Novak
Cover Photos: © Digital Vision, © Brand X,
© Digital Stock, © Photodisc

You can order Llewellyn annuals
and books from *New Worlds*,
Llewellyn's magazine catalog.
To request a free copy of the catalog
call toll-free: 1-877-NEW WRLD,
or visit our website at
http://subscriptions.llewellyn.com.

ISBN 0-7387-0139-4
Llewellyn Worldwide
P.O. Box 64383, Dept. 0-7387-0139-4
St. Paul, MN 55164

# Table of Contents

## Growing and Gathering Herbs

## Culinary Herbs

## Herbs for Health

## Herbs for Beauty

## Herb Crafts

## Herb History, Myth, and Magic

# Introduction to Llewellyn's Herbal Almanac

Welcome to 2005, faithful reader, and a new edition of Llewellyn's *Herbal Almanac*. It's a new year, and time to take a look again at the current research on, and ever-expanding use of, herbs as medicine, as culinary spice, as beautifying cosmetic, and as magical item. This year in particular we tap into some of the world's most ancient knowledge—the garden traditions of medieval monks, for instance, as well as the Japanese art of incense, the herbal healing techniques of India, and the magic and lore of ancient Celtic herbal tradition. And we bring to these pages some of the most innovative and original thinkers and writers on herbs.

This focus on the old ways—on times when men and women around the world knew and understood the power of herbs—is important today. Terrorists, water shortages, hatred, internecine battles, militant religious fervor, war, all seem to be holding sway over the good things in life—beauty, good food, health, love, and friendship. While we don't want to assign blame or cast any other aspersions, this state of affairs perhaps is not surprising considering so many of us—each one of us—is out of touch with the beauty, magic, and health-giving properties inherent in the natural world. Many of us spend too much of our lives rushing about in a technological bubble—striving to make money, being everywhere but here, living life in fast-forward. We forget to focus on the parts of life that can bring us back into balance and harmony.

Still, the news is not all bad. People are still striving to make us all more aware of the magical, beautiful ways that herbs can affect our lives. In the 2005 edition of the *Herbal Almanac*, the various authors pay tribute to the ideals of magic and beauty and balance as they relate to the health-giving and beautifying properties of herbs. This may sound a bit far-fetched, but after all it does not take much imagination to see that a herbal shade garden will bring some much-needed peace to our lives, that making an herbal bouquet for your cousin's wedding will bring joy to all, and that replacing your daily coffee with a healthy herbal substitute will bring health and peace of mind.

Herbs are the perfect complement to the power of the mind, an ancient tool whose time has come back around to help us restore balance in our lives. More and more people are using them, growing and gathering them, and studying them for their beautifying and healing properties. We, the editors and authors of this volume, encourage the treatment of the whole organism—of the person and of the planet—with herbal magic. One person at a time, using ancient wisdom, we can make a new world.

*Note:* The old-fashioned remedies in this book are historical references used for teaching purposes only. The recipes are not for commercial use or profit. The contents are not meant to diagnose, treat, prescribe, or substitute consultation with a licensed health-care professional. Herbs, whether used internally or externally, should be introduced in small amounts to allow the body to adjust and to detect possible allergies. Please consult a standard reference source, or an expert herbalist, to learn more about the possible effects of certain herbs. You must take care not to replace regular medical treatment with the use of herbs. Herbal treatment is intended primarily to complement modern health care. Always seek professional help if you suffer from illness. Also, take care to read all warning labels before taking any herbs or starting on an extended herbal regimen. Always consult an herbal professional before beginning any sort of medical treatment—this is particularly true for pregnant women.

Herbs are powerful things; be sure you are using that power to achieve balance. Llewellyn Worldwide does not participate in, endorse, or have any authority or responsibility concerning private business transactions between its authors and the public.

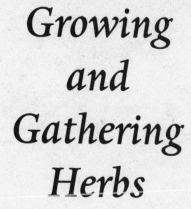

Growing
and
Gathering
Herbs

# Monastic Herb Gardens

by Lynn Smythe

*Spreading herbs and flowerets
  bright,
Glisten'd with the dew of night,
Nor herb nor floweret glisten'd
  there,
But was carved in the cloister-
  arches as fair.*

—Sir Walter Scott,
*The Lay of the Last Minstrel*, Canto II

**M**onastic communities were designed to be largely self-sufficient. The monks grew all the plant material they needed for their daily survival. That is, they grew plants for food, seasoning, medication, dyes, aromatics, pest and insect control, and for strewing. (For details regarding strewing, see my article "Medieval and Renaissance Strewing Herbs" in the 2004 *Herbal Almanac*.)

St. Benedict was the founder of the Benedictine monastic order. He drew

9

up his monastic rule in the sixth century for use by his monastic community in Monte Cassino, Italy. The following passage is from the 66th chapter of the *Regula Sancti Benedicti* (Rule of Saint Benedict).

> *Whenever possible the monastery should be laid out so that everything essential, that is to say water, mills, garden and workshops for the plying of the various crafts, is found within the monastery walls.*

Water was an important element of monastic life. The location of monasteries was usually chosen to be close to a source of water such as a natural spring, pond, or river. The water source could be diverted to various locations throughout the monastery to be used for cooking, bathing, and watering the gardens. Discovering a reliable source of water was an essential element necessary for the self-sufficiency of the monastery, because it ensured the monastery's garden would be successful.

## Types of Monastic Gardens

> *And the Lord God planted a garden eastward in Eden; and there he put the man whom he had formed. And out of the ground made the Lord God to grow every tree that is pleasant to the sight, and good for food; the tree of life also in the midst of the garden, and the tree of knowledge of good and evil. And a river went out of Eden, to water the garden; and from thence it was parted, and became into four heads.*
>
> —Genesis 2: 8–10

### Cloister Garth

The cloister garth was a centrally located courtyard surrounded by the main buildings of the monastery—that is, the church, refectory, and dormitory. The cloister garth contained covered alleys or hallways with a central portion open to the sky. This opening enabled the monks to walk and meditate while partaking of the fresh air. The central courtyard section was sometimes planted with herbs and flowers. This garden was often divided into quadrants thought to represent either the four rivers of the Garden of Eden, or the four elements—air, earth, fire, and water. The cloister garth often included a central fountain or sundial as part of its design.

### Cemetery and Orchard

When monks passed away at the monastery they were buried in its cemetery. The cemetery and surrounding grounds were often planted with various fruit and nut trees such as apples, pears, cherries, walnuts, and almonds. The fruit and nuts harvested from the trees were used for culinary purposes and to make a variety of beverages, such as cider and perry. Perry is a fermented beverage similar to cider but made with pears instead of apples.

### Kitchen

The kitchen garden was known in Latin as the *hortus*. Culinary herbs were grown in the kitchen garden along with many varieties of vegetables. The garden was located very close to the kitchen to facilitate the preparation of meals. Animal pens for poultry and other food animals would have been located close to the kitchen garden, as manure from the pens provided a ready source of organic fertilizer.

In addition to various types of vegetables, numerous culinary herbs such as dill, oregano, and parsley would also be grown in the kitchen garden.

### Physic

The physic garden, known in Latin as the *herbularius*, is the most interesting of all the monastery gardens for anyone interested in herbs. Medicinal herbs were grown in the physic garden. This garden was located very near the infirmary, so that the herbs would be ready to harvest at a moment's notice. The herbs were often grown in raised beds with pathways between the beds. Only one type of herb was grown per bed.

The herbs grown in the physic garden were in great demand throughout the monastery. They were utilized for their healing properties to aid monks that had taken ill and to help heal the sick and poor people that took shelter in the monasteries. The monastery infirmary frequently doubled as the local hospital for travelers and those peasants who could not afford a physician.

The infirmary garden would have also offered a place for convalescents to stroll about in the fresh air while they were recuperating from their illness. A turf seat was an extra feature in some physic gardens. This was a raised bench that had a small planter bed of a hearty herb such as chamomile. The herb's delightful healing fragrance would be released when someone sat upon the seat.

### Sacristan

The sacristan garden was used for the growing various flowers to decorate the statues of the saints and the Virgin Mary through-out the monastery. The flowers would also be used to decorate the altar of the church chapel and to make garlands and wreaths for the various feast days of the saints.

The flowers grown in the sacristan garden could also be used to decorate the guest rooms and refectory. The refectory was the communal dinning hall where the monks took their meals together. This garden was sometimes nicknamed "Paradise," as an allusion to the Garden of Eden. White roses and lilies were among the more popular flowers grown in the sacristan garden.

### Abbot's Garden

Although the monks were forbidden to own any personal prop-erty once they joined the monastery, many abbots had their own personal garden for growing their favorite plant varieties of herbs, roses, and other flowers. The abbot's garden was usually off-limits to the rest of the monastery inhabitants, though the abbot might allow high-ranking visitors to the monastery access to his personal garden.

*Farmland/Forests*

Farmland was usually located outside the monasteries for grow-ing necessary crops such as bread-grain and grapes. These crops needed more space than was contained in the gardens within the confines of the walled monastery. Although some fruit trees may have been grown in the monastery cemetery, any large orchards were usually located outside the monasteries.

Herbs would also have been wild-crafted from the sur-rounding countryside whenever possible. Those plants which could not be found in the surrounding fields and forests or in suf-ficient quantity would be cultivated by the monks in the physic and kitchen gardens. Visiting monks from other monasteries would often bring presents of herb plants and seeds along with them, enabling a monastery to obtain a collection of herbs and plants not commonly available in their area.

# The St. Gall Monastery Plan

A plan of a proposed monastery layout was created around AD 820. that included detailed drawings for the monastic gardens and included a kitchen garden, physic garden, cloister garth, and cemetery orchard. The herbs were meant to be grown in rectan-gular beds separated by narrow paths. A copy of the plan was found preserved in the library at the Abbey of St. Gallen in Switzerland. The plan was addressed to Gozbert, who was abbot of St. Gall from AD 816–836. The St. Gall Monastery plan was never built, but the plan came to be considered the ideal layout for a Benedictine monastery.

The medicinal, or physic, garden of St. Gall was divided into sixteen individual plots and included the following plants:

Cornflag, also called yellow flag *(Iris pseudacorus)*—The leaves were used as a strewing herb, the dried roots were used for chest complaints.

Cumin *(Cuminum cyminum)*—Beneficial to the digestive sys-tem, and especially for sluggish digestion.

Fennel *(Foeniculum vulgare)*—The seeds helped to alleviate hunger (especially useful during the long fast of Lent). It also helped to relieve indigestion and gas and improve liver function.

Fenugreek *(Trigonella foenum-graecum)*—The seeds, when soaked in water, soothed the stomach and digestive tract.

Kidney bean *(Phaceolus vulgaris)*—Monks in the earlier part of the Middle Ages were forbidden to eat the flesh of four-footed animals (such as cows, pigs, and sheep), therefore peas and beans became a staple part of the monks' daily diet. Because beans were known to cause gas, any herbs that relieved gas were treasured. Often, herbs such as savory and fennel were cooked along with the beans.

Lovage *(Levisticum officinale)*—Used for urinary trouble, jaundice, and stomach disorders.

Pennyroyal *(Mentha pulegium)*—Cold remedy, thought to work as a blood purifier and helped alleviate stomach disorders. Pennyroyal was also used as a flea repellent.

Peppermint *(Mentha piperita)*—Relieved gas, diarrhea, and stomach disorders. Mint was also useful as a cold remedy, a breath freshener, and as a strewing herb because of its fragrant aroma.

Rose *(Rosa spp.)*—Rose hips (the fruit of the rose) are very high in vitamin C. Rose hips and rose petals were used by the monks to make a variety of medicinal jams, jellies, and syrups. Rose remedies helped to relieve scurvy, diarrhea, and sore throats and were also thought to help restore strength after a period of illness.

Rosemary *(Rosmarinus officinalis)*—Rosemary was thought to strengthen the memory, and it was burned to purify the air in sick rooms. It was also used as a strewing herb and to repel insects.

Rue *(Ruta graveolens)*—Rue was also known as the herb of grace. A sprig of rue was traditionally used to dip into holy water for sprinkling during Mass. It was used medicinally by monks to promote clear vision and act as an insect repellent.

Sage *(Salvia officinalis)*—Sage was thought to promote longevity, aid digestion, and help eliminate gas. Sage was also used as a blood purifier. An infusion of the leaves helped to relieve sore throats.

Savory *(Satureja* spp.)—Savory aided digestion of gas-producing foods such as beans. It also helped to expel phlegm from the chest and lungs.

Tansy *(Tanacetum vulgare)*—Tansy helped get rid of intestinal parasites. It was used to make cakes called tansies, which were believed to help purify the body after the long fast of Lent. Tansy was also used as a strewing herb to help repel flies.

Watercress *(Nasturtium officinale)*—Watercress aided digestion, cleared toxins, and helped to promote appetite in cases of illness.

White lily *(Lilium candidum)*—White lily is also known as Madonna lily, as the white color was thought to be a symbol of purity. It helped to heal inflamed and irritated skin. It was also known as an ancient cure for various foot complaints and skin problems.

The plan of St. Gall also contains eighteen planter beds in the kitchen garden for the raising of culinary herbs and vegetables. The crops mentioned on the plan were onions, garlic, leeks, shallots, celery, parsley, chevril, coriander, dill, lettuce, poppy, savory, radishes, parsnips, carrots, cabbage, beets, and something called corn cockles.

# Modern-day Monastic Gardens

There are many modern-day recreations of monastic gardens located both in the United States and abroad. Some are maintained on the grounds of ancient monasteries and contain many historically accurate features. Others are maintained at private residences, and although traditional monastery gardens they do recreate some of the features found in such gardens such—raised garden beds, turf seats, and so on.

Author and photographer Mick Hales recently visited and photographed twenty-eight active monasteries in the United States, England, Wales, and France. The photographs he took of the monastery gardens are showcased in his book *Monastic Gardens*, published by Stewart, Tabori, and Chang in 2000.

My own personal garden is similar in layout to a cloister-garth monastic garden (see the illustration on next page). The layout features four sixteen-by-eight–foot raised beds that surround a centrally located raised circular planter.

On top of the planter is a bird bath topped with a rotating decorative sprinkler. There are two benches in the garden that allow for peaceful relaxation among the plants while watching the multitude of visiting butterflies and birds.

The east and west beds are each backed by eight-foot-tall sections of lattice trellis that allow climbing flowering vines and clinging vegetables (such as tomatoes and pole beans) to take hold. Each bed is separated by three-foot-wide gravel pathways interspersed with eighteen-inch-wide slate stepping stones.

This layout allows for quite a vast selection of various plants to grow. I have over ninety varieties of herbs growing in my garden. Many of the herbs in my raised beds may have been found in monastic herb gardens. See the list below (after the herb diagram) for some personal notes on the various plants that I grow in my garden.

# Monastic Herb Garden Diagram

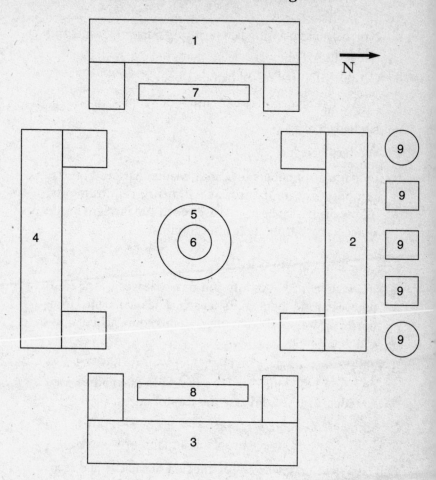

## Diagram Key

1—East-facing planting bed featuring annual herbs and vegetables.

2—South-facing planting bed featuring butterfly plants and annual flowers.

3—West-facing planting bed featuring perennial herbs and vegetables.

4—North-facing planting bed featuring butterfly plants and edible flowers.

5—Centrally located raised planting bed.

6—Bird bath and decorative rotating fountain.

7—Eastern bench.

8—Western bench.

9—Individual containers for exotic plants that need precise temperature, moisture, and lighting requirements. These plants can be moved as needed and brought inside if necessary during the winter months.

## List of Plants in My Garden

Bay *(Laurus nobilis)*—An infusion of bay leaves was used to relieve gas and soothe the stomach. The oil obtained from the leaves was used externally to help reduce aching muscles and joints.

Burdock *(Arctium lappa)*—The dried root of burdock was used as a blood purifier. The fresh leaves could be used to reduce bruises and ease the pain of burns.

Cornflower *(Centaurea cyanus)*—Cornflower was used to help treat various eye problems and minor wounds.

Dill *(Anethum graveolens)*—An infusion of the crushed seeds helped to relieve gas and stimulated one's appetite.

Hyssop *(Hyssopus officinalis)*—An infusion of hyssop leaves could be used to help alleviate fevers, coughs, and colds.

Lavender *(Lavandula angustifolia)*—Lavender was used as a strewing herb and to help repel insects. A relaxing tea could be made from its leaves and flowers.

Self heal, also known as heal-all *(Prunella vulgaris)*—Self heal was used to heal wounds and help stop excessive bleeding.

Sorrel *(Rume xacetosa)*—Sorrel was used to treat various skin problems, and also as a pot (culinary) herb.

## Some Modern Monastery Gardens

### The Cloisters

The Cloisters, in Fort Tryon Park in New York City, is a virtual re-creation of a medieval European monastery such as would have been located in England, France, Italy, or Germany during the Middle Ages. It opened to the public in 1938, and is operated by the Metropolitan Museum of Art.

The Cloisters features the art, gardens, and architecture typical of medieval Europe. There are four gardens on the site: the Cuxa Cloister Garth Garden, the Bonnefont Cloister Herb Garden, the Trie Cloister Garden, and the St. Guilhem Cloister. More than two hundred types of herbs and flowers are grown in the gardens of the Cloisters.

### Michelham Priory

Michelham Priory, meanwhile, is an Augustinian Priory founded on a moated island in 1229. It is located in East Sussex in the United Kingdom. Today the monastery is maintained by the Sussex Archaeological Society. Its features include a mile-long moat walk and seven acres of grounds showcasing a physic garden, kitchen garden, and cloister garden. The physic garden in particular includes over one hundred plants that would have been used in the Middle Ages for medicinal purposes.

The Michelham Priory museum and grounds are open to the public.

### Shrewsbury Quest

The Shrewsbury Quest is located in Great Britain and is a renovated medieval Benedictine monastery that opened to the public in 1994. The gardens are based on a plan of the monastic gardens of Christ Church, Canterbury, from circa 1165. Brother Cadfael is a fictional character created by the novelist Ellis Peter. (Ellis Peter was the pseudonym of the late Edith Pargeter.) Brother Cadfael was a monk, a gardener, and a herbalist featured in the twenty books of Peter's Cadfael Chronicles. As a tribute to Brother Cadfael, the Shrewsbury Quest includes Cadfael's Herb Garden, Cadfael's Private Gardens, and Cadfael's Workshop. Some of the herbs that were grown by Brother Cadfael included gilvers (clove-pinks), gromwell, ginger, columbine, herb of grace, and mustard.

### *Monk Herbalist*

*No joy is so great in a life of seclusion as that of gardening. No matter what the soil may be, sandy or heavy clay, on a hill or a slope, it will serve well.*

—Walafrid Strabo, Hortulus, ca. AD 840

At larger monasteries, one monk was usually assigned the duty of herbalist—as was the case with Brother Cadfael. It was his job to study the many medicinal herbs and to prepare the various ointments, lotions, and other medicines that would have been used by the monastery physician, or infirmerer, in tending to the sick and infirm.

The herbalist may have had a stillroom or workshop where he could dry and store herbs and create the various tinctures, salves, and ointments that were a necessary part of daily medieval monastery life. For this reason, the herbalist was one of the most important members of any monastery community. His contributions to the growing herbal knowledge of a monastery were important to Renaissance scholars who wrote the first popular treatises on herbal healing practices.

# Safety Precautions

*Note:* The herbs mentioned in this article are listed for historical educational purposes only. Many of the herbs mentioned have been proven to be harmful in certain dosages by modern-day herbalists, and they are not meant for internal or medicinal usage. In the event of illness, always be sure to consult a professional herbalist before undertaking any sort of herbal healing regimen.

# For Further Study

Bayard, Tania. *Sweet Herbs and Sundry Flowers: Medieval Gardens and the Gardens of the Cloisters.* New York, NY: Metropolitan Museum of Art, 1985.

Hales, Michael. *Monastic Gardens.* New York, NY: Stewart, Tabori & Chang, 2000.

Peplow, Elizabeth and Reginald. *In a Monastery Garden.* Devon, U.K.: David & Charles, Ltd, 1989.

Whiteman, Robin. *Brother Cadfael's Herb Garden: An Illustrated Companion to Medieval Plants and Their Uses.* Photographs by Rob Talbot. Boston, Mass.: Little, Brown, 1997.

# Additional Resources

The Cloisters
Fort Tryon Park
New York, NY 10040
212-923-3700
www.metmuseum.org

Michelham Priory
Upper Dicker, Hailsham
East Sussex, BN27 3QS
United Kingdom
www.sussexpast.co.uk/mich/michgarden.htm

The Shrewsbury Quest
193 Abbey Foregate
Shrewsbury Shropshire, S42 6AH
United Kingdom

# Starting an Herbal Garden

⤞ by Pearlmoon ⤝

W hen starting an herbal garden, it is important to
decide first which herbs you
want to grow, then to determine where
you want to plant your herbs. Here are
some typical questions you will ask
during the planning stage. Will your
garden be indoors or outdoors? Is
there enough sunlight to support the
herbs you want to grow in your preferred spot? Is the soil loose and with
adequate and good drainage, or is it
very firm and rocky?

Once you have decided which
herbs you want to plant, it is a good
idea to separate them into groups.
That is, you should separate the perennials from the annuals, and separate
the herbs that will need full sunlight
from the ones that will grow well in
partial shade.

It is also a good idea to plan carefully so the taller-growing herbs are placed in the back of the garden, and the shorter ones in the front. This will ensure that all plants benefit from an optimal amount of sunlight.

Be sure to make space between the rows of your garden beds. This is important so that you may reach all the plants for watering and upkeep. I also place stepping stones in these garden rows. They not only look nice, but make it easier to harvest your herbs while still keeping up the planting beds.

## Personal Choices in Your Garden
### *Your Garden's Soil*

When I decided to start my herb bed, I walked out into the yard and looked at the area I wanted to place my garden. I dug up a small portion of the soil. To say it was slightly less than perfect would be a masterpiece of understatement.

My soil was too firm and rocky with a mild to moderate amount of clay. This is a common problem in many areas—you should never fret if you have less-than-optimal planting conditions to start. A good remedy for this is to till up the soil and add equal parts of peat, fertilizer, and compost to what is there. In my case, for reasons I explain below, I also added some perlite and a small amount of sawdust.

Peat is made up of old plant material. It is slightly acidic and comes from bogs. Perlite is volcanic material; it appears as those little white beads you sometimes find in premade planting beds. Compost is made of old plant clippings and food material, mixed together and left to break down naturally into organic material perfect for planting. Fertilizer is usually composed of manure; it is easily found at any nursery.

Mix all of these materials well with your soil, and you should be fairly ready to begin planting. This combination is also good to use in your raised beds along with a bit of top soil or packaged potting soil.

## Clay Pot Planting

Another good idea for coping with poor soil is to plant in clay pots and bury them two-thirds into the ground. An advantage of this practice is you can dig the pots out in the fall and bring them indoors for maintenance during the winter months. A word of caution, though, if you use clay pots. You will want to keep them clean and free of bacteria. You can clean them before use by submerging them in a mix of one part bleach and nine parts very hot (but not boiling) water. After cleaning the pots, paint the inside with a lead-free cement paint. This will prevent water from being absorbed into the pots from outside. There is no need to paint the pots if you will be keeping them indoors full time.

You can, and should, clean your garden tools in much the same way, or you can wipe them with rubbing alcohol before letting them air dry.

## Growing from Seeds

If you are growing seeds, it is best to start in early march, so the seedlings will be ready for planting in early May. Follow the instructions on the seed packages for details such as how deep to plant the seeds. A good way to start your seeds is called "pre-sprouting." Wet a paper towel, then place the seeds on it and cover with another paper towel. Place the towels and seeds in a sealed plastic bag. If kept warm, the seeds should sprout within a couple of days. Once they have sprouted, place them into your pot soil.

Be sure the seed plants have at least twelve to fourteen hours of good sunlight each day. If you live in a cooler area and it is not possible to leave plants outside, then a good plant light will do just as well—unless you have a large window with a lot of warmth and sunlight.

## Miscellaneous Things to Consider

I almost always plant under the Cancer Moon. I think it's a good Moon for planting almost anything.

An important point to be aware of if you are planting herbs for consumption: Never ever use chemical pesticides on them. You could end up eating these chemicals. I always use a natural insecticide soap in my herb garden and in the pots I keep outside. You can find them at most nurseries.

It is also possible to make your own insecticide spray quite inexpensively. Just crush a bulb of garlic, and add it to a cup or two of water. Mix this well in a blender, and allow it to stand for twelve hours. Strain out the garlic with a cheesecloth, and add the remaining liquid to a gallon or so of water—and there you have it.

Another good recipe is to add a teaspoon or two of plain, mild, liquid dish soap to a gallon or so of water. By adding one and a half teaspoons of bleach and a tablespoon of baking soda you can use the mix as fungicide spray. I would apply any of these no more than once a week.

Another problem you might come across in your herb garden, once it is planted, is mildew. If you see a white powder starting to form on your plant's leaves, you will have to pull the plant and some of the surrounding soil as well. Whatever you do, don't throw any of the diseased plants into a compost heap. The mildew will infect the whole thing.

In general, be sure to keep your plants trimmed for good air circulation. Sunlight is important for keeping your plants dry and free of mildew.

Another problem is called "damping off." I didn't know what this was when I first saw it in the garden—but it just looked awful. Damping off is the common name of a fungal infection that kills plants just after they are planted. Like mildew, it is caused by too much moisture.

If this occurs in your garden, you will have to pull the plant along with some of the surrounding soil. If the plant is in a pot, make sure the pot is cleaned again as stated earlier. I spoke to someone at a local nursery, who is also an herbalist. He told me to water the new plants with a combination of chamomile and nettle tea. This will help to kill the fungus until the plants are ready to be planted outside.

# Reaping Your Rewards

### Harvesting Your Plants

It is best to harvest your herbs when they are dry. I find the absolutely best time is just after the morning dew has dried. For harvesting flowers, take them just as they are opening. You will have to be observant, because all flowers on a plant do not bloom at the same time. (The only exception I know of regarding this is lavender; harvest the lavender flowers before the buds are open, if possible.)

For harvesting leaves, try to take them before the flowers start to appear if you can. Before a plant flowers, most of the energy of the plant goes to the leaves. Once the plant flowers, the energy is sent to the flower. When harvesting leaves you will want all the energy in that part of the plant.

When harvesting roots, dig them up in the fall—making sure you leave some of the root to grow for next year. I never harvest roots from a plant under three years old. I like to give it enough time to develop a good strong root system.

To harvest seeds, wait until the seeds are just starting to fall off the plants.

### Drying Your Herbs

When drying your new herbs, just snip off a few sprigs from the plant and tie them into small bundles to hang-dry upside-down in a cool and dry area. I usually tie them with a rubber band— when the stems dry and shrink, the rubber band will shrink with them and stems won't be likely to fall out of the bundle.

Another way of drying herbs is to lay them on a flat rack made of some inexpensive window screening. In this way, air will circulate around all sides of the plant. I recommend the rack method for drying roots. It works much better for them.

Once your herbs are dried you can store them in clean, dark glass jars with tight-fitting lids. If you don't have dark glass jars then just use regular canning jars—sometimes called Mason jars. Another way of storing herbs is in a clean tin can with a tight-fitting lid.

Well, there you are. Now that you have grown, harvested, and dried your herbs you can enjoy them for many months to come. Good luck, and happy gardening.

## For Further Study

Shaudys, Phyllis. *The Pleasure of Herbs: A Month-by-Month Guide to Growing, Using, and Enjoying Herbs*. Pownal, VT: Storey Communications, 1986.

Stuckey, Maggie. *The Complete Herb Book*. New York: Berkley Books, 2001.

# Herbs for Shade Gardens

## ❧ by James Kambos ❧

When I began gardening many years ago, I knew the one thing I wanted to include in my garden were herbs. I spent months reading garden magazines before I put a shovel or hoe into the earth.

I read every garden publication I could find. All the magazines were filled with lush photographs depicting Sun-drenched herb gardens. They featured borders overflowing with such herbs as oregano, and planters with herbs like thyme spilling onto stone paths. Or, they showed lovely clouds of lavender floating above soft silvery foliage.

It was only later that reality set in. Standing in my backyard where my future herb garden would be, I was sheltered by the dappled shade of my beloved elm, pine, crab, locust, and dogwood trees.

It dawned on me then that there was one ingredient my herb garden would never have—Sun. Since I love trees and the way they make me feel connected to the earth, removing them was simply not an option.

I only have two areas on my property that receive nearly full Sun. So, obviously enough, in these few areas I could plant my favorite Sun-loving herbs such as oregano, thyme, and lavender. Unfortunately, about three-fourths of my garden receives only partial Sun, and much of this space is lost in full, deep shade.

I began to seek the advice of experienced gardeners and herbalists. They'd visit my yard and after looking at the shady canopy formed by the trees, they'd look at me and shake their heads. In somber tones akin to a doctor talking to a patient who is seriously ill, they would shake their heads and tell me, "You have too much shade."

Still, I was determined to include herbs in my landscaping plans. One afternoon while watching a gardening program, I heard a wise gardener give this all-too-appropriate advice: "Don't fight the site."

Armed with a feeling of renewed determination, I began seeking shade-loving herbs. I knew they were out there. I obtained garden catalogs from little-known garden nurseries. I visited gardeners who specialized in woodland gardens, and I asked the advice of local garden centers. And what I learned is revealed below.

## So You Want to Have a Shade Garden?

### Starting Your Garden

To start, I had my garden tilled and properly prepared (see "Starting an Herbal Garden" on page 23 for details about how to do this). Then, I began to plant.

It wasn't easy at first. Slowly, many times by trial-and-error, I began to build an extensive shade herb garden. Yes, I had failures, but I also in time had many successes. Over the years, with careful planning, I've been able to fill my difficult areas with herbs.

My garden has in fact evolved over a twelve-year period—not exactly overnight, but well worth the wait. Today I'm able to enjoy a shade herb garden that is every bit as interesting and varied as an herb garden blessed with full Sun.

And actually, so can you. If you love herbs the way I do, but your garden contains large shady areas, this article is written for you. Instead of leaving those hard-to-plant shady places bare, utilize them to create a peaceful, shade-loving herbal retreat.

A shady herb garden is the perfect place to escape a hectic world. It is the perfect place for you to go to find the relaxation and calm you seek in a garden.

## Types of Shade

Before planting, determine how much shade your shade garden has. If an area of your garden receives less than two hours of sunlight, this would be considered a full-shade garden. If your garden receives from two to six hours of Sun each day, this is a partial-shade garden.

Keep in mind, your shade herb garden will receive more sunlight early in the growing season before foliage appears on the trees. If you take advantage of this, you may grow some early spring-blooming bulbs—such as crocuses—which require at least partial Sun to do well. You will also have to observe the light your garden receives through the entire year before you determine what you will be able to plant.

## Site Selection and Preparation

Selecting the site for your herb shade garden is usually easy—nature probably has done this for you. At least that's the way it was for me.

You might want to walk over the area, however, and check for tree roots near the soil's surface that could make ground preparation difficult. If you're not sure about this, you may want to call in a tree service company. They can guide you on deciding where it would be best to dig.

Once you've selected your site and the soil has been tilled, the next critical step is preparing the soil. Most of the shade-loving herbs you'll grow have one thing in common—they prefer a soil that is rich in organic matter. Compost, manure, and peat moss are all good additions for the shade garden's soil.

If your garden is new, spread a layer of organic matter over the soil and work it in. A good rule of thumb here is to work the compost into about the depth of one foot.

To give your shade garden the look of a natural woodland, bring in some rocks or stones. These not only look nice, but after your plants grow, these rocks are convenient places for you to step as you plant and weed.

Another nice touch is a log or two. This will give the look of deadfall wood you see in the woodland. After nature takes its course, moss and lichens will form on your rocks and logs, making your shady niche appear to have been created by Mother Nature.

## Selecting Herbs for a Shade Garden

The following is a list of some of my favorite shade herbs. This list is by no means exhaustive, but includes many of the herbs I've used in my woodland herb garden.

I've observed these plants for many years in my Zone 6 garden, here in Ohio, and can say they've been tough and reliable performers as a general rule. These easy-care plants have returned year after year without special attention.

For each plant I've included information on its size, flowers, and growth habits. Where possible I've given some history as well as magical and medicinal lore.

Any medical information I've given here is for personal enrichment only. Many of the following herbs are quite toxic and are meant to be used for ornamental purposes only. Always consult a qualified herbalist before experimenting with herbal medications of any sort.

Including just a few of these plants in a shady border is a good way to begin learning about shade-loving herbs.

## Herbs for Shade

Bleeding-heart *(Dicentra)*: There are several varieties of this charming herb. The old-fashioned type attains a height of two feet, and blooms with red and white heart-shaped flowers in April and May. It does go dormant in summer. Other cultivars, such as "Luxuriant," reach a height of fifteen inches, bloom most of the summer, and have soft fern-like foliage. Carefree and long-lived, bleeding-heart likes moist, rich soil, and light- to full-shade. Bleeding-hearts also symbolize love.

Bluebells *(Mertensia viraginica)*: Virginia bluebells are a beautiful wildflower from the eastern United States. Plant the roots or potted plants in light to full shade. Bluebells grow to eighteen inches in height. The foliage is soft lettuce-green, and the April flowers first bloom pink, then turn sky-blue. Flowers are bell-shaped and hang in dainty clusters. Since plants die back, overplant with hosta or ferns to prevent bare spots. Plants will self-sow, forming lovely colonies.

Bowman's root *(Gillenia trifoliata)*: The root of this herb was once used by Native Americans as a laxative and overall stimulant. Today this rare herb is the perfect addition to a shady herb garden. Growing to two feet in height, its stems are slender and woody. Its leaves are pointed and grow, as the botanical name suggests, in clusters of three. In early June, the plant is covered by delicate white star-shaped flowers. In autumn, the foliage turns a golden color. This herb is not fussy about soil, and it will take morning Sun. Its growth habit is neat and generally non-invasive.

Boxwood *(Buxus)*: This is one of the few evergreen shrubs suitable for shade and therefore perfect for the shaded herb garden. The boxwood is also an herb itself and was once used to treat high fevers; however, it is highly toxic and can be fatal if ingested. Boxwood does well in Sun or shade, and in any soil. It is long-lived. With an average height of two feet, boxwood may be used to give definition to a herb garden and is easy to prune to any shape. In the home it has many decorative uses, and its stems combine beautifully with other greenery for holiday accents.

Bugleweed *(Ajuga)*: This is an outstanding herb for shade. It is used as a ground cover and is so hardy it can grow even where grass won't. The thick foliage ranges in color from green to burgundy and sends up blue-purple flower spikes four to six inches high, depending on the variety. Bugleweed was once used to treat wounds. Its requirements are shade, rich organic soil, and plenty of moisture. It does spread, so give it some room. Bugleweed is stunning when allowed to creep between stones. It is easy to grow and pest free.

Celandine poppy *(Stylophorum diphyllum)*: One of the joys of spring is seeing the sunny yellow flowers of celandine poppy glowing in the dappled shade of my garden. This woodland herb is easy to grow in shade. It self-sows and pops up at random, but it isn't invasive. The deeply lobed green foliage grows to one-half foot in height. The two-inch-high, cup-shaped yellow flowers stand out against its lush foliage. Celandine poppy blooms from April to June, and if the weather isn't too dry the foliage will last until fall.

Columbine (*Aquilegia*): This attractive member of the crow-foot family is a charming addition to the shaded herb border. The graceful flowers consist of five long, spurred petals. Wild columbine has flowers that are red and yellow. Other varieties available today include blue, yellow, pink, and almost pure white. Bicolors are also an option. The foliage forms a low clump of oval-shaped leaves and the flower stems usually grow two feet high. In my garden I've planted columbine in almost full Sun, as well as in full shade, and they seem to do well in either. When the seed heads ripen after flowering, scatter the seeds to encourage more plants if you wish.

Ferns: There are at least twelve families of ferns—too many for me to go into detail considering the space. So, I'll concentrate on some of the excellent qualities this group of plants has to offer. Of all herbs, ferns may be the most ancient. They thrived on Earth thousands of years ago. Substances found in the rhizomes of certain ferns, such as the male fern, were once used in the treatment of intestinal worms. In the realm of magic, ferns were known to attract fairies, good luck, and prosperity. When planted in the shady herb garden, ferns add grace, color, and texture. They look especially appealing planted near rocks and at the base of trees. Their delicate fronds bring a quiet beauty and softness to the herb garden like no other plant. About three hundred varieties of ferns grow in the United States. If you can include only a few ferns in your garden, may I recommend the following: Lady fern, which grows to two feet in height, takes some Sun or full shade, and is hardy and easy to grow; Japanese silver-painted fern, grows to eighteen inches in height and has outstanding silver and burgundy stems and fronds; ghost fern, which grows to two feet tall, has soft-green fronds that have a touch of silver overtones, and takes some drought. As a general rule, give ferns a moist, woodsy soil, and they'll give you many years of carefree beauty.

Foam flower *(Tiarella)*: In May and early June, foam flower blooms with spikes of tiny white or pink flowers. It grows between four and ten inches high. The real attraction of these tough pest-resistant plants, however, is their handsome foliage. The leaves are similar in shape to a maple leaf and range from soft yellow-green to green veined with burgundy. The leaves were at one time prepared as an infusion and drunk to aid digestion. Plants have a small tidy growth habit and spread no more than two feet. They're beautiful when planted in clumps of three.

Foxglove *(Digitalis)*: There are numerous varieties of foxglove. Many have been developed to take full Sun, but I've found most like part-shade. Their spikes of drooping bell-shaped flowers in soft pastel shade make foxgloves a lovely and romantic plant. Most are biennial to perennial and prefer loose rich soil. Expect them to grow three to four feet high and about eighteen inches wide. The plant has many medicinal qualities, including use as a heart medication, but it is quite toxic. It also has the magical quality of protecting the home and garden from any evil.

Geraniums: I'm speaking of the true perennial geranium, not the Sun-loving common red geranium grown as an annual, which should correctly be called pelargonium. Geraniums are commonly called cranesbill and were used as an herb to treat everything from wounds to diarrhea. They grow happily in light shade and produce a great number of flowers—in pink, white, and blue—from May to June. The plants have a mounding growth habit, reaching from six to eighteen inches in height. Leaves are finely lobed. This group of plants will work well as a ground cover, or in the middle of the border. Two of my favorites are *G. sanguineum* (bloody cranesbill), which has bright-pink flowers and grows one foot high and eighteen inches wide. Also, there is *G. giokovo*, which has delicate white flowers washed with pale pink; its foliage releases a tangy citrus scent when rubbed, and it grows to one foot in height while spreading up to two feet in width.

Ginger *(Asarum europaeum)*: This is the wild European ginger, not to be confused with culinary ginger. Due to the plant's toxicity, it is no longer used as a medication, but at one time was given for headache treatment. Ginger is extremely tolerant of dense shade and is a superb ground cover. Its oval dark-green leaves are held above a three- or four-inch long stem, and in mid-spring insignificant flowers appear beneath the foliage (these can't be seen unless you look for them). Several years ago I planted a ginger root beneath an old crab tree. Today it forms an impressive mat four feet wide and mingles happily with ferns, hostas, and celandine poppies. Ginger requires no care, making it a real winner for any gardener.

Hosta: This member of the lily family is the backbone of the shade herb garden. With at least seventy cultivars to choose from, you can easily find hostas to fit your color scheme and space requirements. Basically, hostas are grown for their lush foliage, which comes in green, blue-green, gold, and many variegated combinations. As a bonus, they send up dramatic flowering stems bearing white or blue flowers—which in my garden are magnets for hummingbirds. Hostas are valuable in the shady herb bed because they can be used to "overplant" spaces where spring-flowering shade herbs, such as bluebells, grow. For example, after the bluebells go dormant, the hostas will begin their growth, hiding the bare area left by the bluebells. Hostas come in a wide range of sizes, growing from around twelve inches high and wide, up to four to five feet high, with similar spread. As an added feature, hosta foliage stays attractive until the killing frost—unlike some perennials that begin to look weary by August.

Jacob's-ladder *(Polemonium caeruleum)*: If you like blue flowers, you must include Jacob's-ladder in your shaded herb garden. This was one of the first shade herbs I ever grew, and immediately I was impressed by its sapphire-blue flowers. Also known as Greek valerian, Jacob's-ladder was once used to treat dysentery, as well as other health problems. This highly ornamental herb spreads about one foot in width; its flower stems rise eighteen inches tall. It is a neat grower and never gets out of hand. It does benefit from a moist soil, some morning Sun, and afternoon shade, and it blooms from May to June.

Lady's-mantle *(Alchemilla mollis)*: For centuries, lady's-mantle was used in love spells and love charm bags. As the Latin name suggests, this herb was thought to possess strong medicinal qualities. For the gardener, this is a refined herb that deserves a place in a good shade garden. The sage-green foliage is large, scalloped, and velvety to the touch. These plants spread eighteen inches in width and grow to a height of roughly eighteen to twenty inches. In early June, lady's-mantle is smothered in frothy chartreuse flower heads that dry very beautifully and make handsome additions to dried floral arrangements and wreaths. After a rain, the soft foliage holds droplets of water like silver beads, further enhancing its appeal. I have planted lady's-mantle in several locations. They seem to do well in part shade to almost full shade.

Lamiums: Also called "dead nettle," lamiums are among the easiest shade herbs to grow. They're an outstanding ground cover that grows six to twelve inches high. One plant can easily spread two to three feet over a period of one to two years. The small leaves can be green and silver, silvery gray, or yellow and white. The flowers are lip shaped and bloom in yellow, white, or shades of pink. Known for producing large amounts of nectar, the flowers were once used as a tea flavoring. Some favorite varieties of lamium include "Beacon Silver," "Herman's Pride," "White Nancy," and "Yellow Archangel." Lamiums are convenient as they grow in difficult areas—such as under trees, in dry shade, and in deep shade. They're striking as a ground cover beneath hostas or ferns. In my Zone 6 garden, lamiums are semi-evergreen and flower sporadically until late fall.

Meadow rue *(Thalictrum)*: Tall, elegant, and graceful are just a few of the terms that come to my mind when I think of this lovely herb. Meadow rue is one of the tallest shade herbs, reaching heights of five to seven feet, depending on growing conditions. It's a slender plant, growing to a width of only eighteen inches. Meadow rue's blue-green foliage is small and resembles that of the columbine. Numerous small lilac-colored flowers bloom in June and are carried on slender stems, giving the plant an airy look. This plant performs in the north or south if given part shade, but it can't handle arid conditions. In magic, meadow rue was used in many love and protection spells.

Monarda *(Monarda didyma)*: This fragrant, showy herb is also called "bee balm" and was used to flavor teas and as a healing agent for wounds. It grows to at least four feet high and one plant can spread to four or feet feet wide. The unusual red or pink flowers bloom in July and attract countless bees and hummingbirds. Monarda grows best in rich soil with part shade. I've found the red cultivars to be the strongest growers in the typical shade garden.

Pennyroyal *(Mentha pulegium)*: If you want to include a mint with your shade herbs, this is the one. Unlike other mints, pennyroyal doesn't spread out of bounds. Strongly aromatic, pennyroyal fills the air with its fragrance when touched. The flowers appear in small pink or lilac whorls along its eighteen- to twenty-inch stems. These flowering stems dry well and are used as an accent in dried floral arrangements. Although the plant's oils are toxic, the small oval leaves have been used around the home to deter fleas. To the magician, pennyroyal is an herb of peace and protection.

Periwinkle *(Vinca minor)*: Periwinkle's glossy evergreen foliage and rich blue flowers help make it one of the most useful ground covers for shade. Its stems form a six-inch-thick mat, which spreads by rooting as it travels. Its flowers, meanwhile, flowers bloom nonstop from March to early June. For a truly exquisite combination, underplant periwinkle in the fall with daffodil bulbs of your choice. The sight of daffodils blooming above the green foliage and blue flowers of periwinkle is one of the delights of spring. Periwinkle has a long association with magic and was known by the charming folk name "sorcerer's violet." It was used to protect against the evil eye and to increase passion.

Primrose *(Primula vulgaris)*: Why this tough, hardy little shade herb isn't used by more gardeners is a mystery to me. The crinkled foliage is neat and remains fresh looking all summer. In early March, when the landscape is still drab, the flower buds of primrose rise just above the leaves and bloom in vivid colors—red, yellow, white, and royal blue. This is definitely a welcome sight after the long winter. The plants grow to ten inches or so in height, with a similar spread. It's also an ideal edging plant. I have several clumps planted along the north side of my house, where they've performed well for years. The flowers and roots of primrose have been used for centuries to treat everything from bronchitis to migraines—it is even useful for treating stress. This is truly an underrated herb.

Sweet cicely *(Myrrhis odorata)*: Of all the herbs I've mentioned, sweet cicely (pronounced like "Sicily") may be the hardest herb to locate at a nursery or seed company. But, I urge you to try. Few herbs have the grace and beauty of this wild European native. The foliage is lacy and fern-like, and when touched it releases a licorice scent. Leaf stems have been used as a dye source, and the oil was used to flavor liqueurs. Leaves can also be pressed and mounted on acid-free paper for framing. In June, it grows flower heads of pure white bloom, similar to Queen Anne's lace. These are followed by upright shiny seed heads. When the seed heads turn black, crush them and scatter the seeds to ensure new plants. The seedlings pop up in unexpected places, but be glad when they do. Sweet cicely reaches a height of three feet and spreads to a width of one-half foot.

Sweet woodruff *(Galium odoratum)*: On summer evenings, when I walk through my woodland herb garden I smell the gentle scent of new mown hay. Actually what I'm smelling is sweet woodruff, a rugged shade-loving ground cover. The pointed green leaves grow in whorls around stems no taller than six to eight inches high. In May, sweet woodruff's starry white flowers glow in the shade. These are especially bewitching when seen at twilight. The famous May wine is flavored with this herb, and its delicate scent has been used to induce sleep. Woodruff is a strong money-attracting herb, ideal for use in prosperity magic. Planted in full to light shade, sweet woodruff will happily ramble around rocks and tree trunks. Once planted, it requires no care.

## In Conclusion

There are other herbs suitable for shade gardens, but the ones I've described are plants I've grown for years in my own garden. They are low maintenance and are easy to grow by the novice or the experienced gardener.

Since most shade herbs originated in the forests or at the edge of the woodland, they're naturally hardy and require little special care once established. In the fall, however, it's a good idea to leave a few fallen leaves on your shaded herb bed. These add protection from drying winds and duplicate the woodland habitat where many shade herbs first grew.

If you don't know what to do with the shady areas of your yard, creating an herb garden for shade and woodland plants is an excellent idea. Not only does it benefit the environment, shade herbs will bring to your garden a calmness and serenity unequalled by other plants.

# Fire in the Garden

### ➢ by Sheri Richerson ➣

T here is no doubt that there is something arousing, mysterious, and magical about fire. Fire is the energy of life. Fire is also nature's cleanser.

Fire is said to change the environment from a mundane, common one to an adventurous and romantic one. The color of fire as it flickers and moves about and the wonderful warm feeling that you receive from being near an open flame add to the magical energy of fire. As a result, many cultures have myths and rites that relate to the origin of fire as well as to its preservation. Fire rituals are an important part of the Baltic religion, for example. During every traditional Baltic holiday a fire is lit—either a bonfire, an altarfire, or a simple candle. To the Baltic people, fire represents the unbroken

lifeline of their family and their ancestry. When a fireplace is lit in a home, everyone is expected to remain quiet and not turn away. Fire was not to be insulted and treated with respect.

## Fire in the Herb Garden

While there are many more stories and myths associated with fire, the properties of fire are important to consider in any herbal garden or greenhouse. The untamed spirit that resides in the flames of a fire is something that many of us would like to learn how to use in our everyday lives. We can tap into this energy through the medium of herbs.

Ayurveda is an ancient Indian approach to health and wellness that has stood up quite well to the test of time (it's roughly three thousand years old). Ayurveda is based on a system of *tridosha*, or three humors, which classifies all individual constitutions of people, diseases, herbs, and other non-herbal remedies and therapies according to whether they are *vata* (air or nerve oriented), *kapha* (water or mucoid type) or *pitta* (fire type). When our doshas are balanced, we function well, but when the doshas are not balanced, a state of disease can set in.

Currently, it may be argued, our society's fire dosha has been thrown out of balance. As more and more empirical evidence reveals, due to the modern diet of refined sugars and simple carbohydrates and excessive fats, this is a time of increased obesity, heart disease, adult-onset diabetes, and other related diseases. As such, it is well worth growing a number of fire herbs. As ayurveda has shown, herbs that have pungent, sour, and salty flavors stimulate fire. These tend to increase digestive fire, and expel and dry excessive fluid build up in the system, including clearing excessive fat from the body, and the accumulation of cholesterol and other fatty deposits in the veins and arteries of the body.

Fire herbs may well represent the perfect way to heal what is currently ailing much of American culture, by bringing balance to its excessively kapha tendencies.

# Philosophies and Associations of Fire

The energy from fire is masculine and its direction is south. The southern direction means that fire represents the Sun at its extreme south declination. This is where the Sun is able to fully warm Mother Earth and infuse her with energy that will bring forth an abundant harvest. The masculine energy is yang, a positive energy. The signs of the zodiac that are associated with fire are Leo, Aries, and Sagittarius. The magical associations connected to fire include power, energy, inspiration, creativity, motivation, leadership, purification, strength, anger, authority, loyalty, health, and vitality.

Fire is the element of strength, change, and passion. The element of fire brings out something in people that causes them to do things they normally would not think of doing.

Fire represents the cycle of life but also destroys anything in its pathway. On the flip side of this, fire does allow for regeneration. When working with fire herbs, the results come about fairly quickly because of the force and passion within the flames.

Fire is the most physical of all the elements. Fire is often used to burn away old desires and bring on new ones.

You can easily experience the magic of fire by trying one of these simple ideas. Watch closely as fire consumes and transforms an object such as paper or wood. Feel the heat of the fire and see the light it creates—how it can both create and destroy.

Candle flames are another great way to experience fire magic. Simply light a candle and meditate on the flame. This could easily be done using a wood burner or fireplace as well. Meditating on the flickering flames can sometimes help one achieve an understanding of the force behind fire as well as a new outlook on life. If you are unhappy with your physical being, fire is especially powerful in allowing you to work transformation. The flames can conjure up creativity and transformative energy that may have been bottled up for some time. Fire can also kindle sexual desires. This is why fireplaces are often used in bedrooms or honeymoon suites. Fire herbs also will serve you well in providing the energy to transform your life. Consider planting the following herbs in your garden or in your greenhouse if you want to tap into the energy of fire.

# Some Fiery Herbs

Holistic medicine was begun as a reaction to the rather narrow, body-focused approach of Western medicine, and is based on ayurvedic and traditional Chinese medical practices. A holistic doctor will look at the whole person— body, mind, and spirit— and use a variety of Western or non-Western techniques to treat illness. Essentially, a holistic doctor enters into partnerships with patients, encouraging them to learn how to reduce risks of illness and how to choose therapies that they're comfortable with. It is an approach to health that emphasizes self-care and personal responsibility for wellness.

Finding balance according to ayurveda involves changing your diet to balance your predominant dosha. With today's fatty diet, heart disease and stroke now account for more than half the deaths in the United States. Fire herbs may be part of a solution. For overweight and sluggish individuals, pitta foods, herbs, and remedies will warm the constitution, raise metabolism, stimulate digestion, clear mucus, and improves circulation. A person afflicted with an imbalance of kapha should avoid meat, cheese, sugar, cold foods and drinks. Weekly fasting may be helpful, and most or all of your daily food should be consumed before 6 pm. Among the warming, or pitta, herbs useful for restoring imbalance are the following.

**Turmeric**
Turmeric has a place of honor in ayurveda. It is considered a cleansing herb for the whole body—treating fever, infections, arthritis, liver problems, and acting as a digestive. Turmeric also may help reduce cholesterol and prevent internal blood clots that trigger heart attack and some strokes. Unfortunately, turmeric is not a garden herb in North America. It is grown from India to

Indonesia, in Zones 10–11. It thrives in rich soil in a warm greenhouse, if you want to experiment. Turmeric is a perennial with pulpy, orange tuberous roots that grow to about two feet long, and that are dried and crushed to create the spice. The flowers are borne in showy spikes. During the plant's dormant state, its soil should not be kept bone dry, or the tubers will shrivel.

## Ginger

According to an old Indian proverb, "Every good quality is contained in ginger." Long used in cooking, ginger also treats digestive, kidney, and liver problems, eliminates body odors, and helps preserve foods. Ginger also helps reduce cholesterol, lowers blood pressure, and prevents blood clots. Ginger is a perennial tropical herb that can be grown in greenhouses in cold climates, and bedding in the summer in warm regions.

## Mustard

Mustard is useful as an appetizer and digestive. It is used in topical oils to encourage blood flow in cases of rheumatism, sciatica, and other internal inflammations. Mustard is a half-hardy annual herb whose leaves are used in salads, and whose seeds are used to flavor foods and as a condiment. Sow mustard seeds in rows twelve inches apart in earliest spring and at weekly intervals until a month before hot weather, and again in the fall until six weeks before winter. For a winter supply, sow from November until March in cold frames or cool greenhouses. Gather by shearing the plants while young and tender.

## Bayberry

In the early nineteenth century, bayberry was popularized as a medicine by Samuel A. Thomson, an herbalist and creator of the earliest patent medicines. He touted it as second only to red pepper for producing "heat" in the body. Today, herbalists recommend the herb externally for varicose veins and internally for cold, flu, bleeding gums, diarrhea, and sore throat. Bayberry is native to the area from New Jersey to the Great Lakes and south to Florida and Texas. It grows from seeds planted in spring or early fall, and prefers peaty soil under full Sun—though it will tolerate sandy soil along streams and in swampy areas. The plants require little care other than pruning. Harvest the root bark after a few years.

## Cayenne

Also known as red pepper, the fiery taste of this plant's fruit makes it one of the world's most noticeable spices. It is also a fiery healing, effective at relieving chronic pain and aiding digestion. Herbalists today prescribe capsules of cayenne powder for colds, gastrointestinal and bowel problems, and externally for arthritis and muscle soreness. Cayenne's active ingredient has also been shown to relieve the severe ankle and foot pain suffered by those who have diabetes. This is a shrubby, tropical perennial with shiny, pendulous, leathery fruit. It grows best in tropical or subtropical areas, but it will also prosper in south-facing windows and greenhouses. In southern states, red pepper seeds may be sown after the risk of frost. In northern states, sow seeds indoors in flats eight weeks before the final frost date, then transplant. Red pepper prefers rich, well-watered, sandy soil and full Sun. When harvesting the peppers, be careful not to break the stems or they may spoil. To dry them, hang them in a warm and dry place for several weeks.

## Motherwort

The ancient Greeks and Romans used motherwort for both physical and emotional problems of the heart—palpitations and heart disease as well as anxiety and depression. In China, motherwort was used to prolong life. Today, studies show the herb is useful in preventing blood clots and reducing blood pressure. Motherwort's perennial roots give rise to red-tinged, stout, square stems that grow to four feet in height. It grows easily, and may actually become a pest in the garden. Plant seeds in spring and thin seedlings to twelve-inch spacing. Motherwort prefers rich, moist, well-drained soil and full Sun. Harvest the entire plant after the flowers blossom.

**Myrrh**

The resin from the stem of myrrh has been used since pre-biblical times in embalming mixtures, as an aromatic for perfumes, as an insect repellent, and to prevent tooth decay and gum disease. Today, myrrh is primarily used for oral hygiene, due to its astringent effect on tissues. It's a common ingredient in European toothpastes. Myrrh may also help prevent heart disease by helping to reduce cholesterol and to prevent blood clots. Myrrh is a small shrub or tree that grows in the Middle East, Ethiopia, and Somalia. It has finely cut leaves and bears small, white flowers. It is hardy to Zone 4, and easily propagated by seed sowing or by root cuttings.

# Fire Essential Oils

For those of you who wish to use essential oils rather than growing your own fire herbs to bring the element of fire to balance your life, you can try the following Fire Essential Oil blend. However, be advised that this is a spicy, hot, and passionate blend, and a little goes a long way.

To make this blend, mix equal parts of the following essential oils: ginger, basil, cardamom, cinnamon, and sweet orange. To use this mixture, try adding it to an essential oil burner. You may also add a few drops to the dryer while drying clothes, or dilute it with some neutral oil (such as sesame or almond) and use as a massage oil or in the tub.

# Fire Rituals

Fire rituals are another popular way of incorporating the spectacular, powerful, and dynamic magic of fire into your everyday life. These rituals are able to connect people with practices that are as old as human spiritual expression.

When creating a fire ritual, make sure that your burning spot is twice as wide as the material that will be burned. This is a basic rule of thumb—more space sometimes is better. It is also a good idea to clear the area of any objects that could catch on fire. The next step is to make sure you have a supply of water in the area, as well as some extra shovels just in case the fire starts to get out of hand. Most importantly, do not use chemical accelerants on the fire.

Finally, remember the embers will be carried into the air but at some point they will come back down. Make sure people watch for these falling embers so that they do not get burned.

Often, fire rituals are done during the harvest season. This not only offers a wide array of burnable products to work with but also opens up farm fields which should give plenty of room to build the bonfire. An especially powerful fire ritual would make use of fire herbs grown in your own garden or greenhouse.

Fire rituals are a physical manifestation of the power of fire. The flip side to using the element of fire is that one must understand that when fire gets out of control it can cause devastation. It is easy to grow out of balance with the humor of fire, and thus experience another set of problems. This is a very important point to remember when working with any type of fire magic. Fire does contain rashness, anger, hostility, and a drying-up capacity. This is why it is so important to focus on the higher qualities that we desire when working with fire.

# Culinary
# Herbs

# Great Herbal Snacks

### ✢ by Dallas Jennifer Cobb ✢

H ave you ever tried to feed a bunch of kids and been met by a chorus of protests? Are you constantly challenged to feed the children in your life healthy snacks that they will actually like? Do you live with picky and impossible-to-please eaters? Then this article is for you.

## The Child/Food Conundrum

It is difficult to get children to eat well, and almost impossible to get them to eat healthy foods. As a mother, I have had lots of experience feeding children healthy snacks. I have also had first-hand experience with several extremely picky eaters. Through it all, I have learned how to shape snacks and meals into yummy adventures that kids will dig into. In particular, I have used

herbs to flavor otherwise nose-turning foods, and well I know their culinary and therapeutic value.

In order to stay focused and on topic, this article focuses primarily on the culinary use of herbs to entice and enchant the finicky eaters in your life. For more information on the therapeutic use of herbs for children, see articles in previous *Herbal Almanacs*. You might also find some interesting information on herbal treatments for children suffering from A.D.D. in Leeda Alleyn Pacotti's article on page 161 of this edition.

The recipes included below have been tested by a small herd of two- and three-year-olds and given a grubby thumbs up. My daughter's playmates return often to our house clamoring for "treats." And believe it or not, my partner even looks forward to leftovers when he arrives home from work.

## Feeding Pitfalls

While herbs are nutritional and therapeutic, kids won't eat them unless they are incorporated into foods that look good and taste great. When you are introducing new foods, avoid the most common pitfalls—those statements that signal a warning to picky eaters. That is, try not to say any of these statements.

*It's good for you.*

*It won't kill you if you eat it.*

Or the dreaded: *Just try it, you'll like it.*

Yes, you know that herbs are good for us, but it won't help to tell your children that. You see, kids have a kind of radar that is constantly scanning for the devious tricks adults use to con them into eating yucky stuff. In the unique language of children "good for you" and "healthy" translate to "yucky" and "tastes bad."

Instead of telling children that the food is good for them, focus instead on making the food look, smell, and taste good. These are the big sellers for the picky palate of children. As sensual creatures, children judge food by look and smell. And if it passes those tests, it may get to their mouth so long as it doesn't feel "funny."

# Pleasing Picky Eaters

Here are some food tips for pleasing picky eaters. Present foods in colorful and creative ways. Kids love a meal they can play with, so encourage them with fun food. For instance, try using animal-shaped cookie cutters to shape sandwiches. Offer sauces for dipping in small, brightly colored tubs. Arrange food in patterns (a clown's face perhaps?) or geometric shapes on the plate. Serve a variety of brightly colored foods that appeal to children (apples, carrots, blue corn chips, tomato wedges, zucchini sticks) and let them choose. Make eating fun by creating a meal or snack around a theme—such as wagon train foods that cowboys used to eat, hiking provisions for a trip to the top of a mountain, a tropical rain forest treat that monkeys and toucans would love to be served, or a tea party for dollies and the March Hare—who of course is running late and due to arrive at any moment.

In particular, fun is appealing to children at eating time, and laughter and games take a child's mind away from the uncertainty of new foods. New foods are often a hard sell with children because they are unfamiliar with them, and therefore suspicious. It is probably linked to a self-preservation instinct handed down through evolution, so don't bother fighting with it.

Choice makes a child feel powerful and safely in control of his or her own feeding. And even if a child only eat two or three of the offered foods, if you serve only healthy things then you know that at least he or she has eaten something healthy.

On the other hand, when you tell your child that some food "won't kill you," rather than reassuring him or her instead you create a deep fear in them—the fear of eating something healthy and yucky. So do yourself a favor, and don't ever catch yourself saying this (even if it's what your mother used to say to you).

# Herbs for Kids

Be aware, there are many herbs that aren't safe for children's consumption. Just because something is a "herb" doesn't mean it is good for all.

Here's a list of herbs safe for children to consume.

Anise *(Pimpinella anisum)*

Basil *(Ocimum basilicum)*

Borage *(Borago officinalis)*

Calendula *(Calendula officinalis)*

Caraway *(Carum carvi)*

Catnip *(Nepeta cataria)*

Chamomile *(Chamaemelum nobile)*

Chives *(Allium schoenoprasum)*

Coriander *(Coriandrum satibum)*

Cumin *(Cuminum cyminum)*

Dandelion *(Taraxacum officinale)*

Dill *(Anethum graveolens)*

Fennel *(Foeniculum vulgore)*

Garlic *(Allium sativum)*

Hyssop *(Hysoppus officinalis)*

Lavender *(Lavendula angustifolia)*

Lemon balm *(Melissa officinalis)*

Lovage *(Levisticum officinale)*

Marjoram *(Origanum majorana)*

Meadowsweet *(Filipendula ulmaria)*

Nasturtium *(Tropaeolum majus)*

Oregano *(Origanum vulgare)*

Parsley *(Petroselinum crispa)*

Peppermint *(Mentha x piperita)*

Rooibos *(Aspalathus linearis)*

Rosemary *(Rosmarinus officinalis)*

Sage *(Salvia officinalis)*

Sorrel *(Rumex scutatus)*

Spearmint *(Mentha spicata)*

Stevia *(Stevia rebaudiana)*

Sweet Basil *(Ocimum basilicum)*

Tarragon *(Artemesia dracunculus)*

Thyme *(Thymus vulgaris)*

Yarrow *(Achillea millefolium)*

In general, try to make foods familiar by having them at the table frequently, consuming them yourself, and offering them as one of the choices that children can select from on their plates. Sometimes getting a child to try a new food is simply a matter of letting him or her see someone else eat it.

Another trick is to involve your children in making food with you, so that they see the ordinary process of preparation. It often helps to demystify individual ingredients.

## The Kid-Friendly Kitchen

There are a few herbs that are so versatile and tasty they are common in many child-friendly recipes. Keep these handy in your kitchen: calendula, catnip, chamomile, lavender, peppermint, and stevia. While not always considered herbs, the spices cinnamon, ginger, and cocoa are also very popular with my ragamuffin herd of experts.

Children love to help in the kitchen, so get them involved in your cooking and baking. You can teach them measurement and mixing, baking and tasting, and have fun at the same time. Children feel a great sense of accomplishment following a simple recipe, measuring out the ingredients, adding them together, and making a "treat" for the whole family.

Herbal treats can be as simple as adding suitable herbs to an already successful recipe, or creating new treats based on the herbs your family likes. And great herbal snacks don't have to be complicated. Try adding a little fresh cilantro to your favorite salsa, adding some mint jelly to your toast, or adding lavender to Christmas shortbread cookies.

Generally, I try to avoid having a lot of refined sugar. It seems to set the kids off and that makes for a difficult time for everyone. I have successfully used maple syrup and honey as sweeteners for many years, and I only recently discovered stevia. This herb tastes great, is easy to bake with, and brings with it no sugar highs and lows.

# Herbalicious Snacks

Below are a few recipes for snacks that will please even the pickiest eaters. Try them, and keep a little list of what works and what doesn't. Soon you will have neighborhood children clamoring to come to your house at snack time.

## *Beverages*

### Lavender Lemonade

    ¼  cup dried lavender blossoms

    2  cups boiling water

    4  large lemons

    1  cup sugar

Steep lavender for ten minutes in the boiling water, then strain. Let the lavender water cool a bit, then combine it with the juice from the lemons and sugar in a pitcher. Fill with ice and with water, and serve cold.

## Baby Bunny's Tummy Tea

Boil some water. Place three tablespoons of dried chamomile flowers and one tablespoon each of dried lemon balm and catnip in a tea pot. Pour the boiling water over them. Cover the tea pot, and let it steep for ten minutes. Strain the tea, and sweeten it with honey or stevia. Chamomile has a soothing effect on the nervous system, and lemon balm and catnip will calm an upset tummy very quickly.

## Fruity Mint Punch

| | |
|---|---|
| 5 | cups strongly brewed Red or Lemon Zinger tea (available from Celestial Seasonings) |
| 2 | cups fresh orange juice |
| ¼ | cup fresh lemon juice |
| ½ | cup boiling water |
| ½ | cup finely chopped mint leaves |
| | Honey or stevia to taste |

Brew and cool the tea, then mix it with the orange juice and lemon juice in a big pitcher. Boil the half cup of water and pour it over the mint leaves. Steep the leaves for five minutes. Strain the leaves, and add the tea to the juice. Sweeten the pitcher with honey or stevia to taste. Cool and serve.

## Herbal Popsicles

At my house, we make our own popsicles out of juices and teas. Buy a plastic popsicle mold at the dollar store and try making your own popsicles. For toddlers, I recommend tea-popsicles from rooibos or Sleepy Time tea (from Celestial Seasonings), or ones made from watered-down juices. For bigger kids, just pour the juice in the mold, and freeze.

When we make lemonade popsicles we often put a little bit of chopped lemon balm, lavender, or mint in the mold and then pour the lemonade in. The kids love to squeal at the results, "Yuck, a bug," and then eat them anyway.

## Sweet Treats

### Ginger Snaps
These delicious cookies are clamored for in my household. They are a little spicier than ordinary ginger snaps, so kids eat a little less (but adults eat a little more).

  1  cup butter

  1  cup sugar

  ¼  cup blackstrap molasses

  1  egg

  1  tsp. vanilla extract

  2  cups all-purpose flour

  ½  tsp. baking soda

  1  tsp. cinnamon

  ½  tsp. powdered ginger

  ½  tsp. powdered cloves

  ¼  tsp. salt

Preheat over to 350 degrees. Cream the butter and sugar, then add the molasses, egg, and vanilla and mix well. In a separate bowl sift the dry ingredients together, then add the mixture to the creamed mix slowly. Drop the resulting dough by table-spoons onto a nonstick cookie sheet, and bake for fifteen minutes or until golden brown.

### Luscious Lavender Shortbread
Shortbread is a favorite in my house because it is so easy to make and easy to eat. We used to make shortbread traditionally at Christmas, but a few years ago we started to make summer shortbread when the lavender was in bloom. We have also created successful rosemary and lemon balm shortbreads using this recipe.

  1  cup butter (do not use margarine)

  ½  cup powdered sugar

3–4 Tbl. fresh lavender, finely chopped

2 cups all-purpose flour

Preheat the oven to 300 degrees. Take the butter from the fridge—it needs to be cold. Cut the butter into small pieces and place them in to a large bowl, then thoroughly cream the sugar and lavender into the butter. Add the flour quickly, using your hands to mix if you have to. Refrigerate the dough for about twenty minutes. Turn the cookie dough out on a board that is lightly floured. Roll it until it is about ¼-inch thick, then cut into shapes. (Kids love shapes—use your imagination.) Bake the shortbread on a nonstick cookie sheet for fifty minutes, or until golden brown. Shortbread keeps well in sealed containers, so make lots to have on hand.

**Natural Licorice Candy**

Licorice helps alleviate cold and flu symptoms, is a natural (yet gentle) laxative, and kids love it.

1 cup blackstrap molasses

1 tsp. ground licorice root

1 tsp. ground anise root

Whole-wheat and all-purpose flour, mixed (two parts all-purpose to one part whole-wheat)

Warm the molasses in a large saucepan on low heat. Add the licorice and anise root. Add flour until you have a dense consistency that you can roll into tubes. Cut the tubes to a desired length. The candy hardens as it cools, and it will keep for a long time in the refrigerator.

**Fragrant Apple Crumble**

½ cup butter

1½ cups rolled oats

¼ tsp. salt

1 cup spelt flour (or whole-wheat flour)

1 cup brown sugar (or ½ cup maple syrup in ¼ cup flour)

5 large apples, cored and sliced

1 cup apple sauce

1 tsp. cinnamon

1 tsp. nutmeg

¼ cup dried rose petals (or ⅛ cup lavender)

Melt the butter, and mix into the dry ingredients. Press half of the mixture into the bottom of a baking dish. Layer apples and herbs and spices, and cover with applesauce. Cover all with the remaining dry ingredients. Bake at 375 degrees for thirty minutes, then turn up to 450 degrees to brown the top.

## Balmy Lemon Madeleines

½ cup butter (plus extra for greasing the pan)

2 large eggs

½ cup sugar

¼ cup plain yogurt

1 Tbl. lemon juice

Dash of vanilla extract

1 cup unbleached all-purpose flour

¼ tsp. kosher salt

3 Tbl. ground lemon balm leaves

½ tsp. freshly grated nutmeg

¼ cup molasses

Grated zest of 1 orange

Grated zest of ½ lemon

Preheat oven to 400 degrees. Generously butter a madeleine pan. Melt the butter, and cool it. In a mixing bowl, mix eggs, sugar, yogurt, lemon juice, and extract, then slowly add the remaining ingredients. Spoon a tablespoon of batter into each madeleine shell, and bake for twelve minutes or until the tiny cakes are golden brown.

## Herb Tea Loaf

This recipe is so easy and satisfying. Make it on a rainy day and play tea party all afternoon. Kids love to have this cake cut into small cubes. It fits on small tea set plates, and they can brag later about how many pieces they ate.

| | |
|---|---|
| 2 | cups unbleached flour |
| 1 | tsp. baking powder |
| ¼ | tsp. salt |
| 2–3 | Tbl. minced mint or lemon balm leaves |
| 1½–2 | tsp. fresh lavender or anise hyssop blossoms |
| ½ | cup milk |
| ½ | cup (1 stick) unsalted butter, softened |
| 1 | cup sugar |
| 3 | eggs, extra large |
| 1 | tsp. vanilla extract |

Preheat the oven to 350 degrees. Combine the dry ingredients and set them aside. Mix then herbs into the milk, and set aside. Cream the butter and sugar and beat in the eggs, one at a time, and the vanilla. Alternately add dry and wet ingredients to the sugar and butter mixture. Mix well. Pour the batter into a nonstick cake pan and bake for forty-five minutes, or until golden brown.

## Lightest Lemony Scones

This is a great winter morning recipe. Get the children to help, and then in the few minutes it takes to clean up the kitchen the scones are baked. Eat with jelly or jam and butter.

| | |
|---|---|
| 3 | cups whole-wheat flour (or all-purpose flour) |
| ⅓ | cup sugar |
| 2½ | tsp. baking powder |
| ½ | tsp. baking soda |
| ¾ | tsp. salt |
| ¾ | cup butter, cut into pieces (do not use margarine) |

1   cup buttermilk or yogurt

1   Tbl. grated lemon zest

1   Tbl. finely chopped lemon balm

Mix all the dry ingredients together, and cut in the butter with
two knives. Keep the mixture cool. Mix with your hands for only
a short time. Add the milk, zest, and herbs, and mix. Roll the
dough to a ½-inch thickness and cut into interesting shapes. Bake
at 425 degrees for ten to twelve minutes on a nonstick cookie sheet.

## Savory Treats

### Wagon Train Biscuits

My mother used to make these biscuits for my brother and I
when we were little. She called them Wooster biscuits, after
Charlie Wooster, the cook on the TV show *Wagon Train*. I
included variations in my recipe, so I renamed them. The tomato
paste variation results in biscuits that are tinged red-pink and
flecked with green. The cheese ones are chewy and a little salty.
The garlic-oregano ones are a bit like garlic bread.

2      cups whole-wheat or all-purpose flour

3      tsp. baking powder

1      tsp. salt

½      cup butter, cut with knives to pea-size pieces

⅔–¾    cup milk, yogurt, or buttermilk

Variations:

1      large clove garlic and ¼ cup finely minced fresh
       oregano (1 Tbl. dried), or

¼      cup tomato paste and ½ cup finely minced fresh
       basil (2 Tbl. dried), or

¾      cup shredded cheddar cheese and ¼ cup minced
       fresh sage (1 Tbl. dried)

Preheat the oven to 450 degrees. Combine the flour, baking
powder, and salt in a large bowl, and blend thoroughly. Cut in

the butter until the mixture resembles a coarse meal. Then mix in the savory flavorings of your choice: herbs, tomato paste, or cheese. Roll out the dough to ½-inch thickness, and cut it into interesting shapes. Bake for twelve to fifteen minutes. Eat these with soups, stews, or gobble them down slathered with butter.

## Presto Pesto

    1   cup fresh basil leaves, removed from stem
    3   large garlic cloves, peeled
    ¼   cup roasted pine nuts
    ¼   cup fresh grated Parmesan or asiago cheese
        Salt and freshly ground pepper to taste
        Olive oil

Purée the ingredients in a food processor, adding just enough olive oil to make a smooth paste. Pesto is great on pasta, vegetables, or on bread. It is easily stored in the freezer. Just thaw it and make your own Presto Pesto dish.

## Oven-Roasted Vegetables with Herbs

Kids love comfort foods, and this is a great cold-day treat. It is easy to prepare and has many variations. Use any combination of potatoes, sweet potatoes, acorn squash, carrots, and parsnips.

    3   large potatoes
    3   sweet potatoes
    6   carrots
    2   onions, peeled and cut into wedges
    1   head of garlic, separated into cloves and peeled
    ¼   cup minced rosemary
    ¼   cup minced thyme
    3   Tbl. olive oil

Cut all the vegetables into into bite-sized chunks. Heat the oven to 400 degrees. In a large bowl, toss all the ingredients together until the herbs are evenly spread. Place the mixture on a large baking sheet and bake, stirring occasionally, for one hour, or until golden brown. Add salt and pepper to taste.

## Herbal Garlic Butter

Garlic seems to be a taste that is often overpowering for children. I have modified garlic recipes so that the kids will eat them, but I usually set some minced garlic aside for adults who want more.

- 2 cloves garlic, finely minced
- 1 Tbl. minced basil
- 1 tsp. minced oregano
- 1 Tbl. minced marjoram
- 1 tsp. minced sage
- 1 cup butter, softened

Finely chop the garlic and the herbs. In a large bowl, combine the herbs with the butter and let the kids mash it up until it is creamy. Spread it generously on bread, rolls, or crackers. Pop them into the oven on a moderate setting until golden brown. This butter keeps well, but makes plastic containers smell like garlic.

## Monster Mash

Let's face it. Sometimes food seems slimy. Guacamole is easy to make, and great for kids—as it is rich in essential fatty acids—but, because it looks yucky, it is often hard to get kids to eat it. Why not get them to make it and learn to associate the weird looking food with lots of kitchen fun?

- 2 ripe avocados
- 1½ cups mild salsa
- 1 clove garlic
- Juice from 1 lime
- ½ cup finely chopped cilantro
- ⅛ cup finely diced red onion

Mash the avocados in a large bowl, add all other ingredients, and mix well. Serve with veggies, corn chips, or pita bread.

## Cream Cheese Please

There are a thousand variations to this cream cheese recipe. Try one of these below or make up your own. Get the kids to squish all the ingredients together until the cream cheese has a smooth consistency. Spread it on bread and bagels, or serve as a dip with sliced veggies and crackers.

In a mixing bowl, combine cream cheese and desired herbs or fruits (see below for suggestions). Mix well. Spread two table-spoons on each piece of bread. Sprinkle with paprika (savory) or calendula petals (sweet). Use a cookie cutter to make shaped sandwiches. As a fancy decoration, spread a little cream cheese on the edges of the sandwiches and then roll the edges in a mixture of chopped herbs or flower petals.

### Pizza Style Cream Cheese

To 1 eight-ounce package of cream cheese add:

½ cup sun-dried tomatoes, finely chopped

1 tsp. minced oregano

1 tsp. minced basil

1 tsp. minced chives

Salt and pepper to taste

### Lemony Orange Cream Cheese

To 1 eight-ounce package of cream cheese add:

⅛ tsp. stevia

Grated zest from 2 oranges

½ cup fresh lemon balm

Calendula petals

### Herbed Cream Cheese

To 1 eight-ounce package of cream cheese add:

½ cup lightly packed, finely chopped fresh herbs (parsley, watercress, basil, chives—in any combination)

1 Tbl. fresh lemon juice

Paprika

## Cucumber Mint Sandwiches

Every tea party needs a special sandwich. When we got tired of peanut butter and banana, we turned to this British tea party standard.

½ stick butter

2 Tbl. fresh mint leaves

8 thin slices whole-wheat bread, crusts removed

2 small cucumbers, peeled and thinly sliced

In a small bowl combine the butter and mint, and mix well. Spread the mint butter on the bread slices. Lay the cucumber on four of the slices and top with the remaining bread to make four sandwiches. Slice them in half diagonally.

# A Great Herbal Snack Life

Fortified with these great herbal snack recipes, you can start trying them out on the children in your life. Be sneaky, and be silent. Don't say a word about what you are making. Don't even whisper that you are trying something new.

Bake some Wagon Train Biscuits and put them out when you next serve soup. Or pack some Lavender Shortbread into tomorrow's lunches. I'm bet the worry will disappear, and all you will hear from your children is "Can I have some more?"

# Making Magical Herbal Teas

## by Jonathan Keyes

Around the Summer Solstice, I often travel to a secluded spot on the Sandy River very near Portland, Oregon. There, I begin my hunt for the elusive native herb known as mugwort. This beautiful plant can be difficult to find, even if you look quite carefully. I am able, however, to draw on years of experience to find mugwort's silver leaves ruffling gently in the breeze.

After locating some small stands, I usually ask permission to collect a few stalks of this gentle, yet powerful herb. I listen carefully to what messages the mugwort offers. It almost always will say what's on its mind. Before harvesting, I pull a little tobacco out of a pouch and give an offering. I always try to give back to the mugwort that I harvest, thus fostering a good relationship

for future harvestings in my favorite secluded and hard-to-find harvesting spots.

A few hours later I am home and brewing up a cup of mugwort tea in my kitchen. I can smell its stimulating, pungent, distinct aroma as the tea brews. The steam envelops me, and I begin to fall into the dreamy state that mugwort often elicits.

I then take a few sips and take in a little of mugwort's essence. It is bitter and strong. I can feel my taste buds and insides start to come alive. The mugwort starts to stir things up, get things moving. A knot of tension in my stomach starts to shift and turn, slowly untying itself and releasing the strain. A few more sips and I can feel my blood moving as a trickle of sweat forms on my brow. A half a cup later and the anxiety and stress in my system dissipates under a calm and even flow of energy that circulates through my body.

With each sip, mugwort draws me into her spell, magically soothing and uplifting me. I can hear her messages to "Be still" and "Unwind." I feel more receptive, more attuned, more open, and more myself. This simple tea has magically helped me transform and become fully present to the moment and the subtle vibrations around me.

## Tea-Crafting and the Four Elements

Herbal teas, when we make them with good intention and a good heart, have the ability to transform us. Each aspect of making a tea, from collecting or buying the herb to how we prepare it and drink it, is vital to whether it is a magical experience or just another activity in our day. Taking the time to truly craft a tea helps us to become wiser, healthier, and more attuned to the world around us.

Crafting tea is a time-honored tradition in places such as China and Japan where rituals are often performed in conjunction with tea making. Timing, presentation, and proper brewing methods are all coordinated to augment a sense of peace and tranquility and to come into harmony with the flow of the natural world.

Making magical teas starts with an understanding of the four basic elements that comprise the natural world—earth, water, fire, and air. Each of these elements is associated with particular aspects and processes of the natural world. Earth is associated with the trees, mountains, hills, valleys, and fields. Water is associated with the rivers, lakes, and oceans. Fire is associated with the Sun and the flame. And air is associated with the currents of wind and the sky.

When we make a magical herbal tea, we are communing with these natural elements and replicating the natural processes of the planet Earth at a basic level. In so doing, we are creating a relationship and harmonizing with the forces of nature through the simple practice of making herbal tea.

### *The Earth Element*

The first step in making herbal tea is to collect or find the best herbal material possible to put in your brew. This first step is vital because it is our initiation into creating a relationship with a particular herb. The best way we can do this is the way I described above with my mugwort: Collect it in its natural state in the wild. Gathering herbs can take some practice and a small amount of botanical knowledge of the plants in your native region. The reason wild plants are the best to work with is that they have evolved and adapted to find the perfect niche to grow and thrive in. This is where they feel most comfortable and at home. Because of this, they resonate with a greater strength and vibrancy. The soil conditions and the amount of light, heat, and moisture are in perfect harmony to allow the plant to grow.

Approaching a herb in its natural environment is similar to approaching any wild creature. It should be done with care and respect. If you can, take the time to learn the ways of the herb you are gathering. Read about it in herbal and botanical books. Get to know its shape, color, fragrance, and appearance.

After developing an alliance with a particular herb, learn what are its best parts to pick. For some herbs you may want to just collect the flowers. For others, you may want to collect the leaves, the roots, or just the root bark. Herb books will give you guidance on this matter.

Before gathering the herb, spend some time in contemplation and appreciation of the powers of the plant. Knowing what it is good for and how you will use it will help the plant give its life more easily. You may want to make prayers, offer tobacco or a strand of hair, or just speak words of appreciation and thanks. Make sure you do not overharvest. Try to limit your gathering to no more than 25 percent of a stand. Leave no trace of yourself behind.

If you are a novice at gathering herbs in the wild, ask an herbalist friend to take you on collecting expeditions. Herbalists have years of experience identifying herbs in the wild and will show you the best methods of collecting each individual herb. They'll also help you avoid poisonous plants when collecting.

Though it can be wonderful to collect a herb in the wild, cultivating and gathering herbs in your own backyard is also rewarding. Many herbs—such as lavender, chamomile, angelica, and peppermint—can be easily grown in the area around your house. Growing your own medicinal plants helps you to have a year-round relationship with them that helps in magical tea making. You can watch as each herb grows day by day, and you can give energy to the herbs through regular watering, pruning, composting, and mulching. Whether cultivated or gathered in the wild, try to harvest the herb before it gets too hot and the Sun starts to wilt the plant. Gather flowers and leaves in the spring or summertime. Gather roots after the energy of the plant has turned inward in the fall or very early spring.

Finally, the next best way to make a magical herbal tea is to buy the loose dried herbs from a reputable source—one that gives tender care to each herb they harvest. Check around and make sure the dried herb looks fresh and full of vital essence.

Avoid leaves that have turned brown or yellow or have splotches on them. Dried herbs should have retained their fragrance and color. You should be able to breathe in their essence.

Get to know the farmers and wildcrafters who gather herbs for you. Make sure they are doing their work in a positive, giving way. The better the herb is cared for, the better will be its effect. Store-bought herbs can sometimes be collected in a machine-like manner with little care and consideration. This diminishes the magical and healing properties of the herbs.

If you have collected a herb in the wild, I highly recommend making a fresh tea soon after you get home. Most herbal teas we drink are from dried plants, but I find that herbs give their most vital essence and best magical qualities when they are prepared fresh as soon after harvesting as possible. It is useful to have a patch of your favorite herbs growing in your backyard.

## Herbal Tea Making and Astrology

To make the herb collection experience more magical, you can pick days that are astrologically associated with the herb. By following the movement of the Moon through the zodiac, one can choose the best day for collecting. Many pocket astrological calendars will tell you what sign the Moon is in each day so you can plan your gathering days accordingly.

| Moon in | Ruler | Herbs to Collect |
|---|---|---|
| Aries, Scorpio | Mars | basil, cayenne, garlic, gentian, ginger, ginseng, hops, juniper, nettle, pine, sarsaparilla, tobacco |
| Taurus, Libra | Venus | burdock, catnip, feverfew, elder, western red cedar, licorice, mugwort, rose, thyme, vervain, violet, yarrow |
| Gemini, Virgo | Mercury | caraway, coltsfoot, dill, elder, fennel, lavender, oats, parsley, peppermint, red clover, valerian |

| | | |
|---|---|---|
| Cancer | Moon | aloe, cleavers, lemon balm, marshmallow, willow |
| Leo | Sun | calendula, chamomile, cinnamon, eyebright, goldenseal, hawthorn, rosemary, St. John's wort, sunflower |
| Sagittarius, Pisces | Jupiter | borage, chicory, dandelion, dock, echinacea, hyssop, maple, Oregon grape, rosemary, sage |
| Capricorn, Aquarius | Saturn | comfrey, horsetail, mullein, oak, plantain |

Along with knowing what astrological sign the Moon is in, it is also helpful to know the phase of the Moon. In general, waxing Moons are helpful for gathering the aerial parts of plants, such as the leaves and flowers. It is better to gather the underground portion when the Moon is waning.

I find that Full Moons are a particularly magical time for gathering herbs, as the energies on the planet are intensely vibrant and full of power. Collecting herbs at the Full Moon can help augment the strength and potency of the herb that is being gathered.

### *The Water Element*

After you have collected the best herb for your magical tea, make sure you have the best quality water as well. Though it may sound strange, not all water is the same. Yes, water may all contain the same one hydrogen and two oxygen molecules, but there is a lot more going on than meets the eye.

Water is the key medium for interacting between the human and the plant world. It is the mediator for helping there to be communication. The plants communicate through their complex chemistry of resins, alkaloids, minerals, and oils. Water helps deliver this message to the human body so that it can assimilate the information in the best possible way.

Water from wild places such as streams and rivers will be highly charged and carry the wildness of the land that it comes from. Often this type of water is more invigorating and helpful for those people who are weak or febrile.

Water that is from deep below the ground, such as from artesian wells, has an earthy quality that is very grounding and healing. This water can be helpful for calming and relaxing people. Oftentimes water contains minerals (this is known as hard water). Mineralized water will be healing in its own right, but will not extract as much nutrients and active constituents from an herb as will soft, or demineralized, water.

Choosing water for a magical tea is a very important part of the process. We wouldn't want to go to all the trouble of getting the freshest herbs and then use tapwater that is rife with pollutants. Either collect your water from a fresh source or use water that is purified in the best possible manner.

Once you have gathered good water, make sure to find a good pot to boil the water and a good vessel to pour the tea into. Cast-iron pots will leech iron into the tea, which can help heal those people who are more anemic and "blood deficient" in nature. Stainless-steel pots work great as well, but avoid anything that is aluminum or has a layer that can peel off.

Finding the right herbal teapot is an important part of the tea-making process. Beautifully designed and colorful pots add to the sense of sensual enjoyment. The best teapots are made of clay and are hand-sculpted by an artisan. The love and care that goes into making the teapot helps make the tea-drinking process more uplifting and magical.

## The Fire Element

Fire is the key alchemical tool for helping the herb deliver its medicinal and healing contents to the water. In traditional Europe, alchemy was known as the science that would transmute baser elements such as lead into precious metals such as gold. On a symbolic level, fire is associated with the spiritual effort and heat required to overcome baser instincts and to develop a mind and heart associated with God. This form of spiritual alchemy is at the root of practices such as tai chi and yoga. Heat generated from postures and movements helps to train the heart toward a goal of "attainment" or oneness with the divine.

In making herbal teas, using the right amount and source of heat is essential for drawing the best qualities from a plant and delivering it to the water. The fire element is instrumental in helping the plant communicate its magical gift to human beings.

In traditional times, tea would be made over a true flame. The type of wood used to make the flame would be important to the process. Cedar wood has different properties from maple, fir, or cherry. Unless you have a wood-burning stove that you can make tea on, it is unlikely you can consider these things. Flame from a gas-burning stove is the next best choice for making a good tea, because it burns efficiently and you can adjust it very easily. Electric stoves are also a good source of the fire element.

When working with the fire element, remember that it is very powerful and has an intelligence of its own. Fire will talk to you if you listen. If the fire gets too hot, the vibration emanating from your stove will seem angry or overly excited. If the heat from the stove is not enough, you will sense that it feels lacking. The proper amount of heat is essential to the process of making tea.

We should always think about the amount of heat we are using in our home environment, and this is especially true of heat for magical teas. Too much heat is wasteful. By connecting with the fire element, we start to be mindful of how much heat we use each day. Using the proper amount of heat helps us to develop a considerate and mindful heart. The process of making tea can then become a meditation for developing integrity when working with the fire element.

### The Air Element

To start the process of making tea, pour a quart of water into a pot and bring it to a boil. Then place an ounce of dried herb into your teapot. Once the water has boiled, pour the water into the tea pot and allow it to steep. While doing this, direct your intention to honoring the herbs and their properties. Give thanks and make prayers of gratitude for their healing powers.

After the water has been completely poured, take a moment to breathe in the aroma of the herbs now that they have been mixed with the water. This is the air element associated with magical tea making. Breathe in the herb's essence as it gently coats your mouth, throat, and bronchial passages. The uplifting qualities found in the essential oils in herbs can be tremendously beneficial to the respiratory tract, nerves, and immunological system.

After breathing in the infusion for ten or twenty seconds, make sure to cap the pot so the essential oils don't evaporate. Then let the tea sit for about ten to sixty minutes. Delicate, flowery herbs such as chamomile and elder flower should be consumed sooner as their properties can fade more quickly. Rooty teas can sit for up to an hour, as it takes a long time for their properties to completely dissolve into the water. The longer a tea sits, the more bitter it tends to become.

## Sun and Moon Tea

Aside from making teas over the stove, there are a couple of other magical ways to make tea. Making a Sun tea is a way of connecting with the original source of the fire element, the Sun. Sun tea is made by simply placing your herbs and water in a quart glass jar that sits out under the Sun. The water heats up with the Sun's rays. The herb delivers its medicinal and healing properties to the water, though it usually takes a little longer than making tea on a stove. You should generally wait about four to six hours before you drink this brew. Sun tea is especially helpful for those people who tend to be fatigued, cold, and depressed.

One of my other favorite ways of making tea is to utilize the magical power of the Moon. On the night of a Full Moon, follow the same directions as for the Sun tea, except place the glass jar out under the Moon. If you can, choose a time when the Moon is in the same sign that rules the herb (see table above).

Steep the tea for an entire night, and then drink it in the morning. The tea will be cold but will have taken in some of the essence of the Moon's energies. This is especially helpful for people who run too hot and tend to be anxious and "wired." Moon tea helps you to become more relaxed.

## Drink Your Tea!

After making tea, pour yourself a delicious cup. Use a strainer to strain out the herb and allow the tea to come through. Take some time to enjoy this sensuous and sumptuous experience. Find a favorite chair or relax into a bath and breathe in the aroma of the tea. Sip slowly and delicately. Never hurry your tea!

Taste the flavor of the tea, and feel how it affects you as you drink in its essence. Notice your change in mood. Allow the tea-drinking process to be slow and relaxing. This is not something to be rushed. After sipping a couple cups of tea, notice how you feel. The tea should have imparted its best medicinal qualities to you, and the alchemical process of harmonizing with the elements will have helped to transform and harmonize your spirit.

Making magical tea is simply the process of bringing mindfulness and good intention to every part of the tea-making process. It involves attention to detail along with respect for the herb. Through care and consideration, tea-making becomes a full-body and full-spirit experience that helps us to transform and become more fully alive and present.

Compare steeping a store-bought tea bag to going through the more involved process of crafting a magical cup of tea. See if you notice a difference. I know I have!

# Savory Herbs for the Crock Pot

### ❧ by Elizabeth Barrette ❧

Nothing says "cozy kitchen" quite like a crock pot. This slow-cooking kitchen device combines a level of convenience and versatility equaled by few other appliances. There's a special satisfaction in coming home to a house redolent with mouth-watering scents of bay, sage, oregano, beef stew, pork roast, or vegetable medley. Best of all, the crock pot is perfect for working a bit of herbal magic.

## What Is a Crock Pot?

Today, you can find a wide variety of appliances intended for slow-cooking recipes. The brand name Crock-Pot, also generically called a crockery cooker, refers to an upright appliance with a ceramic bowl, either removable or fixed. (If you can, get the kind with

the removable liner; they're much easier to clean.) The heating element usually wraps around the sides of the bowl, with a controller marked "high" and "low," and sometimes also "medium." The original Crock-Pot comes from Rival, and this company still makes some of the best available.

There are also some related devices that work similarly to the crock pot. A "slow cooker" or "multi-cooker" is an upright or horizontal appliance, usually with the heating element situated under the bowl. These often have a real thermostat. A "Dutch oven," meanwhile, refers to a large, horizontal appliance that is usually oblong or rectangular in shape. They may have a thermostat or a simple high/low setting, and usually have the heating element under the bowl. *Note:* Don't confuse the cheaper modern electric version of this device with the older, better-quality, cast-iron type of Dutch oven.

All of these devices run on electricity and can be used for almost anything—from relatively short recipes like soups that only need to simmer for a half-hour, on up to all-day recipes where you pack in the ingredients and ignore it until the day has passed. They deliver a steady heat with minimal risk of burning. For this article, the term "crock pot" covers all of the above devices. The same herbs work in any appliance intended for leisurely recipes.

## The Modern Cauldron

In researching this article, I discovered that magical cookbooks have largely overlooked the crock pot in their discussion of equipment for heating or cooking recipes. In his excellent volume *Wicca in the Kitchen*, Scott Cunningham covers various devices in chapters labeled "Cups, Bowls, and Pots" and "The Cauldron," but there is no info on the old crock pot. Karri Ann Allrich offers a wonderful chapter on "Using Herbs and Spices Magically" in her *Cooking by Moonlight*. But she too ignores what could well become a key device for the modern Pagan.

The crock pot is the modern cauldron. After all, almost every kitchen has one. It serves exactly the same function as the historic cast-iron cauldron, which is to cook a substantial amount of food slowly and gently. Plus, the crock pot benefits from technological advances—it runs on electricity instead of requiring a fire, and as such offers better control of temperature and is easier to clean.

You can safely leave a crock pot unattended too—something that is not advisable with a cauldron. The crock pot represents the great Goddess and the feminine principle. In elemental terms, it balances fire and water. And although you can find plain ones, most crock pots are decorated with discreetly magical designs: Greek key patterns, apple boughs, cornucopias, and so forth.

Used regularly for magical or spiritual purposes, a crock pot builds up a respectable aura of energy, just as with any altar tool. Every ritual feast and Pagan potluck include at least one crock pot recipe. What's more, it's easy to match herbal correspondences and flavors to the intent of your sabbat, spell, or other ceremonies. Set your intent when you fill the crock pot, and it keeps working for you all day.

And if you are worried about the lack of "tradition" behind this modern cauldron, don't be. When the cast-iron cauldron was first introduced, it was considered the cutting edge of technology too!

## Crock Pot Stars

Certain herbs have a well-earned reputation for holding up their flavor through long cooking and for working in a medley of other ingredients. These make the best choice for crock pot recipes, although you can round them out with other herbs and spices.

The list includes everything from ubiquitous seasonings like sage to unusual ones like juniper. You can charts that show which herbs go well with which foods—these will be helpful if you wish to experiment with herb recipes. Consider also making your own chart for magical correspondences (or use the chart I've provided at the end of this article).

Now let's take a close look at our crock pot stars.

## *Basil*

Basil grows as a small bushy plant. Dried basil leaves typically work best in a crock pot, as fresh basil turns to mush when cooked. However, some recipes rely on basil paste or pesto, best made from fresh leaves immediately before use.

Basil's sweet, spicy scent soothes frayed tempers and brings happiness. It also sweetens the breath and aids digestion. Its flavor defines spaghetti sauce and other Mediterranean foods. Basil also goes well with chicken, lamb, rabbit, carrots, mushrooms, and potatoes. It actually intensifies during cooking—a real asset in leisurely recipes. Serve basil-based recipes for Beltane or Lammas, or for crescent Moon esbats.

This herb is ruled by the planet Mars and the element Fire. Use it in spells for love, prosperity, or protection.

## *Bay*

Bay leaves come from a tree. Always use one dried, whole leaf rather than a crumbled batch of leaves. Bay grants courage and purifies the area. Priestesses of Apollo chewed bay leaves for prophetic visions, and the branches are still used in Yule decorations.

The powerful taste of bay leaves goes well with dark meats and robust stews like beef, venison, potatoes, and tomatoes. Serve it for Mabon or Yule. This herb is ruled by the Sun and by the element of fire. Use it in spells for healing, protection, success, or enhancing magical abilities.

## *Chives*

Chives look like miniature onions. The leaves serve equally well fresh or dried, and the pink flower heads make an attractive garnish. Magically, chives help ward off negative energy and hostile entities.

With a more delicate flavor than onion, chives complement chicken, pork, carrots, and tomatoes. The connotations of spring inherent in the growth of chives make it a good choice for Imbolc or Ostara. Chives also work nicely for esbats held at the crescent Moon. This herb is ruled by Mars and fire. Use it in spells for prosperity or protection.

## Coriander

Coriander is the round seed of the cilantro plant. If you use whole seeds, be sparing in their use—as their taste is sharp and sour. For a more milder, more blended effect, use powdered coriander.

Pregnant women may eat coriander to make their child more intelligent. Coriander also stimulates the appetite and soothes upset stomachs. Some consider it an aphrodisiac, and so serve it at Beltane or Midsummer, or for Full Moon esbats. Its tangy flavor makes coriander a fine match for beef, chicken, mushrooms, or tomatoes. This herb is ruled by Mars and fire. Use it in spells for healing or love.

## Garlic

Garlic grows as a plump bulb underground. You can get dried garlic either chopped or powdered, but fresh garlic is far superior. Garlic is sacred to Hecate. It repels all manner of negative spirits or energy.

When eaten before a contest or confrontation, garlic grants its consumer an extra dose of courage. Its potent flavor complements strong foods such as beef, pork, and potatoes. Garlic also is used in numerous world cuisines to flavor vegetable dips and other dishes. Consider garlic dishes for Samhain or Yule, and for use during dark Moon esbats. This herb is ruled by Mars and by fire. Use garlic—sparingly—in any spells intended for healing, for protection, or for success.

# Ginger

Ginger is a knobby root, available in many forms. Ginger powder is convenient in recipes, but the freshly grated root yields by far the best flavor. Ginger soothes digestion and reduces flatulence. Eat ginger before spellwork to increase your power.

Ginger's sweet, intense heat accents chicken, lamb, pheasant, and carrots. Take advantage of its warming quality for winter events like Yule and Imbolc. This herb is ruled by Mars and fire. Use it in spells for love, prosperity, success, or for general magical enhancement.

# Juniper

Juniper bushes yield small, wrinkled black berries that are used as an occasional flavoring in some dishes. Always remove the berries from your dish before serving. Also note, a little bit goes a long way.

Juniper stimulates the appetite nicely. Men may carry the berries to increase their potency and fertility. The unique resinous taste goes well with pork and venison; it also adds interest to barbecues and soups. Serve juniper dishes for Samhain or Yule. This herb is ruled by the Sun and fire. Use it in spells for healing, love, or protection.

# Marjoram

Marjoram is a low-growing plant with rounded leaves. You can use it fresh, but the dried leaves crumble very nicely to make a rub for meats. Sacred to Aphrodite, marjoram promotes happiness and affection. Historically, it played a key role in wedding feasts.

Serve marjoram dishes at handfastings to sanctify the union. Marjoram dishes also work well for Beltane or Midsummer rituals. The herb's sweet, charming flavor combines well with just about everything.

Marjoram herb is ruled by Mercury and air. Use it in spells for healing, love, prosperity, or protection.

## Onion

Onions form round bulbs underground, though with green onion you can also use part of the stem. Onions holds up especially well in a crock pot, becoming tender without turning to mush. Although often considered a vegetable, this herb has potent properties of its own, with magical uses going back for centuries.

The Egyptians painted onions in their tombs, so consider serving this herb for Samhain. Also, round white onions are perfect for Full Moon esbats. Hot onion intensifies the flavor of many dishes, while sweet onion has a mellower effect. Cook onion with beef, lamb, pheasant, or beans. This herb is ruled by Mars and fire. Use it in spells for healing, prosperity, or protection.

## Oregano

Oregano grows into a luxurious, small-mounded plant, with soft oval leaves pointed at the end. The dried or fresh leaves of oregano both work nicely in cooking, especially if you save some fresh sprigs for a garnish on roasts.

Oregano fosters a sense of peace and well-being, and helps prevent indigestion. It has a more robust flavor than marjoram, its close relative, and combines well with beef, pork, upland birds, tomatoes, and broccoli. Oregano is a good choice for Lammas or Mabon dishes. This herb is ruled by Mercury and air. Use it in spells for healing, love, or protection.

## Parsley

Parsley comes in two forms, flat leaved and curly leaved. Dried parsley flakes often retain their nice green color even after cooking, so they are often a good choice in crock pot recipes. Fresh curly parsley sprigs layered under a roast help keep it from sticking to the bottom of the pot.

Parsley also has a breath-sweetening quality, and so is often added to garlicky, oniony dishes. It promotes fertility and wards off misfortune. Ironically, parsley also appears in funeral feasts and decorations; therefore, serve it at Ostara or Samhain.

Parsley's delicate green taste complements chicken, rabbit, and any vegetable. It particularly helps blend other flavors around it. This herb is ruled by Mercury and air. Use it in spells for love or protection.

## Pepper

Pepper comes in a rainbow of colors, each with a subtly unique flavor. This is the quintessential crock pot herb, as it appears in most recipes. Whole peppercorns are ideal if you remove them after cooking. Use fresh-ground pepper in recipes for a more blended effect.

Pepper banishes evil and adds kick to magic and food alike. Suitable for any sabbat, it works especially well for dark Moon esbats. Its hot flavor enhances beef, lamb, venison, beans, and potatoes. Pepper is ruled by Mars and fire. Use it in spells for protection or success.

## Rosemary

Rosemary is a spiky little plant with narrow leaves like evergreen needles. The whole leaves, fresh or dried, hold their shape well when cooked. They convey a sense of uplifting youthfulness.

Rosemary also aids the memory. Its sharp, resinous flavor brightens dark meats such as beef and various types of water-fowl. It also accents potatoes and tomatoes. Serve rosemary dishes for Mabon or Samhain. This herb is ruled by the Sun and fire. Use it in spells for healing, love, magical enhancement, or protection.

## Sage

Sage begins as a soft plant but turns itself into a low, woody shrub with leathery leaves over time. Dried sage imparts a robust, slightly musky flavor. Fresh sage has the same depth but with a delightful lemony note. Crumble dried sage leaves when you add them to recipes. Fresh leaves may be chopped or left whole if you want to remove them later.

Sacred in some Pagan traditions, sage is ideal for feast foods or altar offerings at any sabbat. It also aids digestion. Its complex taste enriches chicken, venison, waterfowl, beans, carrots, and tomatoes. This herb is ruled by Jupiter and air. Use it in spells for healing, protection, or success.

### *Thyme*

Thyme forms a dense mat of tiny leaves and stems, making an excellent ground cover. Its diverse types yield a range of flavors, from the robust and musky English thyme to the milder mother-of-thyme and the sprightly lemon thyme. Thyme works well either fresh or dried, but take care to chop it finely or the stems can stick in your teeth.

Legend says that eating thyme enables you to see fairies. It soothes stomach upsets as well. Serve thyme-flavored dishes at Ostara or Midsummer. It also serves well for esbats at any phase of the Moon. The flavor of thyme combines nicely with chicken, lamb, upland birds, beans, mushrooms, or potatoes. This herb is ruled by Venus and water. Use it in spells for healing, love, protection, or enhancing magical power.

## Combinations and Correspondences

You can apply the above herbs in various ways. One is to add the herbs directly to the other ingredients when you put everything in the crock pot. Another option is to combine herbs in a mortar or food processor, and then rub the blend into the meat before cooking.

A perfect crock pot trick is to tie the herbs in a muslin bag, called a sachet, which you can easily remove after cooking. This works especially well with bay leaves, juniper berries, peppercorns, and other herbs that are no fun to bite into.

The following lists give a general rundown of good herbal combinations and their magical and other correspondences. Feel free to begin experimenting; just be ginger any time you add a new herb to an old recipe.

## Meat-Herb Combinations

**Beef:** bay, coriander, garlic, ginger, marjoram, onion, oregano, parsley, pepper, rosemary, thyme

**Chicken:** basil, bay, chives, coriander, garlic, ginger, marjoram, oregano, parsley, rosemary, sage, thyme

**Lamb:** basil, chives, coriander, garlic, ginger, marjoram, onion, oregano, pepper, rosemary, thyme

**Pork:** basil, garlic, juniper, marjoram, onion, oregano, pepper, rosemary, sage, thyme

**Rabbit:** basil, bay, marjoram, parsley, rosemary, sage

**Upland birds:** basil, ginger, marjoram, onion, oregano, pepper, thyme

**Venison:** bay, juniper, marjoram, onion, pepper, rosemary, sage

**Waterfowl:** bay, marjoram, rosemary, pepper, sage

## Vegetable-Herb Combinations

**Beans:** garlic, marjoram, onion, oregano, parsley, pepper, sage, thyme

**Broccoli:** basil, garlic, marjoram, oregano, parsley

**Carrots:** basil, chives, ginger, marjoram, parsley, sage, thyme

**Mushrooms:** basil, coriander, garlic, marjoram, oregano, parsley, rosemary, thyme

**Potatoes:** basil, bay, chives, marjoram, oregano, parsley, pepper, rosemary, sage, thyme

**Tomatoes:** basil, bay, chives, coriander, garlic, marjoram, oregano, parsley, rosemary, sage, thyme

## Herbs for Various Types of Cooking

**Barbecue:** basil, garlic, ginger, juniper, oregano, pepper

**Chili:** coriander, garlic, onion, oregano, pepper

**Roasting:** bay, garlic, onion, pepper, rosemary, sage, thyme

**Sachets:** bay, coriander, juniper, marjoram, pepper, thyme

**Soup:** garlic, juniper, marjoram, onion, parsley, rosemary, thyme

**Spaghetti sauce:** basil, garlic, onion, oregano, pepper, sage

**Vegetable medley:** basil, chive, ginger, marjoram, onion, thyme

## Herb Correspondences for Esbats

**Dark Moon Esbats:** garlic, juniper, pepper, sage

**Crescent Moon Esbats:** basil, chives, ginger, parsley

**Full Moon Esbats:** bay, coriander, marjoram, onion

## Herb Correspondences for Sabbats

**Samhain:** garlic, juniper, onion, parsley, rosemary

**Yule:** bay, garlic, ginger, juniper, pepper

**Imbolc:** chives, ginger, pepper, sage

**Ostara:** chives, parsley, thyme, sage

**Beltane:** basil, coriander, marjoram, sage

**Midsummer:** coriander, marjoram, thyme, pepper

**Lammas:** basil, oregano, pepper, sage

**Mabon:** bay, oregano, rosemary, pepper

## Herb Correspondences for Spells

**Healing:** bay, coriander, garlic, juniper, marjoram, onion, rosemary, thyme

**Love:** basil, coriander, ginger, juniper, marjoram, rosemary, thyme

**Magical power:** bay, ginger, rosemary, sage

**Prosperity:** basil, chives, ginger, marjoram, onion

**Protection:** basil, bay, chives, garlic, juniper, onion, rosemary, sage

**Success:** bay, garlic, ginger, pepper, sage

# A Crock Pot Conclusion

Bring a little witchery into your kitchen by taking advantage of the modern cauldron—the crock pot. Its convenience and versatility can add a lot to your spells and ritual feasts. By studying the herbs most compatible with crock pot cooking, you can learn how to combine them for best culinary and metaphysical effect.

When people step into your house, breathe deeply, and exclaim, "Mmm! That smells wonderful. How do you do it?" You can smile and reply, "Magic."

# For Further Study

The following books are listed for your further research and enjoyment. I've also annotated some notes about particular chapters and sections that may be most interesting and appropriate to your culinary and magical crock pot creations. Enjoy!

Allrich, Karri Ann. *Cooking by Moonlight: A Witch's Guide to Culinary Magic.* St. Paul, Minn.: Llewellyn Publications, 2003.

See especially: "Using Herbs and Spices Magically," pp. 31–42.

Bremness, Leslie. *The Complete Book of Herbs: A Practical Guide to Growing & Using Herbs*. New York: Viking Studio Books, 1988.
Features generous description of herbs and their processing. See especially "Culinary Herb Gardens," pp. 30–31; "A Roman Cook's Herb Garden," p. 34; "A Witch's Herb Garden," p. 35; "Herbs in the Kitchen," pp. 163–193; and instructions for harvesting and storing herbs, pp. 269–270.

Cunningham, Scott. *Cunningham's Encyclopedia of Magical Herbs*. St. Paul, Minn.: Llewellyn Publications, 1991.
Offers extensive listing of herbs and their magical properties, including correspondences.

———. *Cunningham's Encyclopedia of Wicca in the Kitchen*. St. Paul, Minn.: Llewellyn Publications, 2003.
See "The Cauldron," pp. 15–16; the author also discusses many aspects of magical cooking throughout the book.

Kowalchik, Claire, and William H. Hylton, eds. *Rodale's Illustrated Encyclopedia of Herbs*. Emmaus, Penn.: Rodale Press, 1987.
Features an extensive guide to herbs and their uses, with a special chapter, "Cooking with Herbs," pp. 114–124, that lists what herbs go best with which vegetables and meats.

Pillsbury Company. *One-Dish Meals Cookbook: More than 300 Recipes for Casseroles, Skillet Dishes, and Slow-Cooker Meals*. (Maureen Rosener, ed.) New York: Clarkson Potter Publishers, 1999.
See "Slow-Cooker Meals," pp. 233–309; includes tips for successful slow-cooking and some other basics.

———. *Pillsbury Doughboy Slow Cooker Recipes: 140 New Ways to Have Dinner Ready and Waiting!* New York: Clarkson Potter Publishers, 2003.

Weatherstone, Lunaea, ed. *Soul Stirrings: The SageWoman Cookbook.* Point Arena, Calif.: Blessed Bee, Inc., 1999. Includes some crock pot and herb recipes, plus magical essays.

# Dandelion and Chicory Coffee

### ✤ by Tammy Sullivan ✤

**B**elieve it or not, the humble dandelion, especially when mixed with a bit of chicory, makes a nice and healthy substitute to your daily cup of joe. These two plant items can be brewed singly, blended together, or added to coffee for medicinal benefits and a gourmet flavor.

## The Story of Two Misfits

While both dandelion and chicory are generally thought to be troublesome weeds, they in fact have quite a pedigree in medicinal and culinary use.

### The Dandelion

The dandelion is known as *taraxacum officinale*, lion's tooth, piss-a-bed, monk's head, puffball, priest's crown, and swine's snout. The dandelion grows in fields, meadows, roadsides, and waste places.

As to vital statistics, the dandelion is a perennial that grows between two to twelve inches in height. Its flower is a golden yellow, one to two inches in diameter, and solitary atop a smooth, hollow stem. It opens in full daylight and closes at dusk. The leaves form a rosette on the soil surface and are between one to eighteen inches in length, jagged, grooved and emerge directly from the root. The dandelion flowers from June to October.

In general, the dandelion's leaves are used to make a magenta dye, and its flowers are used to make a yellow dye. Once the flower matures, the petals wither and it forms a puff-ball seed head that disperses with the wind.

The dandelion has an auspicious history in the medical field and was classified a drug for more than one hundred years in the United States. Ancient Egyptians knew and used the plant, but it was Arabian physicians of the Middle Ages who first officially recognized the healing properties of the dandelion. It is used for cleansing purposes, to treat obstructions of the liver, gall bladder, and spleen, and as a diuretic.

European women have rinsed their faces in dandelion water for centuries, due to its ability to fade freckles and its refreshing effects. Dandelion water has been used to treat eczema, scurvy, and other skin problems. Today a tonic made from dandelion is a common ingredient in European herbal baths. Dandelion, if rubbed about a person's body, is said to have the ability to make one feel welcome wherever one goes. It is also thought to grant wishes. Dandelion does have the ability to predict the weather to a degree. If rain is coming, the flowers close up tight.

Surprisingly, dandelion leaves are edible and delicious. They are often added raw to spring and summer salads. They are also boiled and steamed with seasonings for a side dish. The leaves and flowers are commonly brewed into wine.

## Chicory

Chickory, also spelled chicory, is known as *Cichorium intybus*, suc-cory, wild endive, and blue sailors. Like the dandelion, it is also a perennial. The name "blue sailors" stems from a legend about a beautiful young girl whose true love abandoned her and went off to sea. Left alone, she waited by the roadside for his return. The Gods took pity on her and turned her into the chicory flower, so she may forever be a delight for all to see.

The chicory grows from two to five feet in height. The leaves are jagged, groovy, and hairy, and they grow directly from the root, forming a rosette on the soil surface up to twelve inches in length. The flowers are generally blue, but also sometimes pink or white, and they look similar to those of the dandelion.

The greens of the chicory are not only edible, but highly desirable and marketed in many supermarkets as endive. Radicchio is a curly leafed, reddish type of chicory. The chicory root may be treated as a vegetable and boiled and eaten with butter. This plant grows wild on roadsides and waste places, and flowers from June to October. If you boil the leaves of the chicory plant a vivid blue dye is produced.

Chicory roots were used for making a hot beverage similar to coffee, in France, long before coffee was introduced there. The French have used a mixture of chicory and coffee for hundreds of years. Chicory is said to be a counter stimulant for caffeine and is used to decrease the bitterness of coffee.

Magically known as an herb of love, chicory, when used in secret, is said to enflame the lover of your choice with passion. For a thriving romantic life, wear a chicory flower on your person. Be sure to replace it every fifteen days or so. Like its counterpart the dandelion, chicory has a long history in medicine. It is used to treat digestive disorders as a cleansing agent, and Culpepper recommended it for swooning of the heart. Bach lists it as a corrective for those who love selfishly.

Legend states that chicory, when eaten in certain ceremonies, has the power to render one invisible. It is also thought to have the ability to open locks, and if gathered on the night of July 25 at midnight, holds special power. Both the dandelion and chicory are endowed with a long taproot. The root is used for the coffee making process. If a piece of root is left when harvesting, a new plant will grow.

# Harvesting Tips

Harvesting chicory roots should be undertaken in late spring or early summer, before the roots become too hard. It is best to cultivate the plants in your own garden, as chicory roots become increasingly bitter after two years, but be prepared for a battle. Left on its own, chicory sets itself firmly in place. The taproots of these plants are long-reaching and strong. It is much easier to harvest this plant after a heavy rain. Pulling chicory from your garden, on the other hand, tends to be simpler due to the looser, cultivated soil.

Dandelion roots are best harvested in the fall of the year. They should be harvested before the plant flowers. Because they are very juicy you need to take extra steps with dandelion to improve the drying procedure. Begin by scrubbing and peeling the root, then slicing it, being very careful not to bruise the root. You should steam the root pieces until the milky juice no longer seeps from them. Alternately you may choose to use a dehydrator before the roasting process.

# Roasting Tips

To roast these herbs, the roasting process is the same for dandelion as it is for chicory. Gather the roots and scrub them vigorously with a stiff brush. Slice and roast slowly at 200 degrees Fahrenheit. When they are a dark brown color all the way through, set them aside to cool, then store in a tightly closed container. You might wish to grind the roots fresh each time you use them, for premium taste.

Dandelion coffee, on its own, has a slight chocolaty taste, while chicory alone may have a bit of a caramel taste. At the last third of the roasting process, pay special attention to the smaller pieces. If they seem to be getting a bit too brown, spray them with cool water to stop the roast. Be careful not to char the roots.

The benefits of using chicory and dandelion as a substitute for coffee are that you are reducing your caffeine intake and cleansing your system. Chicory is known to lower blood sugar. Both dandelion and chicory are known for curing digestive disorders, and both are known for being helpful to the liver and digestive system. Adding chicory and dandelion to traditional coffee, however, is a flavor explosion, and a good way to stretch your coffee supply.

# Brewing Tips

You will want to use whatever measurements suit your palette, but a good rule to follow is to use one level teaspoon of total ingredients per cup of boiling water. If you grind the roots finely you can use the mixture as you would use an instant coffee. For more coarsely ground roots, you may use any traditional coffee brewing method. It is important to use only fresh, clear water when brewing your coffees. Coffee is 98 percent water, and bad water means bad coffee.

My favorite recipe, is to use three parts dandelion, two parts chicory, and two parts coffee. Since chicory has a tendency to darken the color of coffee, many people mistakenly assume that the resulting flavor will be stronger. You can sweeten your brew, no matter the proportions, with sugar and cream as you would traditional coffee, or you may wish to use flavored syrups. The addition of chicory and dandelion enhances the flavor of espresso and other coffee drinks.

Another recipe: Take twelve ounces of cold leftover chicory and coffee, and place it in your blender. Add about one-half cup of whole milk, and a good dollop of flavored syrup, and blend. You may also add a few chocolate chips or fresh fruit to the mixture.

## Chicory Café au Lait

This beverage requires no more than a cup of warm milk and a small piece of roasted chicory root. Combine the two in a small saucepan and heat on low, stirring constantly, until it is heated thoroughly. Pour into a cup and enjoy. The great thing about this drink is since there is no caffeine, you may drink it anytime of the day or night with no worry of losing sleep.

### The Absolute Best Cup of Coffee Recipe

Coarsely grind two parts coffee, two parts chicory, and three parts dandelion. Boil four cups of water in a pan. When the water is boiling, turn off the heat and add eight tablespoons of your coffee mixture. Add eight tablespoons of sugar, and stir slowly until the sugar is dissolved. Let it rest for about five minutes. Strain the mixture into cups using a fine strainer or sieve.

This coffee will have some grit in the bottom, so don't stir it and don't drink the last sip. The coarser the grind, the less grit. If you wish to add milk, heat it separately to the point of boiling. Take the strained cup of coffee and pour it and the hot milk into another cup at the same time, allowing it to bubble and mix itself perfectly. One sip and you will see why I call it the Absolute Best Cup of Coffee.

### Iced Coffee

Whisk together two tablespoons of your brewed coffee mixture and one cup of cold milk. Pour this mixture over ice cubes. You may garnish with whipped cream and sprinkles if desired.

*Note:* Any and all of these recipes can be made using chicory and dandelion only, if your goal is to eliminate coffee completely from your diet.

# An Herbal Thanksgiving Celebration

### ❧ by Lynn Smythe ❧

You can wonderful herb-and-spice-infused dishes to serve at your next big traditional Thanksgiving dinner. Or, you may choose to enjoy the recipes by hosting a Mabon celebration. Mabon is the time-honored Witches' Thanksgiving feast, otherwise known as the Fall Equinox, occurring around September 21 each year. Consult Llewellyn's *Moon Sign Book* for the exact date.

To me a Thanksgiving feast is all about the side dishes and other accompaniments, while the turkey is a bonus. This article features a variety of appetizers, salads, side dishes, and dessert recipes to add to your turkey.

## Obtaining Herbs

I have the luxury of living in southeastern Florida where my Zone 10 organic garden provides me with fresh herbs year-round. If you have a garden and grow your own herbs, you could harvest extra and freeze or dry them so they are ready to use whenever you need them. Also, many grocery and health food stores now stock packages of fresh herbs on a continual basis in their produce sections. Or you could start an indoor herb garden by growing herbs in containers, which will be available even through the cold winter months.

Although I prefer the taste of fresh herbs, dried herbs can be substituted for fresh if necessary. Use approximately one teaspoon of dried crushed herb to replace each tablespoon of fresh herb.

# Herb and Spice Blends

I have included some classic herb and spice blends that work well to flavor many holiday recipes. You may be able to find some of these blends in the spice section of your local grocery store. You can also experiment and make your own blends to lend a unique flair to your own recipes.

### Pepper Blend

Sprinkle this blend into soups, stews, sauces, and gravies as a nice change from regular black pepper. Place all the ingredients into a peppermill and grind as needed.

1   tsp. black peppercorns

1   tsp. white peppercorns

1   tsp. allspice berries

1   tsp. juniper berries

### Pie Spice Blend

Add this mix to pumpkin, apple, or other types of pie. It can also be used in hot mulled apple cider. I use preground spices to put this blend together. This recipe makes approximately two and a half tablespoons of pie spice blend.

2　tsp. cinnamon

1　tsp. cloves

1　tsp. ginger

1　tsp. nutmeg

1　tsp. allspice

### Poultry Seasoning

Use this seasoning blend to flavor chicken, turkey, duck, or Cornish game hen. It also makes a great addition to any kind of stuffing that is served along with your poultry dishes.

1　tsp. celery seed

1　Tbl. fresh marjoram, minced

1　Tbl. fresh sage, minced

1　Tbl. fresh savory, minced

1　Tbl. fresh thyme leaves

# Thanksgiving Recipes

Depending on the actual number of guests coming to your Thanksgiving dinner you may choose to make all or just a few of these dishes. A variety of appetizer, side dish, entrée, and dessert recipes have been included for you to choose from.

### Pre-Meal Delights

**Hot Mulled Cider**

This wonderful brew can be left on the stove throughout the duration of your holiday meal if desired. It imparts a wonderfully aromatic scent that permeates the house and adds to the festive mood. I like to serve this to my guests as soon as they arrive.

1　gallon apple cider

2　whole cinnamon sticks, broken into pieces

2　star anise pods

1　Tbl. whole cloves

1   one-inch piece fresh ginger root, peeled and sliced

Peel from 1 orange

Unsalted butter

Ground nutmeg for garnishing

Pour the apple cider into a large stock pot, and place the pot on the stove over medium heat. Place the broken cinnamon sticks, star anise pods, cloves, ginger, and orange peel onto a piece of cheese cloth. Fold the edges of the cloth over, and tie it with a piece of string. Place the spice bundle into the pot of apple cider, and let it come to a boil. Immediately reduce the heat to low, and simmer for thirty minutes. To serve, fill a mug with the cider, add a teaspoon of butter, and sprinkle with a little bit of nutmeg.

**Potato Leek Tart with Nutmeg and Chives**

This tart is a wonderful dish to serve as either an appetizer or entrée depending upon what other foods are being served at your Thanksgiving celebration. Spreading the cheese onto the bottom of the tart shell after prebaking it helps to prevent the crust from becoming soggy.

For the crust:

1½   cups whole wheat flour

½   tsp. ground nutmeg

½   tsp. salt

½   cup (1 stick) butter, chilled

1   egg

2   Tbl. water

1   cup Swiss cheese, shredded

Preheat your oven to 375 degrees. Place the flour, nutmeg, and salt in a large mixing bowl. Mix the butter into the flour using a pastry knife or two knives until it has the texture of coarse corn meal. In a small bowl, whisk together the egg and water, then add it to the flour mixture, using your hands. Thoroughly mix all the ingredients together. Press the dough into the bottom and sides of a greased, ten-inch tart pan. Prick the bottom and sides of the crust a few times with a fork. Place the pan in the oven and bake for ten minutes. Remove it from the oven, and immediately spread the cheese over the bottom of the crust.

For the filling:

    2   Tbl. olive oil
    2   cups potatoes, peeled and diced
    2   cups leeks, chopped
    3   eggs
    ¼   cup milk
    ½   cup heavy cream
    ½   tsp. ground nutmeg
    ⅓   cup chopped fresh chives
    ½   tsp. salt

Add the olive oil to a large frying pan set over medium heat. Add the potatoes and cook for five minutes. Add the leeks and cook for another ten minutes. Place the potato and leek mixture onto the bottom of the prepared tart shell. In a mixing bowl whisk together the eggs, milk, cream, nutmeg, chives, and salt. Pour the egg mixture into the tart shell. Place the tart pan in the oven and cook (at 375 degrees) for forty to fifty minutes until the eggs are set and no longer runny. Remove the tart from the oven, and let it cool five to ten minutes prior to cutting. Cut the tart into wedge-shaped pieces. This recipe makes approximately sixteen appetizer or eight dinner-size servings.

## *Breads and Rolls*

### Buttermilk Sage Biscuits

The sage in these biscuits makes a wonderful flavor enhancer to complement your Thanksgiving turkey.

    1¼   cups all-purpose flour
    2    tsp. baking powder

½   tsp. baking soda

½   tsp. salt

1   tsp. granulated sugar

6   Tbl. butter, chilled

2   Tbl. fresh sage, finely chopped

¼   cup buttermilk

Preheat your oven to 450 degrees. In a large mixing bowl sift together the flour, baking powder, baking soda, salt, and sugar. Cut the chilled butter into the dry ingredients using a pastry blender or two knives until it has the appearance of coarse corn meal. Add the sage and buttermilk and stir until well blended. Spray a twelve-compartment muffin pan with nonstick cooking spray. Fill each compartment approximately halfway. Place the pan in the oven and bake for twelve to fifteen minutes until golden brown. This recipe makes twelve biscuits.

### Cranberry Basil Muffins

I like to eat these muffins along with turkey salad with sage (recipe below) the day after Thanksgiving.

1   cup all-purpose flour

1   cup cake flour

½   cup granulated sugar

1   Tbl. baking powder

1   tsp. baking soda

6   Tbl. butter, chilled

1   cup buttermilk

1   cup fresh sweet basil, minced

1   cup dried cranberries

Preheat your oven to 400 degrees. In a large bowl, sift together the all-purpose flour, cake flour, sugar, baking powder, and baking soda. Cut the butter into the flour mixture using a pastry knife or two knives until it has the texture of coarse cornmeal.

Stir in the buttermilk, basil, and cranberries. Spray a muffin pay with nonstick cooking spray then evenly divide the dough into each compartment of the pan. Place the pan in the oven and bake twelve to fifteen minutes until golden brown. Makes twelve muffins.

## Popovers

I remember the first time I experienced popovers. I was eight years old and visiting my grandparents in Florida. We were eating at a fancy steak house when the waiter brought out a basket of these delights. I've been a convert ever since. The savory version can be made as a dinner accompaniment, whereas the sweet version can be served as a dessert along with sweetened butter or whipped cream on the side. The directions are the same for either version, though the ingredients are slightly different.

Savory popover ingredients:

| | |
|---|---|
| 2 | eggs |
| 1 | cup milk |
| 1 | cup all-purpose flour |
| 1 | Tbl. melted butter |
| 1 | Tbl. fresh thyme leaves |
| 1 | tsp. paprika |
| ½ | tsp. salt |

Sweet popover ingredients:

| | |
|---|---|
| 2 | eggs |
| 1 | cup milk |
| 1 | cup all-purpose flour |
| 1 | Tbl. melted butter |
| 1 | Tbl. granulated sugar |
| 1 | tsp. ground cinnamon |
| 1 | tsp. ground allspice |

Preheat your oven to 450 degrees. In a large bowl, whisk together the eggs and milk. Sift in the flour and stir well. Stir in the remaining ingredients. Grease and flour a muffin pan. Fill nine of the muffin compartments half full with the batter. Bake at 450 degrees for twenty minutes. Without opening the oven turn the heat down to 350 degrees and continue to bake for another twenty minutes. Remove the popovers from the muffin pan and serve immediately. If they remain in the muffin pan for more than a minute or two they have a tendency to become soggy. Makes nine popovers.

## Sweet Butter

Whisk together a half stick of room-temperature butter, one cup confectioner's sugar, and one teaspoon of vanilla extract. Serve with the sweet version of the popovers if desired.

### Salads

## Cranberry Clove Orange Salad

This dish is a cranberry salad variation, served at Thanksgiving. My kids also like it as delightfully fruity snack any time of the year.

> 2 three-ounce packages of raspberry gelatin
>
> ½ tsp. ground cloves
>
> 1 cup boiling water
>
> 1½ cups cold water
>
> 1 eleven-ounce can mandarin oranges, drained
>
> 1 sixteen-ounce can whole berry cranberry sauce

Place the gelatin and cloves into a medium mixing bowl. Pour in the boiling water, and stir until the gelatin is dissolved. Stir in the cold water, and place the bowl in the refrigerator until the gelatin is partially set (about one hour). Remove the bowl from the refrigerator, and stir in the mandarin oranges and cranberry sauce. Cover the bowl, and return it to the refrigerator until the gelatin is fully set (about four hours).

## Cranberry Pecan Salad with Basil, Mint, and Orange Dressing

This makes a wonderful green salad which can be served as part of your Thanksgiving dinner.

For the salad:

    6   cups mixed greens (iceberg, romaine, butter greens, spinach, and so on)

    1   cup dried cranberries

    1   cup pecans, chopped

    1   cup carrots, peeled and shredded

Tear the lettuce into bite-sized pieces, and place them in a large salad bowl. Add the cranberries, pecans, and carrots, and toss well. Prior to serving, drizzle on some of the dressing and toss well. Offer additional dressing on the side, if desired.

For the dressing:

    1   cup sour cream

    1   cup rice vinegar

    ½   cup orange juice

    1   Tbl. fresh basil leaves, minced

    1   Tbl. fresh mint leaves, minced

    ½   tsp. salt

    1   cup vegetable oil

    1   Tbl. Dijon-style mustard

Whisk together all the ingredients in a small bowl until well blended, or pour all the ingredients into a canning jar and shake well. Makes approximately one and a half cups dressing. Left-over dressing can be stored in the refrigerator for up to one week.

## Side Dishes

### Creamed Onions with Thyme and Nutmeg

This recipe makes a wonderful side dish. Pearl onions are deliciously sweet and not at all pungent like regular onions.

    1   pound pearl onions

    3   Tbl. butter

    3   Tbl. all-purpose flour

½ tsp. ground nutmeg

½ tsp. salt

2 cups milk

2 Tbl. fresh thyme leaves

½ cup dry bread crumbs

1 Tbl. butter, melted

1 Tbl. freshly grated Parmesan cheese

Slice the ends off the pearl onions. Add water to a small saucepan and bring it to a boil. Add the onions to the pan and blanch them for five minutes. Remove the pan from the heat, drain off the hot water, and cover the onions with cold water to slightly cool them. Drain off the cool water, peel off the onion skins, and place them in a glass, 1½-quart baking dish. Preheat your oven to 350 degrees. Melt the butter in a small saucepan set over medium heat. Whisk in the flour, nutmeg, and salt, and cook for one minute. Whisk in the milk, and continue heating while whisking until the sauce begins to thicken. Remove the pan from the heat, and stir in the thyme. Pour the sauce over the onions. In a small bowl mix together the bread crumbs, melted butter, and parmesan cheese. Top the onions with the seasoned bread crumbs, place the dish in the oven, and bake for thirty minutes. Let it cool slightly before serving, as this dish will be very hot.

## Garlic and Parsley Mashed Potatoes

The amount of garlic that you add to these potatoes depends upon your personal preference. My husband and I love garlic so we always add at least ten cloves of garlic when making this recipe. You may want to use fewer cloves.

5–10 whole cloves garlic

½ cup (1 stick) butter

2 pounds potatoes, peeled and cut into quarters

½ cup milk

½ tsp. salt

1 tsp. white pepper

1 cup fresh parsley, finely chopped

Blanch the unpeeled garlic cloves in boiling water for three minutes. Drain the hot water, pour cold water over the cloves, then peel off the skins. Smash each garlic clove with the flat side of a large kitchen knife. Melt the butter in a small sauce pan and add the smashed garlic, then simmer on low heat for twenty minutes. Fill a large stock pot with water and bring to a boil, then add the potatoes and cook for twenty minutes, until the potatoes are tender. Drain off the water. Add the garlic/butter mixture, milk, salt, and white pepper to the potatoes and mash well. Add the parsley and serve immediately. Makes six to eight servings.

## Lemon Balm Stuffing with Fruit and Walnuts

Using vegetable broth in place of the chicken broth in this recipe makes it suitable for vegetarians.

2 Tbl. vegetable oil

2 cups celery, diced

2 cups apples, peeled, cored, and chopped

2 cups mushrooms, chopped

1 fifteen-ounce package unseasoned bread cubes

⅓ cup fresh lemon balm, finely chopped

2 Tbl. fresh sage, minced

2 cups chicken broth

1 cup (2 sticks) unsalted butter, melted

1 cup walnuts, chopped

1 cup dried cranberries, chopped

Preheat your oven to 375 degrees. Add the oil to a large frying pan over medium heat. Cook the celery and apples in the oil for five minutes. Add the mushrooms, and cook for another five minutes. Place the mixture in a large bowl. Add the bread crumbs, sage, and lemon balm to the bowl. Stir in the chicken broth and melted butter, and mix well. Stir in the walnuts and cranberries. Place the prepared stuffing into a greased three-quart baking dish. Place the dish in the oven and bake for forty-five minutes, stirring occasionally to keep it from burning on the bottom.

## Minty Carrot Bites

This is one of my favorite cooked-vegetable recipes, and I usually don't like the taste of cooked carrots. The mint and honey add a nice refreshing flavor to these carrots.

>     2   Tbl. butter
>     ½   cup honey
>     2   Tbl. water
>     4   cups carrots, peeled and sliced into ¼-inch pieces
>     ⅔   cup fresh spearmint leaves, finely chopped
>     2   Tbl. lemon juice

Place the butter into a large frying pan on a burner set to medium. Add the honey, water, and carrots, and bring to a boil. Reduce the heat to medium-low, cover the pan with a lid, and simmer for five minutes. Remove the lid, turn the heat up to medium, and cook for five to ten minutes while stirring occasionally. When the carrots begin to caramelize and most of the liquid has evaporated from the pan, remove the pan from the heat, and stir in the chopped mint and lemon. Serve this dish immediately.

## Sweet Potato Cakes with Nutmeg

>     ½   cup heavy cream
>     ½   tsp. ground nutmeg
>     2   eggs
>     ½   cup all-purpose flour
>     4   cups sweet potatoes, peeled and shredded
>     ⅔   cup vegetable oil

Sour cream (optional)

Maple syrup (optional)

In a medium bowl, whisk together the cream, nutmeg, eggs, and flour. Stir in the sweet potatoes, and mix well. Heat one-third cup of the oil in a large frying pan over medium heat. Make individual potato cakes by pouring in approximately one-quarter cup of the batter and flattening each cake by pressing down with a spatula. Add the additional oil to the pan if needed. Cook until the cakes are well browned on both sides (approximately three minutes per side). Place the finished potato cakes on a paper towel–lined plate to absorb any excess oil. Serve with sour cream or maple syrup on the side if desired. Makes approximately ten sweet potato cakes.

## Entrées

### Oven Roasted Turkey with Tarragon Orange Sauce

This recipe is a change from the traditional roasted turkey. This dish can also be made with a large roasting chicken or duck instead of turkey.

For the turkey:

1   turkey

2   Tbl. olive oil

1   recipe Poultry Seasoning (see recipe located in the "Herb and Spice Blends" section of this article on page 100)

Remove any giblets or other organs from inside the turkey. Rinse off the turkey, and pat it dry. Place the turkey on a rack in a large roasting pan. Rub the olive oil over the turkey using a pastry brush or paper towel. Spread the seasoning over the top of the turkey. Cook the turkey according to the package directions.

For the sauce:

1   cup butter

1   cup all-purpose flour

2 tsp. orange zest

2 cups orange juice

½ cup white wine

1 Tbl. fresh tarragon, minced

½ tsp. salt

1 Tbl. heavy cream

In a small saucepan, melt the butter over low heat. Whisk in the flour and cook for one minute. Whisk in the orange zest, orange juice, wine, tarragon, and salt, and bring the sauce to a boil over medium heat. Turn the heat down to low, and simmer until the sauce has thickened. Remove the pan from the heat, and whisk in the cream. Serve this sauce along with the prepared roasted turkey.

## Turkey Salad with Sage

This is a tasty way to use up your leftover turkey. Serve it along with the Cranberry Basil Muffins (on page 104) if desired. This salad can also be made with leftover chicken.

2 cups leftover cooked turkey, chopped

½ cup celery, diced

½ cup walnuts, chopped

½ cup mayonnaise

1 Tbl. fresh sage, minced

½ tsp. salt

1 tsp. pepper blend

Mix all the ingredients together in a bowl. Chill the salad in the refrigerator until ready to serve. This recipe makes three cups of salad.

## *And Last, But Certainly Not Least—Dessert*

At our house, we are usually so full after eating such a large Thanksgiving meal that we have little room for dessert. For those of you still desiring a sweet treat after you've finished your big Thanksgiving meal, here is the recipe for one of my favorite holiday desserts.

## Carrot Cake with Cream Cheese Frosting

This is one of my favorite desserts to serve during the holidays.

For the cake:

- 2 cups all-purpose flour
- 2 tsp. baking soda
- 2 tsp. baking powder
- 1½ Tbl. Pie Spice Blend (see recipe in the "Herb and Spice Blend" section of this article on page 100)
- ½ tsp. salt
- 1⅓ cups vegetable oil
- 2 cups granulated sugar
- 4 eggs
- 2 Tbl. fresh cinnamon basil, minced
- 3 cups grated carrots
- 1 cup chopped walnuts

Preheat your oven to 325 degrees. In a large mixing bowl sift together the flour, baking soda, and baking powder. Stir in the pie spice blend and salt. In a another bowl mix together the oil, sugar, eggs, and cinnamon basil using a hand-held electric mixer. Stir this mixture into the flour mixture. Add the carrots and walnuts and stir well. Place the batter into a greased and floured 13 x 9-inch baking pan. Place the pan into the oven and bake for one and a half hours or until a caketester inserted into the middle comes out clean. Let the cake cool before frosting.

For the frosting:

- 1 eight-ounce package of room temperature cream cheese
- ½ cup (1 stick) room temperature butter

2 tsp. vanilla extract

4 cups sifted confectioner's sugar

Mix together the cream cheese and butter in a bowl using a handheld electric mixer. Stir in the vanilla extract. Mix in the confectioners sugar one cup at a time until the frosting is well blended. Makes approximately three cups of frosting, a perfect amount for the carrot cake.

Herbs for
Health

# Rejuvenating Rosemary

## ❧ by S. Y. Zenith ❧

Rosemary (*Rosmarinus officinalis*) is one of the most versatile herbs used in the traditional folk customs of many countries. The therapeutic use of rosemary can be traced back to Greek and Roman times. Ancient Greeks burned rosemary on their shrines, and their great classical writers Dioscorides and Theophrastus mentioned its use for stomach and liver problems. Rosemary is one of the most rejuvenating herbal medicines available to us today, and its long history is testament to its worth as a healing herb.

## Ancient Rosemary

Rosemary is a very ancient herb. Hippocrates, the "Father of Medicine," prescribed rosemary for cooking along with vegetables to overcome liver and spleen disorders. The Romans used infusions of rosemary for weakness of the heart, poor circulation, anemia, and nervous exhaustion. The infusion was also used for cleansing wounds, easing coughs, and soothing chest ailments. Greek and Roman students once wore wreaths of rosemary during their exams as a brain stimulant for energizing alertness and memory recall, and heightening sensory perception.

Revered as a symbol of remembrance, rosemary was used during weddings as decorations especially during the Middle Ages in Europe. Traditionally, rosemary was included in the bride's bouquet or worn on her hair as an indication of fidelity. Later, it was customary for female members of bridal parties to each hold a sprig of rosemary in their right hands during a wedding ceremony as testimony that the bride was still a virgin. Nuptial bed linen was scented with rosemary. Brides who wanted to ensure their husband's fidelity would present grooms with a sprig of rosemary on the wedding night.

One of the components associated with funeral rites for ancient Egyptians included the use of rosemary in embalming processes. Prospero Alpini, a renowned archaeologist, discovered rosemary sprigs within the wrappings of a mummy in Cairo. Some traces of rosemary have also been found in Egyptian tombs dating back to the civilization's First Dynasty, circa 2000 BC.

In the Anglo-Saxon *Leech Book of Bald*, from circa AD 1000, rosemary is mentioned as a protection against evil spirits and a remedy for toothache. In a French treatise of the thirteenth century, Arnauld de Villeneuve mentioned the distillation of rosemary plants into essential oils for use as a remedy. An old French name for rosemary is *incensier*, indicating its use as an incense. During World War II, French nurses used rosemary leaves and juniper berries for fumigating hospital wards.

The legendary "Queen of Hungary Water" utilizes rosemary as a principal ingredient. This detoxifying and regenerative "water" was said to have transformed a fourteenth-century paralytic and gout-ridden seventy-two-year-old monarch into a blooming beauty. While there exists many so-called "original" recipes for Queen of Hungary Water, the basic mixture consists of the flowers and flowering tips of the rosemary plant macerated and steeped for one month in alcohol. The plant is then strained through fine muslin, and the resulting decoction is consumed in small doses of less than a teaspoon to alleviate rheumatism and other related aches and pains. See page 126 for an alternative recipe version of Queen of Hungary Water.

Rosemary has not been limited to use only in ancient European healing practices. Chinese herbal doctors traditionally mix rosemary with ginger for treating headaches, indigestion, insomnia, and malaria. Topically, the herb is also used for treating baldness.

In modern times, an aromatherapy study claimed that a mixture of rosemary, thyme, lavender, and cedar wood massaged into the scalp generates hair growth and slows the process of balding. Known also to calm palpitations and strengthen the heart, rosemary is noted in the official German pharmacopoeia in a recipe for rosemary massage oil that can be rubbed over the heart region. Napoleon was fond of large quantities of eau de cologne containing the oil of rosemary. Arabs traditionally sprinkled fine rosemary powder on the umbilical cords of newborn infants as an astringent antiseptic.

## The Rosemary Plant

Shrubby and aromatic rosemary grows well near salt water and prefers light, well-drained soil. Like lavender, rosemary can be trimmed to make excellent hedges. It is one of the easiest plants to propagate. The plant layers and grows from either root division or heeled cuttings. Rosemary grows wild in many rocky locations of the Mediterranean. It is woody and evergreen. Rosemary shrubs thrive well in areas with copious light and year-round warmth.

Rosemary is lovingly cultivated in many countries throughout the world for its aromatic and volatile oil, the most important active principle of the herb. Apart from valuable oil, the plant also contains bitters and tannins.

## The Magical Uses of Rosemary

The name of the rosemary plant is derived from the Latin *ros marinus*, which means "dew of the sea." It is of the family of *Labiatae*, and its ruling planet is the Sun. When utilized in magical rituals, rosemary is known to enhance mental powers, love, purification, protection, exorcism, and healing. Rosemary is burned to dispel negativity and other impure vibrations or presences. Sleeping with a sprig of rosemary under the pillow at night prevents nightmares. When placed underneath the bed, rosemary sprigs protect from harm, malevolent thought-forms, and foreign entities.

Spaniards referred to rosemary as *romero*, or "pilgrim's flower." In both Spain and Italy, rosemary has been a time-honored safeguard against sorcery and baneful spirits especially while undertaking long journeys. The herb's connection to the sea is evident in some of its folk names—such as "compass plant," "polar plant," and "compass weed." Perhaps it is no coincidence that the diagram on the background of compasses—the one that shows all directions relating to the north—is still referred to as "mariner's rose."

After an exhausting day of negative occurrences, a warm bath taken with Epsom salts and some fresh rosemary, or drops of rosemary essential oil, purifies personal energy fields. Before and after healing sessions, healers wash their hands with rosemary infusions to remove unwanted vibes.

Rune masters, tarot card readers, and other practitioners of divinatory arts and sciences also benefit from the use of rosemary in their work. Powdered rosemary can be strewn on floors to expel bane. For discharging the energies of oft-used crystals, place them in a bowl with powdered rosemary, cover with a cloth, and leave overnight before washing the crystals in salt water. Rosemary makes a good substitute for frankincense in spell work.

### Properties of Rosemary

The properties of rosemary are numerous. The herb is an adrenal cortex stimulant, analgesic, antiseptic, antispasmodic, astringent, carminative, cephalic, digestive, diuretic, and hepatic. Rosemary is prescribed for a whole host of complaints including asthma, arteriosclerosis, baldness, cirrhosis, colds, colitis, debility, dyspepsia, fainting, flatulence, gall stones, gout, headache, hepatic disorders, hysteria, influenza, jaundice, mental fatigue, nervous disorders, palpitations, rheumatism, scabies, skin care, whooping cough, and simple wounds.

### The Side Effects of Rosemary

Generally, all medicines, whether natural or synthetic, have side effects. When trying out a new herb for the first time, it is essential to pay attention to any uncomfortable or unusual physical symptoms. If experiencing unpleasant reactions such as dizziness, nausea, or headaches, it is important to reduce dosages or stop taking the herb altogether. If it does not feel right, do not take it any longer.

It is known that pharmaceutical medicines may sometimes interact adversely with each other or with certain foods. Interactions differ from person to person. Herbal medicines and herbal byproducts are no exception. It pays to be careful and mindful when taking more than one medication and herb or combinations of both.

Pregnant women and persons suffering from epilepsy or high blood pressure should take special precautions. For temporary relief of morning sickness, use direct inhalation from an essential oil bottle or try the vaporization method (a few drops of rosemary essential oil dissolved in a spray bottle of water), but take care not to use more than five drops of oil. If ever in doubt, consult an appropriate medical professional such as your family doctor, herbalist, naturopath, aromatherapist, or other competent health-care practitioners before using any of the rosemary recipes herein.

# Rosemary in Health, Beauty, and in the Kitchen

### Rosemary Hair Care

Add a few drops of rosemary essential oil to your hairbrush or use in rinsing water or shampoo. Rosemary, when massaged into the scalp, discourages dandruff and assists in healthy hair growth. An alternative to using rosemary oil is to simmer rosemary leaves in boiling water for half an hour for use as a hair tonic (after it cools). A simple hair rinse can also be made by putting a half cup of rosemary leaves in a cheesecloth bag and soaking it in two cups of boiling water.

### Rosemary Infusion

For an aromatic and mild infusion to settle the stomach, clear a stuffed nose, relieve rheumatic aches, or assist with indigestion, use one teaspoon of crushed fresh rosemary per cup of boiling water. Steep the infusion for ten to fifteen minutes. It is recommended that no more than three cups of this infusion be drunk per day. An infusion made from rosemary leaves can be bottled and stored in the refrigerator for use as an antiseptic and mouth gargle.

### Flower Water Decoction

A decoction is an extract of herbs produced by boiling the herb in water for a longish period of time. This method is especially used for the hard seeds, roots, and barks of herbs. It produces a liquid stronger than an infusion as a result of prolonged simmering. Decoctions are recommended for children and those with weak constitutions. They can be drunk on their own, made into syrups or douches, added to honey or to baths, floor washes, and laundry rinsing.

Rosemary water decoction is a great astringent for improving the complexion. It also makes a revitalizing body spray during lethargic periods in winter, and a cooling one in summer when stored in a spray bottle. Put four tablespoons of fresh rosemary and one and a half cups water into a steel saucepan, and bring to a simmer. Cover the pan and allow the contents to simmer for thirty minutes. Remove from heat, cool, strain the mixture, and squeeze any remaining liquid from the herbs. If a stronger scent is preferred, repeat the process and add more rosemary to the liquid. Remember to top up if required.

### Rosemary Compress

Soak a pad in a hot rosemary infusion and use for sprains. Be gentle, and alternate the warm pads with cold ice packs every two or three minutes.

### Rosemary Herbal Liniment

Apply this herbal liniment in massage to ease sore muscles and joints. It is also helpful for warming muscles before exercising. Gather one-half cup chopped rosemary leaves, one-half cup of chopped peppermint leaves, two tablespoons chopped cayenne pods, two tablespoons grated fresh ginger, six bay leaves (broken into pieces), and two cups olive (or other oil of personal choice).

Immerse the herbs completely in the oil, then put the oil into a double boiler with the lid on. Boil on very low heat for one hour. Remove the pan from heat, and let the herbs steep for another two hours. Strain the herbs and bottle the oil. Store it in a cool place.

### Insect Repellent

Dried rosemary is effective for repelling moths, fleas, and other winged pests. It can be used alone or combined with other herbs such as lavender, southernwood, mint, or woodruff. For a more potent mixture, add orris root, crushed cinnamon, or crushed cloves. Put the mixture into small bags, and place the bags in the wardrobe, linen cupboard, or drawers. Protect favorite clothing on hangers by attaching a decorative bag to the hangers with pieces of ribbon or silken threads. These also make appealing gifts to those fond of rosemary. Rosemary bags hung around the house also help deter insects. When it is mosquito season, rub a few rosemary leaves on your skin.

### Foot Massage Oil

A handful of freshly cut rosemary stalks used with safflower oil and one teaspoon cider vinegar are soothing for tired feet after a long day. Pack the rosemary stalks into a small glass container with the safflower oil and seal it. Shake the container daily for three weeks. Strain the oil into a bottle and use whenever you need it.

### Rosemary Bath Oil

Thirty minutes spent in a hot bath perfumed with rosemary bath oil and Epsom salts is greatly invigorating. To make the oil, pack one cup of chopped fresh rosemary into a glass jar. Gently warm one and a half cups of sunflower oil in a saucepan on very low heat for fifteen minutes, then pour the oil into the jar and seal. Place the jar in a sunny spot for two weeks, and shake each day. After this period, pour the jar's contents into a saucepan again to warm slightly. Strain through a double layer of muslin, discard the rosemary, and pour the oil into a bottle.

### Aromatic Herbal Bath

This is a seventeenth-century bath recipe that uses several aromatic herbs—including rosemary. When using fresh herbs, a handful of each is enough. For dried herbs, one teaspoonful of each is sufficient. The herbs are rosemary, bay leaves, peppermint, marjoram, lavender, wormwood, mint, lemon balm, and thyme. Boil the herbs in a saucepan of water for ten minutes. Remove the pan from heat, and set aside to cool. Strain the mixture into a clean jar, and add half a bottle of brandy to it. Put the lid on, and shake the jar a few times before pouring into a special bottle. Use no more than two tablespoons in each bath.

### Rosemary Body Lotion

A basic but useful rosemary body lotion when chilled in the refrigerator, gives a soothing effect during warm weather. Ingredients are simply one-third cups rosemary infusion or flower water and two tablespoons of glycerin. Whisk rosemary water and glycerin together in a small glass bowl then pour into a small jar and seal. Shake well before using.

### Rosemary Facial Sauna

A facial sauna, or "steam bath," activates perspiration necessary for the skin's pores to expel impurities. This refreshes the skin and improves texture. Rosemary also possesses astringent qualities and is therefore beneficial for oily skin. Pour one to two quarts of boiling water over a handful of rosemary leaves in a basin or large glass bowl. Position your face directly over the steam. Drape a towel over the head to form a "tent" to prevent steam from escaping. Take care not to overexpose your skin to the temperature of the hot water. Inhale for five to ten minutes. When the steam subsides, pour more hot water into the bowl if you wish. This facial sauna is not only beneficial to the skin but also helps clear sinuses. After a facial sauna, wash your face with cool water before applying your usual toner and moisturizer. This facial sauna is not recommended for very dry skin, overtly sensitive skin, and those with dilated red veins. If in doubt, consult a beautician.

### Rosemary Aftershave Splash

A rosemary aftershave is refreshing and mildly antiseptic. As one of the appealing ingredients of the classic eau de cologne, it also makes an ideal gift for men. To a glass container, add ten drops rosemary essential oil, six drops bayberry essential oil, five drops lemon essential oil, and two drops lime, sage, and sandalwood essential oils. Dissolve and blend well the combination of essential oils in one-third fluid ounces of tincture of benzoin, then add one-half fluid ounces of witch hazel to the same container. In another glass container, add two fluid ounces of rosewater and two fluid ounces of cider vinegar, and mix. Pour the oils from the first container into the second container. Ensure that the mixture is thoroughly blended before pouring the whole into a glass bottle with a nonmetallic lid.

### Queen of Hungary Water, Alternate Version

This modern version Queen of Hungary Water is based on a traditional variant of the original formula thought to be in the handwriting of the Queen of Hungary, dated AD 1235. It is preserved in a museum in Vienna. Gather four tablespoons of crushed fresh rosemary, three tablespoons crushed fresh mint, three tablespoons of crushed rose petals, one tablespoon of lemon rind, three and a half fluid ounces of orange flower water, two fluid ounces of purified water, and five fluid ounces of perfume base alcohol or pure vodka.

In a saucepan, combine the herbs, flowers, lemon rind, orange flower water, and purified water. Cover the saucepan with a lid and bring the mixture to a boil. Reduce heat and let simmer for thirty minutes. Remove from heat with saucepan lid intact, and let it cool.

Using fine muslin, linen, or cotton, strain the flowers and herbs from the fragrant water. Those who prefer a stronger mixture can repeat the process with the same water, adding more flowers and herbs. When satisfied, add alcohol to the fragrant water, pour it into a bottle, and seal and store it away from heat and sunlight. The concoction generally takes two weeks to merge and mature.

## *Four Thieves Vinegar*

This particular vinegar contains rosemary as one of the ingredients, and has its unique place in history because of its use during the days when bubonic plague epidemics were rife in Marseilles, France. "Four Thieves Vinegar" gained its name and notoriety from four real-life rogues who robbed the dying and the dead, often stealing directly from their helpless victims. Having doused themselves with an ingenuous liquid concoction, the four thieves were immune to the epidemics.

After their capture and during subsequent interrogations by the authorities of the time, they were given an opportunity to escape execution if they would disclose their "health secret." The respected French medical historian Jacques Dupreau discovered the old recipe in the archives of Marseilles. He graciously shared it with John Heinerman, a widely traveled medical anthropologist who penned *Heinerman's New Encyclopedia of Fruits and Vegetables* and several other books.

The method—according to the "old recipe"—for making Four Thieves Vinegar involves using one quart of red wine vinegar, preferably obtained from the second pressings of red grapes. Add two chopped garlic cloves, two chopped shallots, and one tablespoon each of powdered cinnamon, cloves, and nutmeg. Then add one teaspoon each of rosemary, sage, and wormwood. Put all ingredients in a bottle and seal. Place it in a cool place for seven days and shake the bottle once a day.

## *Rosemary Mead*

Queen Elizabeth I of England was believed to have been fond of metheglin, a rosemary-flavored alcoholic mead. A modern variation is easily concocted using a handful of fresh rosemary tips and a generous serving of dry white wine in a medium to large glass jar. Soak the rosemary tips in the wine for at least three days before straining and storing in a dry, clean bottle.

As a general tonic, rosemary wine is prepared by steeping a handful of fresh or dried herb for one week in a good quality dry red or white wine. Alternatively, you can use sherry or port instead of wine. After the curing period of one week, strain the rosemary-flavored wine into a decanter or bottle. No more than three small glasses a day should be consumed half an hour after a meal.

### Rosemary Vinegar

Herb vinegars are simple and inexpensive to make. They are also delightful gifts for the culinary inclined. A basic rosemary herbal vinegar is made by putting washed sprigs into a jar and filling it with vinegar. White wine vinegar is the best, but plain white vinegar or cider vinegar is also commonly used. Store the vinegar in a dry, cool, and dark cupboard for two to three weeks. Shake the jar each day to ensure that the rosemary flavor steeps into the vinegar. When the required flavor and strength is achieved, strain and pour into a bottle. Add a fresh sprig for enhanced decoration, and seal.

### Rosemary with Olives

In a jar, place some rosemary leaves, black olives, a few cloves of garlic, and one strip of lemon peel, and fill the jar with virgin olive oil. Seal the jar, and leave it in the larder to marinate for three to six months before using.

## Some Other Uses of Rosemary

### Rosemary-Scented Stationery

Personal stationery can be decorated and scented with rosemary. One way to add this little extra delightful touch is to make a slit in the back of a greeting card and insert a sprig of rosemary for both decoration and fragrance. Dried rosemary can be gently glued to writing paper and envelopes, just be sparing with the herb. Springs of rosemary inserted into cotton pouches or sachets placed in a writing compendium or stationery box infuses the paper with a gentle fragrance.

## Some Further Culinary Tips

The flavor of rosemary leaves is strong when added to dishes. A little goes a long way, thus it is advisable to use it very sparingly in stews, casseroles, and sauces. For those fond of meat, rosemary goes especially well with lamb. It also helps digestion when a touch is eaten with rich dishes such as roast duck and pork.

A sprig burned on the barbeque while grilling sausages and chops will lend a nice flavor to the meat. For fish and poultry, adding a bit of rosemary provides zest and sumptuousness. Keep a jar of sugar containing rosemary sprigs for sprinkling over fruit pies. Rosemary flowers can be frosted by dipping them in egg whites and fine sugar and then leaving to dry. Use these as edible garnishes in salads.

# For Further Study

Cunningham, Scott. *Cunningham's Encyclopedia of Magical Herbs.* St. Paul, Minn.: Llewellyn Publications, 1994.

———. *Magical Aromatherapy: The Power of Scent.* Scott Cunningham. St. Paul, Minn.: Llewellyn Publications, 1994.

Fisher, Kathleen. *Herbal Remedies: Dozens of Safe, Effective Treatments to Grow and Make.* Emmaus, Penn.: Rodale Press, 1999.

Garland, Sarah. *The Complete Book of Herbs and Spices: An Illustrated Guide to Growing and Using Culinary, Aromatic, Cosmetic and Medicinal Plants.* Pleasantville, N.Y.: Reader's Digest Association, 1993.

Hedley, Christopher, and Non Shaw. *Herbal Remedies: A Practical Beginner's Guide to Making Effective Remedies in the Kitchen.* New York: Smithmark Publishing, 1996.

Heinerman, John. *Heinerman's Encyclopedia of Fruits, Vegetables, and Herbs.* West Nyack, N.Y : Parker Pub. Co., 1988.

Le Strange, Richard. *A History of Herbal Plants.* London: Angus & Robertson, 1977.

Thomson, William A. R. *Healing Plants: A Modern Herbal.* London & Basingstoke, U.K.: Macmillan London Ltd., 1978.

Tisserand, Robert. *The Art of Aromatherapy.* London: C. W. Daniel, 1977.

# Ginger Compresses

### ❧ by Chandra Moira Beal ❧

G inger is a herb with many useful and healing qualities. The
roots are readily available at
most supermarkets, and a ginger compress is easy to make. A compress is the
name for a piece of cloth that has been
dipped into a liquid, wrung out, and
then applied to the surface of the body.
Compresses can be hot or cold.

## Ginger Facts

The use of ginger dates back 4,400
years to Egypt in the time of Cheops,
when people first made gingerbread.
The Chinese imported ginger for tea
to act as an aid to indigestion or colds.
The yang/heat-generating qualities of
ginger make it a masculine herb ruled
by Mars. Ginger is all about fire.

Carried in your purse or pocket,
ginger can ensure prosperity. It draws

adventure and new experiences, and promotes sensuality, sexuality, and personal confidence. Ginger draws power, success, and love. Ginger adds to the strength and speedy effectiveness of any mixture in which it is included.

## How a Ginger Compress Works

The purpose of a ginger compress is to increase the circulation of blood and body fluids, especially where stagnation exists. Strong heat dilates the blood vessels and melts mucus and fatty accumulations. It also helps break up mineral crystallizations. The strong heat of ginger can penetrate deep into the body, even into organs.

Use ginger compresses to alleviate pain from arthritis, backaches, cramps, or a stiff neck. Ginger is especially useful in dissolving hardened accumulations of fats, proteins, or minerals in cases of kidney stones, gall bladder stones, cysts, and benign tumors. Ginger can also help speed up recovery from inflammatory conditions such as bronchitis, boils, and abscesses, and it relieves the congestion of asthma after an attack.

The ginger compress works because of the energetic, or chi, activities of the heat in the ginger root. According to yin-yang theory, ginger root has strong yang activity by virtue of being a root. This more yang activity means the energy of the ginger has a strong, downward, penetrating movement.

Whenever you grate ginger you will notice how its aroma immediately fills the room, attesting to a strong dispersing, expansive movement of energy. Ginger root grows sideways, meaning it is more influenced by yin activity than, say a carrot root, and so this yin-dispersing action is further enhanced.

The heat activity of a ginger compress stimulates the blood and tissue circulation in the area being treated, and as a result the dispersed toxins can be excreted. The tissues receive clean, healthy blood and become revitalized, leading to a regeneration and restoration of their proper, harmonious function.

The main purpose of a ginger compress is to increase blood circulation and body fluids at areas where stagnation exists. This stagnation usually manifests itself in the form of pain, inflammation, swelling, or stiffness. Strong heat will dilate the blood vessels and activate the movement of stagnated fluids. Strong heat will also melt or soften mucus stagnations. Thus a ginger compress can exert its influence deep inside the body, even within solid organs such as the kidneys and liver, or within the lungs.

### A Few Compress Cautions

Because ginger works through its thermal properties, be careful handling it and applying it to your skin. A good way to test whether it's too hot is to bring it near your face. If you can stand the heat, it's probably okay to apply.

Never apply the ginger compress to your scalp or over your brain. You may use a mild compress on the face to aid sinusitis. Never apply ginger compresses to babies, to elderly people, or to pregnant women. Don't apply ginger to an inflamed appendix or to the lungs if you have pneumonia, and do not use one when you have a fever.

Fresh ginger roots are not hard to find these days. Natural food stores and supermarkets carry them. If you buy a large quantity of ginger, store the roots by burying them in dry sand—in a flowerpot, for instance. Keep this pot in a cool, dry place. If you cannot find fresh ginger, use about four tablespoons of ginger powder to one gallon of water.

## How to Make Your Compress

Several large ginger roots
1   large, heavy (enameled if possible) pot with a lid
1   gallon of water
1   large, thick bath towel

2–3   smaller cotton kitchen towels

1   small cotton bag with a string tie (or you may use a
small cotton towel or cheesecloth and a piece of
string, some rubber bands, or a white cotton sock)

Bring the water to a boil in the pot. Wash the ginger and dry. Grate the ginger and wrap it in the cotton bag or cheesecloth, tying it closed. There should be enough space inside to allow water to circulate throughout the contents. When the water is boiling, turn down the heat to a simmer and add the ginger.

(Never boil ginger water! The active ingredients in ginger are destroyed at boiling point temperatures.)

Let the ginger simmer for about five minutes. The water will turn yellowish and smell strongly of ginger. While you are applying compresses, the ginger water tends to cool off gradually. Keep the heat on low under the pot, so the water remains fairly warm while you make repeated applications. To be effective, a ginger compress must be warm.

## Applying the Ginger Compress

To apply the compress, fold a hand towel so it forms a long rectangle. Dip the center of the towel into the pot, holding the dry ends with your hands. Wring out the towel so that it no longer drips rapidly, but still retains saturated moisture in the towel. Unfold the towel for a moment and notice the steam. Quickly refold it and apply the compress to your affected area. As for how hot it should be: The compress should be as hot as you can bear without burning.

Place a bath towel over the hand towel to keep the heat in the compress. It will stay hot for five to ten minutes. As soon as the heat dissipates, you should apply another one. Keep applying compresses until the skin shows a deep and lasting red color. This can take from twenty to thirty minutes or three to six compress exchanges.

In some cases it is necessary to continue treatment much longer than just one or two sessions. To treat a chronic condition, one twenty- to thirty-minute compress treatment may be sufficient, but to relieve acute situations such as an asthma crisis, or a discharge of a kidney stone, the treatment can be continued much longer—over the course of several days.

Ginger water is most potent for only two to three hours. If two or three treatments per day are necessary for a serious condition, you should prepare fresh ginger water for every one of your treatments. For a less serious condition, you can use the same ginger water several times during one day (that is, during a twenty-four-hour period), but the next day you should prepare fresh ginger liquid.

Additionally, whenever you finish with your ginger water do not discard it. You can reheat it and then add it to a bath or use as a footbath. Soaking your feet in hot water (either ginger water or just plain hot water) and washing them with soap before going to bed helps secure a good sleep. You can also use day-old ginger water in the morning to vigorously wash or scrub the body. This is very stimulating.

## After the Treatment

As a result of doing the ginger compress treatment, mucus deposits are gradually dissolved and toxins flushed into the bloodstream. The body may show signs of detoxification or may show no overt signs of cleansing other than passive weight loss, increased urination and bowel movement, and some fatigue.

More active signs of cleansing include nasal mucus discharge, sore throat, coughing and sneezing, fever and flu-like symptoms, temporary constipation or diarrhea, various aches and pains, skin eruptions on various parts of the body, and headaches. If these are accompanied with a healthy appetite, normal sleep patterns, good vitality, and no nausea, these signs indicate the healing process is going well. If not, immediately discontinue your ginger compress treatments, and seek medical advice. You may have ginger sensitivities or allergies that were undiagnosed.

Ginger is a wonderful addition to anyone's herbal treasure chest. It's inexpensive, abundant, and effective. Stock up and enjoy.

# Herbs for Menopause

≈ by Leeda Alleyn Pacotti ≈

W omen today live in an exciting time. Our mothers have
outlived their expected life
span of seventy-two years, and we ourselves will exceed the expectations of
longevity for our generations.

While the true length of a natural
human life is undetermined, we now
suspect there are unimaginable possibilities for our bodily life expectancy.
Only recently has medical science discovered that men, if they eat properly
and maintain active exercise, can keep
the robust, strong body of their adult
maturity well into their eighties. Men,
however, don't undergo kaleidoscopic,
almost cataclysmic, physical transformations as do women. As women age
and science progresses, we will have
increased opportunities to observe and
understand the strength and potency
of the fully bloomed woman.

# What the Experts Don't Know

Prior to the twentieth century, not so many women lived beyond their thirties. Their bodies, ravaged by continuous pregnancy and weakened by insufficient harvests or depleted winter resources, became vulnerable to periodic epidemics of contagion—many of which are remembered only in oral histories. Rare was the woman whose age advanced her into the physical changes of midlife. From this incomplete record and the rare experiences of middle-aged women arose many common misconceptions about the physical transition of menopause.

In the last hundred years or so, as medical science advanced, its practitioners who treated women during their menopausal years erroneously concluded that the transition at midlife was a disease. After all, some of the symptoms, such as abrupt changes in body temperature, the interruption of rhythmic menstrual flows, and sexual disinterest, had the appearance of illness. The thought was here was some sort of pandemic common to old women. And this misconception became somewhat insidious, as any sign of emotion or uneven temperament in women was attributed to this imagined illness.

Men, of course, were exempt from physical transitions of this other—except for "natural" aging transformations. Men died early, usually from the stress and strain of labor and overwork, as they shouldered the entire economic burden of providing for a family. Because they wore out, there was no need for science to consider that men might also have a midlife transition akin to a woman's. Only recently, with men's life spans lengthening, has biological science begun to question that assumption.

In all the scientific and popular literature, only one thing is certain about menopause: It is an observable condition. Otherwise, menopause does not come on at any fixed age. Its symptoms vary from woman to woman. Along with the cessation of a woman's ability to conceive a child, fluctuations in hormonal output or deliveries throughout the body are known. But what the ultimate physical reasons are for menopause and how a woman's body may be differently utilized after menopause are unknown.

## An Elusive Chase

Medical science was not to be deterred by unknowns regarding menopause. As long as it was viewed as a disease, menopause had to have a cause. In its most narrow and isolating of manners, research noticed that the production of estrogen, later dubbed the "feminine" hormone, was reduced as true menopause approached.

The problem with such isolated research is that it caused doctors and other health practitioners to believe that estrogen was solely responsible for this life transition. In fact, a woman's body is affected by a wide variety of hormonal interchanges, including progesterone, testosterone, cortisol, and DHEA (dehydroepiandrosterone). Because production of these other hormones differed little during the menopausal years, estrogen replacement became the preeminent hormonal therapy for women undergoing menopause.

Research in the last ten years has shown that when estrogen is in too great a quantity in the body or overwhelms other interactive hormonal production it acts as a precursor for deleterious health effects. Starting in the 1970s, doctors found a 500 percent increase in uterine cancer among women on estrogen replacement therapy. Estrogen was known to thicken the walls of the uterus, and when taken in quantity estrogen caused the uterine walls to thicken continuously, making them ripe for infection and eventual cancerous growth.

Also during the 1970s, medical science introduced a modified hormonal therapy—estrogen along with progestin, which balances estrogen's effect on the uterine walls. While uterine cancer decreased, women still had all the symptoms of perimenopause, the first stage of the menopause transition.

As the secrets of the body have gradually unfolded under scientific scrutiny, we have learned that hormonal replacement programs cannot fulfill all possible hormonal deficiencies. Because hormones work synergistically, any replacement therapy of an isolated hormone will have little positive effect, since the body does not or cannot produce other necessary hormones.

At this time, severe health risks derive from modified hormonal replacement therapy—in particular, cancer of the breast and uterus, high blood pressure and stroke, fibroid growth in the uterus and endometriosis, fluid retention, premenstrual symptoms, weight gain, and yeast infections. To the rational mind, it is a wonder that any practitioner of medical science would inflict such risks on a healthy woman, but unfortunately many still consider menopause itself a disease.

## The Known Stages of Menopause

We can speak of the known stages of menopause, as they have long been observed and detailed. However, we may not know the full picture for some time yet. Until enough women live long enough for us to understand the role of menopause in the evolution of a woman's body, we must content ourselves with our current understanding.

First off, it should be known that often what women note of their experience is not itself menopause. Beginning during her thirties and forties, perimenopause begins—a lengthy process of physical adjustment toward menopause. Until about fifty years ago, this phase was called the "climacteric" (suggesting that a woman's physical life had climaxed and thereafter was now on the decline). During perimenopause, women first notice changes in their menstrual cycles—its regularity is altered by becoming irregular or spaced further apart. This occurs as hormonal production begins to fluctuate. For some, the character of the flow dramatically varies, shifting from profuse to minimal. Those who have been clockwork-regular often begin to notice staining between the menstrual periods.

As perimenopause progresses, hormonal imbalances produce further effects. Periodically, the body loses its ability to regulate temperature, sending rushes of heat to the face and neck and blotching the skin. These episodes are infamously known as "hot flashes," and they typically last from a few minutes up to a half hour. In the past, it was not known that hormones affect emotions and cause mood swings. Sleep, also regulated by hormones, is often erratically disrupted, resulting in bouts of fatigue during waking hours.

Besides observable physical effects, perimenopause changes woman's sexual organs and drive. The vaginal walls, because of decreased estrogen, became thinner, dryer, and less elastic, making sexual intercourse uncomfortable, if not outright painful. Worse, the dryer conditions of this normally moist tissue increases risk of infection. As with the shifts in emotions, women unfortunately discover a loss of interest in sex.

Changes within the body during perimenopause doesn't stop with the reproductive organs or the emotions. Some women develop patterns of migraine, fluttering palpitations in the heart, joint pain in response to fluctuations in body temperature, or the more unusual incidence of a burning mouth. Adding insult to injury, women sometimes experience digestive changes, with queasiness and morning sickness reminiscent of pregnancy.

Obviously, those little chemical carriers, the hormones, are playing some dirty tricks!

In the second stage of these changes, which is more properly known as menopause, the woman gets her reprieve. Her menstrual flows return after long interruptions that sometimes last more than eighteen months. Eventually, she has one last mother-of-all-flows—presumed to be characteristically different from the others of perimenopause. The exact difference depends from woman to woman. Afterward, the seemingly lifelong cycle of ovulation, menstruation, and gestation simply stop.

As a point of caution, though, during the menopause stage women must be careful. Infrequent as they are, the menstrual flows mean that the ovaries are still releasing an ovum. A woman enjoying sexual activity during this time must continue to take precaution against an unwanted pregnancy. That is to say, despite a long cessation of the menstrual cycle, take care not to have a false sense of security and an unguarded attitude, or you may end up with a late-life child.

The third stage of this transition is called post-menopause. There really is no description of this phase, except that a woman no longer has any menstrual flows. At this time, the term simply addresses the condition of a woman's body from a reproductive standpoint. It is possible that the full interval of development after the second stage has not been adequately observed to draw any true or complete conclusion.

Still, medical science has delineated certain observed physical conditions that are common to women who have passed through the second stage. Because estrogen helps bones retain calcium, the body's decrease in production leads to osteoporosis. Calcium is a major component of teeth, and many women who previously enjoyed excellent dental health experience abrupt changes—including periodontal disease, cracked or broken teeth, and increased decay. Tendencies to cardiovascular disease increase due to lower estrogen levels, resulting in atherosclerosis, or hardening of the arteries, hypertension, and stroke.

An effect of lowered estrogen is also experienced in the urinary system, in which the walls of the bladder become thinner. Consequently, the bladder cannot withstand certain physical strains from exercise, lifting, or abdominal movement from coughing or laughing. What a disappointment it must be to know that hearty or joyful laughter, after such a difficult passage, can bring on social embarrassment.

# At the Threshold of the Wise Woman

While scientists, psychologists, and health practitioners rack their brains to label appropriately the post-menopausal life, we can look back to a more poetic description of the woman in later life. These few women were the survivors of a marriage, and likely to be great-grandmothers. They were wizened, with papery network of lines on their faces and and long, untamed white manes flowered from their heads. In old parlance, these women were hags.

But a kinder, more enlightened term befits the older woman of the modern day—Wise Woman. She no longer is a casualty of pregnancy, child-bearing, or child-rearing. As a grandmother or great-grandmother, she enjoys her distance from youth and willingly respects her daughter's responsibilities of motherhood. The Wise Woman has an acquired authority, gleaned from age and experience. She is at the threshold of a greater adventure into life and living.

In the post-menopausal stage, this woman experiences another change in hormonal production. At this time, the level of androgens increase, igniting the sex drive. More appropriately, these hormones generate creative appetites and drives. The post-menopausal woman, freed of procreative obligations, is poised for the development of new interests, explorative behavior, and adventurous opportunities. She can come to full stature and adorn herself with the trappings and appointments of a new life. All women who have and will surpass menopause are on the verge of extraordinary discovery.

## Vitality for the Happy Hag

More and more, women are questioning the validity of hormone replacement therapies, understanding that the involvement of an isolated biochemical component is an incomplete solution. Fortunately, with some considerate lifestyle changes and the occasional assistance of alternative remedies, you can healthily traverse the feminine transformation of menopause, and remain strong and able for the exciting life ahead.

## *Diet*

If your estrogen levels are a concern, build your diet around vegetables that carry phytoestrogens. Almost all have some estrogenic content, but some of the best are broccoli, brussel sprouts, cabbage, garbanzo beans, greens, humus, kale, miso, radishes, soy beans and soy milk, spinach, tofu, and watercress.

Only a few cautions apply. If you have a thyroid condition, always cook to tender broccoli, brussel sprouts, cabbage, and kale. When eaten raw, these vegetables have a goitrogenic effect, disrupting proper thyroid activity. If you were given soy milk in infancy formula or for long periods as a child, resumption of a steady diet of soy beans or soy milk can also disrupt thyroid regulation. Consequently, use soy products intermittently.

Muscle tissue becomes more important with age, helping to support the skeletal system. Eat beans, fish, nuts, range-fed poultry, and low-fat plain yogurt. Find out from your meat department whether the animals received steroidal hormones to induce growth. If they did, find another meat producer or go to a health food store. Your body will become more hormonally deranged if you eat hormonally inoculated meat. Your liver will store these animal hormones and attempt to combine them with your body's.

You'll want to limit simple sugars, but continue eating complex carbohydrates, which help keep your energy levels smooth. Include beets, corn, green peas, parsnips, sweet potatoes, pumpkin, and yams in your diet. Eat a variety of grains for breakfast or dinner—try amaranth, which is very high in calcium; quinoa; steel-cut oats for your heart; whole-grain rice; whole-grain or rice pasta, and cracked whole wheat.

Your sweet tooth will be satisfied with fresh or squeezed fruits of all kinds. Fruit salads, juices, and smoothies help between-meal cravings. A well-rounded diet provides plenty of natural fiber for healthy intestinal function. Reducing or eliminating meat fats, salt, sugars, and caffeine will help stave off cardiovascular complications.

Your body's nutritional demands will change frequently throughout the stages of menopause. Take a daily multi-mineral/vitamin complex to keep your reserves at optimal levels. Essential fatty acids plump your skin with suppleness, and either of two types will meet your objective. If no health conditions interfere, you can take them together. If you have a cardiac history, consume fish oils only, which contain EPA, or eicosapentaenoic acid. Otherwise, use vegetable oils, which contain GLA, or gamma-linoleic acid, especially if you are primarily suffering menopausal symptoms.

### Exercise

If you have maintained a regular exercise or athletic program since childhood, your body is accustomed to motion and you can continue. However, if your exercise plan has been less than ideal, start with walking, swimming, and pool bouncing for cardiovascular problems and weight loss. Stretching and dancing at your own speed, of course, are very low impact.

Exercise does more than help you lose weight. Expect a reduction in diabetic symptoms, less insomnia, an elimination of depression with the release of endorphins, and a renewed interest in sexual relations as your body tones.

If you have fancied more strenuous programs, such as aerobics, weightlifting, or yoga, consult a qualified physical trainer or work with a class instructor, before plunging in. These people will assess your muscular strength and its ability to support your bone structure.

### Herbs

Certain herbs have been traditionally used to treat symptoms of the menopause stages. Black cohosh is widely used for common physical menopausal symptoms. Chaste berry balances estrogren-progesterone levels and reduces mood swings. Raspberry leaf helps the feminine reproductive organs at any age. Wild yam root is an estrogenic precursor, helping to reduce menopause symptoms. If you have cardiovascular problems, take garlic to protect your heart and include it as a meal chaser to help break down consumed fats.

Herbal remedies are available as teas, capsuled powders, and concentrated extracts. Follow the manufacturer's suggested dosage. At first, avoid combining the herbs to observe how your body reacts to them individually.

### *Flower Remedies*

Runaway emotions demand the help of flower remedies. Usually, these extracts are taken by mouth or stirred into a glass of water. If you choose to use them together, be sure to combine no more than five. Flower remedies, however, can be used simultaneously with herbs.

In the list of the remedies below, North American plants are indicated (NA) and those of the English countryside are marked (E). The symptoms addressed are precise, but the abundance of available flower remedies will help you regain discipline over your emotional tapestry.

**Alpine lily (NA):** Helps deal with the physical changes and fluctuations of menopause.

**Black cohosh (NA):** Treats gripping tension at or around the reproductive organs.

**Black-eyed susan (NA):** Encourages acceptance of the natural transitions of menopause.

**Borage (NA):** Lessens grieving over halted menses.

**Buttercup (NA):** Treats poor self-image of older woman.

**Crab apple (E):** Treat toxicity or congestion from interrupted menstrual flow.

**Easter lily (NA):** Treats pronounced disturbances or toxicity in the reproductive organs.

**Echinacea (NA):** Restores lost feminine identity.

**Fuschia (NA):** Treats strong emotional reactions and debilitating bodily symptoms.

**Hibiscus (NA):** Helps redefine sexuality, unrelated to producing children.

**Lavender (NA):** Treats erratic energy levels during menopause.

**Olive (E):** Treats severe physical drain and fatigue.

**Pink yarrow (NA):** Lessens emotional excesses.

**Pomegranate (NA):** Lessens urgent desires to conceive a child.

**Sage (NA):** Encourages acceptance of the Wise Woman or Hag self-image.

**Self-heal (NA):** Encourages view of menopause as a healthy transition.

**Zinnia (NA):** Encourages view of menopause as the advent of freedom.

### Homeopathic Remedies

These remedies should not be combined with each other; however, they can be used in tandem with the flower remedies. Use homeopathic remedies when your symptoms are more pronounced or less controllable with herbs. Follow the manufacturer's recommended dosage until your symptom subsides or alleviates. If the homeopathic remedy has no effect, it is the wrong choice for you at the moment.

**Cimicifuga racemosa:** Works on the uterus and ovaries, pain around ovaries, pain across pelvis from hip to hip.

**Gelsemium:** Treats nervousness, excessive emotional excitement, sensation of uterus being squeezed.

**Ignatia:** Usually useful for the woman with darker complexion and mild disposition; treats sensitivity, excitability, changeable moods, melancholy and grief, sexual frigidity.

**Lachesis:** Primarily useful for perimenopausal symptoms; treats excessive talk, sadness in the morning, depression, deranged sense of time, painful left ovary, sacral pain when rising from sitting, and a bluish appearance of the breasts.

**Nux moschata:** Treats contradictory bouts of emotion, impaired memory, irregularity of rhythm and quantity of menses.

**Nux vomica:** Treats pronounced irritability, sensitivity to noise, odor, light, or touch, sullenness and irritability, prolapsed or fallen uterus.

**Pulsatilla:** A preeminent woman's remedy, especially for blondes with a mild, gentle, yielding disposition; treats timidity and fear, dread of men, suppressed menstruation.

**Sepia:** Works well on women; treats indifference to love, sensitivity, bearing down of the uterus, clutching pains, stitching pain from the uterus to the navel, painful vagina, morning sickness.

For several generations, menopause has loomed like a forbidding specter as a woman reached her best years of maturity. Hopefully, with greater circumspection on the part of researchers and more forthright portrayals from women, we can unlock the mysteries of this physical transformation and the new life phase to which menopause leads.

# The Aromatic Treasures of India

### ≈ by Stephanie Rose Bird ≈

Our need to find additional tools to enrich our minds, bodies, and spirits has led to the discovery of what were once considered "exotic" herbs. East India and its environs in particular offer a treasure chest of healing aromatic herbs. Intoxicating and delightful on their own, Indian herbs have been processed for thousands of years, yielding some of the world's finest perfumes and incenses.

This article focuses on the history, myths, and lore connected to a select group of distinctive Indian fragrances. Suggestions, recipes, and rituals are provided to encourage your use of these fascinating aromatics.

## Ayurveda

Before beginning to use Indian oils and herbs, it is important to understand the basic concepts of ayurveda, derived from the words *ayu* ("life") and *veda* ("science"). The ancient concepts of ayurveda continue to influence and direct the use of healing herbs and aromatic treatments. Ayurveda is rooted in cherished scriptures called Vedas that date back to 1500 BC. This sacred literature includes the Rig-Veda, which contains 1,000 hymns, written between 1700 and 800 BC. The Rig-Veda asserts considerable influence over Indian healing traditions. While ancient, the vedas still influence the contemporary interest in holistic healing, since they stress care of the entire being.

According to ayurvedic practice, the mind exerts profound influence on the body. A well-balanced, tranquil mind can free the body from illness. Acute awareness is central to achieving this necessary balance. Stones, flowers, water, trees, herbs, talismans, amulets, and symbols play important roles in ayurvedic healing.

Aromas released by fire or captured in oils are key as well. When I write, for example, I dab my chakras with my favorite Indian *ruhs* and essential oils. I usually have a *dhoona* (sacred fire), in the form of a sandalwood candle, burning on my desk, while a stick of *dhoop* (incense) wafts its smoke overhead.

## Fragrant Blessings from India

The current interest in aromatherapy has facilitated a wider public appreciation Indian scents. There are now many commercial enterprises that sell delightful scents used for cleansing, health, beauty, ritual, prayer, and magic. Presented below is a terminology key and ingredient listing for a few of my favorite Indian fragrances.

### *Terminology*

**Attar:** Essential oils of precious flowers or herbs, obtained through hydro-distillation. In India, attars are often extracted into a sandalwood base.

**Essential oil:** Concentrated extract of plants usually derived from herbs, flowers, resins, bark, moss, roots, or berries.

**Hydrosol:** A term coined by aromath... what were once referred to as... to Rose's website for the ... word "hydrosol" comes fr... (or solution). Hydrosols are th... through steam distillation of p... Hydrosols contain essential oils. H... feature sandalwood, orange blossom, a...

**Incense:** Blends of dried aromatic plants, res... that have been smoldered; this brings togeth... ments of air and fire.

**Champas:** Incenses that contain the Indian flower called ... *maddi*, a sweet, fragrant blossom from the plumeria tree...

**Chandan:** An incense featuring sandalwood.

**Dhoop:** The general Indian term for a pure herbal incense, created without a bamboo core.

**Dhoona:** A sacred fire that aids in the enlightenment of the spirit on the life-long journey

**Dubars:** Sweet and complex floral masala incenses in a gummy base.

**Masala:** Indian incense created from a blend of aromatic plants that have been dried, ground, and rolled around a bamboo core.

**Otto:** Plant material that undergoes a process similar to attars.

**Ruh:** Extracted essences of flowers in concentrated form.

## Some of India's Fragrant Herbs

### *Tulsi* (Ocimum sanctum), *or Sacred Basil*

The word *basilicum* translates roughly to "royal or princely." In India, the herb commonly called tulsi is also referred to as *bhutagni* (destroyer of demons). Tulsi is thought of as a divine

the goddess. Worshippers of Vishnu perceive the
goddess Lakshmi, while devotees of Rama see it as Sita.
*ktas* view the herb as Vrinda, Radha, or Rukmani.

are numerous legends in India that revolve around
sil. The actual word "myth" is nonexistent in Indian
ry; instead the term *pura-katha* ("ancient tale") or *divya-*
"divine story") is used. In the divya-katha "Churning of
smic Ocean," Vishnu obtained tulsi from the rough ocean
s as an aid to the health of all beings. In Sanskrit, the sacred
b is regarded as Tulasi. Tulasi was the wife of a celestial being,
ssed by Lord Krishna so everyone could worship her.
Offerings are not complete unless they include Tulasi's blessings.
Many incenses are named Tulsi, Tulasi, Lakshmi, or Laxmi.

## The Healing Qualities of Tulsi

The herb serves as a deterrent to snakes and mosquitoes. Tulsi
helps the earth by preventing soil erosion and enriching the
health of humans and animals. It keeps the body healthy and the
mind free from worry, enabling concentration on spirituality and
inner peace.

The vedas also praise the abilities of tulsi to cure blood and
skin diseases, to act as an antidote to poisons, to cure kidney disease, and to treat arthritis. Typically, sacred basil is prepared as a
tea or poultice in medical treatment.

## Growing Tulsi

Tulsi thrives in the pleasant climate of India. In temperate zones,
it can be grown from seed beginning indoors during April in a
moist, peaty soil. This herb is a vigorous grower, usually reaching eighteen inches in height. It should be placed outdoors in
mid-June in pots, window boxes, or directly in the garden.
Pinching back the top of the plant ensures healthy growth and
prevents an unattractively tall, leggy appearance. Clippings from
the plant work well tied in a bunch with a green ribbon for healing or purple ribbon for spirituality and hung about the home.
Tulsi bundles attract prosperity, health, and good spirits. The

plant is very attractive, with mauve to pink flowers and striking deep purple stems.

## *Menhadi* (Lawsonia inermis)

This is a perfume oil created from what is commonly called the henna plant. Henna comes from the Persian word for the plant. In India, it is called by many names depending on the dialect: menhadi, mehendi, mehedi, mendi, hina, and mendika. Many readers are familiar with menhadi (henna) as a hair colorant or dye used for creating temporary tattoos, but it is also a useful medicine and revered perfume.

The flowers and leaves from this plant have been used as a refrigerant, cooling people for centuries in the hot climates of India and North Africa. Menhadi is also astringent, treating headache, fever, insect bites, and painful joints. Its pungent, earthy fragrance, with a slight hint of floral, is processed using sandalwood oil. The oil-based perfume is referred to as mehndi attar, hina, or gulhina. Mostly men wear gulhina oil; it is also used in worship and ceremony.

The symbolic power of menhadi rises from its association with Lord Shiva and his consort Parvati. Lord Shiva is the most powerful of all deities and the god of destruction. Parvati decorated herself with henna to please him and win his affections. Lord Shiva responded favorably to her charms, and ever since the herb is associated with sensuality. Since Shiva is a feared god, menhadi is also associated with protection of women. The herb is also associated with marriage and relationships, hence its central role in marriage ceremonies and rites of passage.

## *Jasmine* (Jasminum officinale)

Jasmine has an intensely sweet, almost narcotic perfume with hints of honey, fruit, and green undertones. Its sweet, romantic scent eases anxiety and aids sleep. This is a perfect plant for a fragrant summer garden. Try planting jasmine in window boxes or pots, or on verandahs. Jasmine is a fragrant hair accessory, worn fresh, pinned to the hair. Motia is the Indian name for jasmine attar. To use motia, apply to your pulse points (use sparingly).

## *Kewda* (Pandanus odoratissimus)

Kewda is a superb mind, body, and spirit medicine with a mysterious, penetrating scent. The top note is reminiscent of hyacinth, yet it quickly fades to a gentle, rejuvenating scent. The Ganjam district has ideal conditions for growing Kewda. There are 300,000–400,000 Kewda trees in the Ganjam district, but it has trouble growing under different weather conditions. Apply a dab of kewda attar to chakras or pulse points.

## *Lotus* (Melumbo nucifera)

In the Hindu faith, the lotus, particularly the pink flowered variety, is associated with the goddess Lakshmi. In art, Lakshmi is often featured standing on or holding lotus pods. Buddhists associate the lotus with purity, since neither the leaves nor the petals show traces of the mud from which it grows. This mythology about the plant grows from the fact that the stem and roots vanish beneath muddy water, while its delicate blossoms open up towards the sky.

The white lotus, *Nymphaea lotus L.*, only blooms at night, evoking an additional sexual metaphor. The lotus symbolizes the awakening of the soul as it reaches toward enlightenment and moves away from ignorance. Across the globe, the lotus symbolizes the duality of nature—the flower exists in two realms, above and beneath the ground. It is a symbol of grace, beauty, womanhood, opportunity, and sensuality. The image reflects the divinely feminine and represents the female sex organ, the yoni. Ultimately, the lotus also symbolizes the bounty and abundance of the Earth. Wearing the oil, or a tattooed image or amulet of the lotus, sparks creativity and love, and enhances sexuality.

The scent of the lotus is moist and watery, suggestive of the fecundity of the Great Earth Mother. Lotus oil comes from blue, white, and pink flowers—each has a distinctive scent. Blue or white scents are great for an introduction to lotus. The plant is slightly narcotic, causing sedation and deep relaxation. The lotus is believed to have been a gift from Egypt to India. The type commonly available today is the *Nymphaea lotus*. Reputable sources for lotus oil are listed in the appendix. Apply pure lotus oil neat to pulse points or chakras for grounding and centering or to enhance sexuality.

## Mitti (Baked Earth Attar)

Mitti is distilled earth—an attar with an exquisite, rich, deep, mysterious smell. The perfumers of Kannauj gather the earth from dried lakes, ponds, or wells, moisten it, form dough, and make coarse vessels that they bake in handmade kilns with straw. When half baked, the vessels are moistened and then the lengthy distillery process begins. The scent is used by pregnant women to smooth the transitioning of the reincarnated souls of fetuses. The smell is evocative physically, spiritually, and metaphorically to all who encounter it, as it is a reminder of the bountiful gifts of our planet.

## Orange (Citrus spp.)

Bitter orange flowers (*C. auranthium*) is used to make the multipurpose elixir called orange flower water. Orange flower water is a hydrosol, useful in perfumery, aromatherapy, and health and beauty recipes; it also has culinary uses.

Neroli is an expensive, intense, orange-scented oil derived from the same blossoms as the hydrosol. Neroli is known to alleviate stress and anxiety that may arise during sexual encounters. This intoxicating oil is quite complex, fresh, sweet, green, and floral with a hint of spice. Neroli is used on mature and sensitive skin to fade scars and stretch marks, and it is used to ease depression.

## Patchouli (Pogostemon cablin)

Patchouli is a base for many perfumes. It is sultry, earthy, dark, and noted for its ability to attract love. Connoisseurs of patchouli's fine fragrance complain that far too often the essential oil is adulterated or aged improperly. Aging in proper containers, they say, produces a much more subtle and complex scent. Patchouli intensifies other botanical ingredients, and acts as a preservative and scent fixative. This earth-kissed herb has many useful functions including: treating reduced libido, promoting healthy skin, treating wrinkles, tightening pores, and easing eczema. Patchouli also heals cracked skin, fungal infection, and athlete's foot.

Patchouli is a tender plant that grows quite successfully during the summers in temperate zones. It is perennial in Zones 11 or above. Patchouli plants require humidity, a peaty-composted soil, regularly watering, and an attentive eye. Harvest and dry patchouli leaves during the summer season. Patchouli leaves are useful all year; add them to potpourris, dream pillows, and wool or cashmere storage containers.

### *Ruh khus* (Vetiveria ziazaniodes)

Ruh khus is called the "Oil of Tranquility." It is created from the distilled, wild-crafted vetiver grass grown in Uttar Pradesh, Haryana, Madhya Pradesh, and Rajasthan. Ruh khus has fixative or scent-preserving qualities in botanical blends and perfumes. It is a natural refrigerant, useful in cooling fevers or returning lovers to balance after a passionate interlude. Ruh khus is excellent perfumed oil, used neat, and applied to pulse points or chakras. The oil cools the body during hot, steamy summer months.

To wear ruh khus is to be enveloped in the sweet embrace of the Earth Mother in her numerous incarnations. The smell suggests earth, roots, and dampness, and it sparks creativity, fecundity, inspiration, and fertility. Ruh khus is an excellent scent for striking balance in our chaotic world and for bringing us into the inner sanctum of creation. The grasses that yield ruh khus, vetiver, are also used to create thick mats that are misted with water to emit a cooling fragrance. Hand-held fans made from vetiver grass are doused with water and used for cooling as well.

In some places, a basic type of air conditioning is created by surrounding the home or temple with vetiver mats. Shri Nathji's palace for example, is sealed with thick mats created from the grass.

## *Rose otto* (Rosa damascena)

The rose is one of the most revered flowers of India and is considered to be an incarnation of the Mother Goddess. Whatever you need—calm, balance, stimulation, an aphrodisiac, or cooling off after an argument—rose otto, or attar of roses, can help. Bulgarian or Damask roses are widely available in East Indian shops and health food stores prepared as a rose water. This is used in a sprayer-topped bottle. Rose water is an anointment oil that purifies the environment and is used for cleansing and blessing. Rose otto and rose attar are very expensive but also very powerful—a few drops are all that is needed for most recipes.

## *Sandalwood* (Santalum album)

Wood from the sandal tree has been used for at least 4,000 years. It is mentioned in the oldest vedic scripture, the Nirukta. Sandalwood is called *chadan* in Hindu; it symbolizes mystery, sanctity, and devotion. In India, the heartwood of sandal trees has divine status. The oil is used to anoint sacred deities images, as it is considered pleasing to the gods. Sandalwood is used in the last rites of Hindus. The fragrance is used on funeral pyres to carry the soul to its eternal abode.

Sandalwood is beloved in numerous cultures as an aid to meditation and as an aphrodisiac, emollient, anti-inflammatory, and mild astringent. It is also known for its ability to break insomnia. The mellow scent of sandalwood eases inhibitions, builds self-confidence, induces a calm sedate mood, and assists in achieving a meditative state.

Incense enjoys a central role in the Hindu faith. According to Hindu religious writing, worship must include burning fires of fragrant woods at the four cardinal points. Though sandalwood hails from India, the three-hundred-year-old Baieido Company from Japan makes a incense from sandalwood chips, called *byaku-dan* (Japanese for "old mountain"). This is a high-grade incense suitable for mixing with other incense ingredients or burning on a charcoal block alone. Sandalwood blends well with many herbs and resins, particularly frankincense and myrrh. Sandalwood is also an aphrodisiac that builds self-confidence and generates well-being within the environment. Sandalwood embodies the profound relationship between fragrance and spirituality in India and elsewhere. The pure oil is becoming increasingly more precious and is protected by the government of India. Experts feel that the best type currently comes from Tamil Nadu, though a high quality sandalwood also comes from Mysore.

# Rituals and Recipes

## *Neroli*

Add a few drops of neroli (orange blossom) essential oil to your bath for an aphrodisiac bath. Try adding three drops of neroli essential oil to unscented shampoo or conditioner. Add three drops of neroli to a half cup of safflower, sweet almond, grapeseed, or sunflower oil. Use this on your scalp for a tantalizing scent before a date. During a date, you can use this same oil as stimulating massage oil.

Put some orange blossom water in a spritz bottle. Mist your bedroom before or after lovemaking. Mist yourself after bathing.

## *Sandalwood Massage Oil*

Sandalwood is wonderful applied to the body in massage when diluted with sweet almond oil. Use one-quarter teaspoon to eight ounces of oil. The oil can also be applied to pulse points or chakras neat before going out or at bedtime to induce peaceful sleep.

## *Cooling Herbal Treats*

On a hot summer evening, add a teaspoon ruh kus or gulhina to the bath. Mix well. When finished, gently blot your feet with a towel, but do not dry your body. Stand in front of fan or open window; enjoy the cooling energy of either plant.

Alternately, fill a misting bottle with rose water. Place the bottle in the refrigerator. Mist your face, hair, and neck as needed throughout the day for its calming influence and cooling effect on the body.

### Jasmine Tea

Add a teaspoon of dried jasmine flowers to a cup of very hot water, and sweeten with honey. Serve as a fragrant dessert tea or without honey at bedtime.

### Love Pillow

Crush enough fragrant rose petals, patchouli leaves, and jasmine blossoms to fill a six-by-eight-inch muslin bag. Sprinkle one-half teaspoon ruh khus and sandalwood essential oils over herbs. Add two drops attar of roses. Mix, and store for forty-eight hours in a capped stainless-steel or glass container. Refresh herbs with ruh, attar, and essential oils every other month or as needed.

### Tulsi

Steep tulsi leaves in wine overnight to create a brew that acts as a stimulant and aphrodisiac. Many Indians place a tulsi leaf on their chest as they are about to fall asleep to ensure pleasant dreams and protect against evil. Try this nighttime ritual if you suffer from nightmares. Another interesting tradition to try is placing a tulsi leaf on a grave to please the ancestors or recently departed loved ones.

### Diwali Lakshmi Ritual

Diwali is a two-week long celebration in late October through mid-November. The Hindu people use Diwali as a period to vanquish ignorance by driving away the darkness that engulfs the light of knowledge. Diwali is a festival of lights, as the word is derived from the Sanskrit words for "row of light." Set up hanging lamps or as many candles as possible to encourage the presence of Diwali. Welcome Lakshmi, goddess of prosperity. Lakshmi is embodied in basil, rice, coins, and other symbols of prosperity and fertility. To invoke the blessings of Lakshmi during Diwali infuse a cup of basil leaves in four cups of water, then strain. Add one-quarter teaspoon of peppermint and one-quarter teaspoon of basil essential oil. Wash your floors and walls with this basil spiritual wash. Place rice in a small dish on your altar along with an array of coins. Sleep each night for two weeks with a basil leaf under your pillow.

## Suppliers of Indian Scent Products

Lakshmi International
    843 Shuttleworth Dr.
    Eric, CO 80516

Liberty Natural Products, Inc.
    8120 SE Stark St.
    Portland, OR 97215
    Phone: 503-256-1227
    www.libertynatural.com

White Lotus Aromatics
    801 Park Way
    El Cerrito, CA 94530
    www.whitelotusaromatics.com

# Herbal Remedies for A.D.D.

### ❧ By Leeda Alleyn Pacotti ❧

S o, you're hard at work, mulling over a major snafu or rushing to finalize details on a deadline that's arriving too soon. Puncturing your concentration comes a phone call from little Johnny's or Janey's school. A school administrator, you've probably not met, says your child has something called "A.D.D." As you bring full focus to the conversation, you're told the teacher has done everything possible to help your child, and nothing has helped. You now have a choice: Either put your child on medication, or be prepared for an expulsion from school.

While this may sound like a drastic situation, nowadays it's an all-too-common scenario. Some parents receive a call at home or a letter from the school. No matter how the ultimatum is delivered, you're caught between concern for your child's welfare and your responsibilities to provide for his or her education.

## A National Disorder

Attention deficit disorder, or A.D.D., and its cousin attention deficit hyperactivity disorder (A.D.H.D.), are not new terms in the American vocabulary. For the last twenty years, school administrators, psychiatrists, and psychologists have espoused an unusual rise in these mental conditions, which they say has caused disruptions smooth educational operations and goals. At present, children with problems in school are quickly designated A.D.H.D. Recently, a third variant, A.D.H.D. with impulsiveness, has made its entry.

Nonetheless, these disorders are hard to pin down. The descriptions from the *Diagnostic and Statistical Manual of Mental Disorders* lists nine symptoms for inattention and nine symptoms for hyperactivity/impulsivity. The disorder and variants are confirmed if a patient exhibits at least six symptoms in the appropriate categories. In the last three years, A.D.H.D. has moved into the arena of adult disorders and is thought to be a disruption in family situations.

Interestingly, all of the mental descriptions start with the word "often," and the language of these categories is subject to a broad range of interpretation, in which a severe opinion could easily intimidate a parent. In the category of inattention, for example, you will find: often fails to give close attention to details or makes careless mistakes in schoolwork, work or other activities; often has difficulty organizing tasks and activities; often very easily distracted by extraneous stimuli. And under hyperactivity/impulsivity, the symptomatology suggests: often fidgets with hands or feet or squirms in seat; often on the go; often blurts out answers before questions have been completed.

Even a casual reading of these symptoms of the various disorders raises questions, because none are qualified by age, maturity, or distinctive personality traits. Expectations regarding these symptoms differs when read in terms of the expectation for a six-year-old, as opposed for a sixteen-year-old or a forty-five-year-old. As a matter of objectivity, the descriptions of these conditions raise more questions than they answer. Although a psychiatric manual may sound definitive and educated, the average parent deserves to know some hard facts.

The National Institutes of Health has stated in its reports there is no valid diagnosis of A.D.H.D. and no data whatsoever that says this condition results from a brain dysfunction. When a diagnosis is performed, generally there is no objective testing. Diagnosis, instead, starts from a questionnaire given to parents and teachers. The opinions expressed in a questionnaire, no matter how structured, are subjective and easily manipulated, depending on whether a parent attempts to minimize the situation or a hard-pressed teacher is looking for a solution.

## When Common Sense Becomes Nonsense

At this stage in the treatment of these disorders, psychiatrists, psychologists, school officials, and teachers have learned one common cure—drug it!

Before 2001, treatment for A.D.H.D. focused on the pharmaceutical Ritalin. Although some other depressants are being used more extensively now, many children and teenagers in the 1980s and 1990s were introduced to this drug. Today, unlike the children of the past, we benefit from knowing the severity of Ritalin. Among psychotropic treatments, Ritalin is a Schedule II drug, falling in the same category as cocaine, opium, morphine, and heroin. Pharmacologically, it is similar to cocaine, with both drugs going to the same receptor sites in the brain. The similarity is so dramatic, scientists often exchange Ritalin for cocaine in medical studies to identify specific areas of the brain. Ritalin has in fact been illegally distributed as a cocaine substitute. The Drug Enforcement Agency's Drug and Chemical Report of 1995 advised "neither animals nor humans can tell the difference between cocaine, amphetamines, or methylphenidate [i.e., Ritalin], when they are administered the same way in comparable doses. In short, they produce effects that are nearly identical."

Considering the psychotropic nature of Ritalin, it is likely the drug should never have been offered as treatment to children. Once the word was out about the similarities between Ritalin and cocaine, older children learned to crush their dosages and snort the powder. Teens and college students suggested to their physicians that they experienced problems with attention and concentration in the classroom, thus yielding a prescription to the drug, from which they launched a tidy business, selling it to their peers.

As with cocaine, Ritalin users can develop a dependency. Even though prescriptions of this pharmaceutical are no longer as widespread, some parents and physicians are concerned that former Ritalin users will turn to cocaine as a safety valve. Ritalin also produces a high potential for cardiac debility. That the heart was severely affected was a known side effect, but that prolonged use of the drug could produce multiple cardiac symptoms and complex deterioration beyond the term of dosage was not known then, as it is now.

In an attempt to stave off Ritalin use, other curative pharmaceuticals have been introduced for treatment, specifically Adderall, Catapres, Dexedrine, Luvox, Norparmine, Paxil, Prozac, Wellbutrin, and Zoloft. All of these drugs have a common effect on the body—cardiac difficulties and deterioration, in some cases leading to death, depending on how long they are prescribed.

## Why the Dedication to Medication

If these pharmaceuticals are potentially lethal, why aren't educators more enlightened about the irreversible emotional, physical, and psychological harm potential inherent in prescribing them?

In simple terms, it's a matter of money. Under the Americans with Disabilities Act, A.D.H.D. qualifies as a disability. Consequently, every diagnosed and treated child flags the school district for extra federal funds.

Effectively, school administrations and teachers have turned a blind eye to the overall welfare and well-being of the child, focusing specifically on behavior and performance in the classroom and ignoring possible effects on other activities in the child's daily life. In some states, school districts have even resorted to charging allegations of negligence, sending Child Protective Services after parents who refuse to drug their children.

Being an educator or administrator does not confer some all-encompassing knowledge of anything, so these professionals, in turn, rely on intelligent information to make their recommendations. In one specific situation, the organization Children and Adults with Attention Deficit Disorder advocated the use of psychiatric drugs for children—even though clinical trials of these drugs never included anyone under the age of sixteen. A lawsuit in Texas petitioned against this organization and its primary donor, the pharmaceutical company Novartis, which was the manufacturer of Ritalin, for fraud, conspiracy, and collusion. Both the organization and the drug manufacturer were accused of complicity in developing and promoting the diagnosis of A.D.H.D. and its variants.

When school personnel make recommendations or demands on the basis of biased information, how is a parent expected to make an informed decision?

## Parents Have Rights Too

In the face of pressure, you, as a parent, have to become cool and level headed. Your child's welfare is at stake, and you're his or her only protection. Starting with the first notification of your child's difficulties in the classroom, take a deep breath and think about how you will respond.

You may be given paperwork for your child to be tested for learning disabilities. If so, read it carefully or have it reviewed by someone familiar with any unusual jargon, such as your attorney or your health-care provider. Frequently, documentation carries an all-pervasive permission to test your child psychologically. If a specific learning skills test seems wise, let the school know that you will only sign a document for that test.

Sometimes, the school asks to give your child psychological testing. No matter whether the school suggests it bears a responsibility to test, you are under no requirement or obligation to give permission for it. Be aware, if the school ordered a psychological test with your permission, its psychological expert will be in a stronger position than another you bring in. Get to know the federal and state laws and regulations regarding school's authority.

As a rule, questioning is always good. Does the administrator who notified you personally know or interact with your child? Is the teacher experiencing something in his or her personal life that's being transferred to the classroom? Is there a difference between the mental style or approach between your child and the teacher? Does the teacher have poor teaching skills? These and other interpersonal considerations should be investigated. Specifically, though, it's absolutely illegal for any teacher, school administrator, or other nonmedical personnel to say or write a recommendation for a child to be medicated. Not only is this outside their professional purview, it's also practicing medicine without a license!

Reading carefully and thoughtfully, withholding permission, and questioning are all good reactive stances. Proactive approaches, though, force the school personnel to be reactive. At the minimum, you can take steps to slow and possibly thwart the entire medication process.

As a responsible parent, inform the school you will take your child to his or her own physician for a complete health evaluation. The opinion of school personnel does not stands well against the evaluative advice of your own health-care professional.

You may want to obtain more than one opinion, if you believe your school district will question the results. Ask the physician to test for some specifics, beyond those normally proposed.

Toxicity from mercury, which builds up from continuous vaccinations, causes restlessness and hyperactivity. Other toxic metals and environmental pollutants can congest organs. Appropriate testing reveals any accumulations.

Obtain a thyroid test for your child. Hyperthyroidism causes restlessness and overactivity, while hypothyroidism generates fatigue and poor memory.

Determine whether school officials are misinterpreting the physical development of a teething child. Children, after all, are growing beings. At age six, the six-year molars erupt at the back of a small mouth and can cause a lack of concentration or attention from irritability, jaw pain, or headaches. The replacement of baby teeth with permanent teeth and the eruption of additional molars continues from this age through as late as sixteen.

Remember, the head is a complex of sensory organs, all interacting with a common nerve system in the brain. Eye, ear, and nose organs, when disturbed through inflammation, stress, or injury, can all affect each other. Any complaints of persistent headache should be checked for migraine patterns.

Digestive and urinary systems need review for any upset. Most teachers don't want to address this problem. Perhaps, your child suffers a small bladder or cannot properly digest the foods prepared in the school cafeteria. Constant urinary and bowel urges disrupt concentration and deter attention to studies. Worm infestation of the intestines can make the child jittery.

While physical evaluations are going on, suggest a temporary educational link to your home through mobile communications and the internet. If the school system takes a severe or nonnegotiable stance, investigate home schooling.

Of course, if the situation becomes so severe that the school refuses to wait for your physician's evaluation or threatens notification to Child Protective Services, go public. When you, as a concerned and involved parent, are hampered from taking steps to determine the real cause of your child's learning difficulties, a hard-nosed, superior posture by a noncustodial governmental jurisdiction, such as a school district, will look very bad in the press and on the news. Your proactive response can cause the school to back off or give you time to finish your own health evaluations.

## Reinforce Your Child's Everyday Health

All of us derive our good health from excellent nutrition and adequate activity. By attending to these two health factors, you can eliminate several impediments to your child's ability to learn.

### *Diet and Nutrition*

First and foremost, stop the sugar! This false food alone contributes to the majority of childhood hyperactivity and inattention problems—via the abrupt energy high as simple sugar metabolizes and the crashing low as the body tries to absorb sugar from the bloodstream.

Unfortunately, stopping sugar in the form of candies and desserts is not enough in our marketplace of prepared foods. Simple sugars abound in most frozen and packaged preparations. Read the ingredients, and purchase only pure foods—such as peanut butter with peanuts and salt only, and no added sugar or dextrose. Refuse to purchase items with sugar—even natural cane, corn syrup, fructose (separated fruit sugars), galactose (dairy sugars), malt syrup, maple syrup or sugar, molasses, or sorghum. When encountering an ingredient you don't know, err on the side of caution; don't buy it. This method puts you in control of how much sweetener your child ingests.

Food additive manufacturers have long resisted any extended research on chemicals introduced into foods. Interestingly, 80 to 90 percent of children diagnosed with A.D.D., and A.D.H.D. have allergies to red, blue, and yellow food dyes. Primarily, these dyes are added to snack foods. Lately, as a marketing ploy aimed at "fun" eating, condiments have been loaded with dyes. Think carefully before you give in to purple ketchup, green mustard, and blue mayonnaise. The chemicals depress the assimilative action of the small intestine, preventing absorption of nutrients.

When it comes to feeding your child, be a purist. Skip the prepared luncheon meats. Instead, acquaint your child with proteins from beans, fish, and nuts. Nuts are an easy after-school snack. (Avoid almonds, however, until your child's body has stabilized.)

Fruits, such as melons, pears, kiwi, lemons, and limes, can be given in abundance. These help regulate consistent digestive activity and promote the release of toxins from the body. However, certain fruits are either too acidic or difficult on young livers. Refrain from giving your child apples, apricots, berries, cherries, currants, oranges, plums, and prunes. As with nuts, fruits can be eaten as snacks. Melons are ideal at breakfast along with other food or drink.

Almost all vegetables are excellent. Until your child's system is cleansed, withhold cucumbers, peppers, and tomatoes, which digest poorly in an immature intestinal tract. For after-school snacks, prepare raw beet slices, carrot and celery sticks, raw jicama slices, and whole radishes. Refrigerate them in a water-filled container within easy reach. If your child is diagnosed with a thyroid condition, don't prepare raw broccoli or cauliflower for snacks. These vegetables in raw form are goitrogenic, suppressing the proper activity of the thyroid.

Complex carbohydrates from whole grains supply your child with slowly released sugars, necessary for good brain function and even energy. Whole grains provide vitamins and digestive fiber. Look for amaranth, whole barley, raw buckwheat, corn grits, millet, steel-cut oats, quinoa, rye berries, and cracked whole wheat at health food stores. Whole grains are filling. Expect your child to eat a smaller quantity of these than you expect.

Children reach for and eat what is available. Invite your child to help with food preparation and storage. Of course, caution them that all food preparation must be supervised by you. Within a week, you'll have good feel for your child's appetite.

When a child has eaten predominately prepackaged or canned foods, he or she may suffer a vitamin or mineral insufficiency. In the immature and developing body, any deficiency may exhibit more dramatically than in an adult's. Give your child a daily vitamin and mineral complex until good eating habits are restored. For the child who suffers restlessness or hyperactivity, a child's dose of calcium and magnesium, in a 2:1 ratio, about one hour before bed, serves as a calmative.

### Exercise

Play and movement are mainstays for children. Through activity, their bodies break down and slough off tissues, which are then replenished during recuperative sleep. Exercise is crucial.

Each day, the average adult requires thirty minutes of physical activity to keep the body functioning properly. Total exercise time increases for younger children, which is why they are often on the move. Turn off the television and computer. Create joint play times after you come home from work. You and your children will be more calm and relaxed in the evenings.

### Herbs

Your child's body may take longer to adjust to a healthier diet, but specific calmative herbs will balance physical energies during the transition. Herbal extracts are the easiest to administer—just place a few drops in a glass of water. If herbs are purchased in capsule form, these capsules can be opened to make into tea. Despite the form you purchase, adjust doses according to age. For children ages six to twelve years, give one-third to one-half the adult dose. For children aged twelve to fifteen, give one-half to two-thirds the adult dose. For fifteen years and over, give the full adult dosage.

Calmative herbs include catnip, chamomile, lemon balm, oats, passionflower, skullcap, St. John's wort, valerian root extract, and wood betony. All of these herbs will induce sleep. Valerian root extract, a muscle relaxant, has a strong smell, which small children may refuse. Wood betony works directly on the pineal gland, nourishing the nervous system and stopping patterns of migraines within a few days.

## *Flower Remedies*

Flower remedies are homeopathically prepared, and work directly on the emotions. Children have the same emotions and complexities as do adults. Uncontrollable emotions interfere with classroom conduct and study habits. Up to five remedies can be combined at once, though singular remedies are best for trial and error. Place two to four drops in a small glass of water, stirring clockwise and counterclockwise for one minute. Give your child this dosage upon arising and in the early evening.

The following remedies specifically address learning difficulties and are listed by the observable behavioral trait. The original remedies are from English (E) plants, while North American (NA) botanicals have recently been introduced. A child in North America may respond more quickly to plants from that continent.

**California wild rose (NA):** Treats lack of interest in study materials.

**Chamomile (NA):** Treats emotional hyperactivity that interferes with learning and concentration.

**Chestnut bud (E):** Treats repetitious errors that impede learning.

**Clematis (E):** Lessens inattentiveness, daydreaming, and fantasizing.

**Cosmos (NA):** Treats speech difficulties from information overload.

**Gentian (E):** Mitigates tendency toward surrender and disappointment in the face of difficulties.

**Impatiens (E):** Treats nervousness, lack of focus, and restlessness.

**Madia (NA):** Mitigates a short attention span.

**Milkweed (NA):** Lessens emotional immaturity.

**Peppermint (NA):** Treats dullness or a sluggish temperament.

**Self-heal (NA):** Lessens a lack of confidence in the ability to learn.

**Yarrow (NA):** Treats environmental distress that interferes with concentration and focus.

### *Homeopathic Remedies*

Two particular homeopathic remedies help children. When a child's anticipation of school or the classroom environment creates anxiety, give gelsemium. The nervous, upset child, whose symptoms have progressed to anger and tantrums, needs ignatia.

Give small children one pillule or small tablet in a 6x potency every four hours until symptoms subside. Teenagers receive the same dose and frequency, but in a 30x potency. Expect to observe these symptoms over the weekend, and especially the day before school.

*Herbs*
*for*
*Beauty*

# Natural Body Care

### ❧ by Pearlmoon ❧

I n these modern times, it is possible to walk into any department store at the mall, or go down a beauty aisle at the supermarket, and find any number of high-priced body-care products. In doing so, it can become easy for us to forget that our Mother Earth has created so many natural ways to help us care for our bodies—so we don't need high-tech chemical emollients and shampoos and so on.

Centuries ago, our ancestors used herbal teas, floral oils, and bath salts to scent their baths. Certain teas were also used for skin care. They used particular types of mud to draw out impurities from the skin and other parts of the body, and so on. Today, these products are still very much available, though we often end up paying a rather high price for them. But we don't have

to. That is, at boutique stores you might find a jar of bath salts for maybe five or seven dollars. For that same amount of money, you could purchase the raw ingredients and make five times the amount for less money. There is a clear advantage in making your own body-care products.

# Skin-Care Recipes

Below are a few recipes for body-care products that are far less expensive and easier to make than any you can buy in a store. Most of the ingredients can be found right outside your door, especially if you're a gardener, or at your local supermarket.

### *Basic Bath Salts*

1   cup sea salt or table salt

½   cup Epsom salt

½   cup baking soda

Mix the ingredients thoroughly. You may add a few drops of food coloring for color, or add a few drops of your favorite essential oil. Add one cup of bath salts to each tub of water.

### *Relaxing Bath Tea*

1   part rose petals

1   part orange blossoms

1   part lavender flowers

1   part chamomile flowers

1   part Epsom salt

Follow the same directions as above.

### *Wake-Up Skin Lotion*

½   cup cocoa butter

¼   ounce beeswax

1½   teaspoons lanolin

1   cup almond oil

3   drops lemon verbena oil

Melt the cocoa butter, lanolin, and beeswax in the almond oil. Remove the pan from the heat, and allow it to cool slightly. When the mixture is slightly warm to the touch, add the lemon verbena oil. Whip mixture to a creamy consistency, and store in clean glass jar.

### Herbal Shampoo

You can make your own herbal shampoo by adding a few drops of your favorite essential oil and favorite dried herb to an inexpensive bottle of regular or unscented baby shampoo.

### Milk Bath

You can make your own milk bath by combining a cup of powdered milk with a few drops of your favorite essential oil. Add a cupful of the mixture to a tub of hot water and enjoy.

### Rose Perfume

2   cups distilled water

3   Tbl. vodka

10   drops rose essential oil

5   drops rose geranium essential oil

Combine the ingredients in a glass jar, and allow to stand for twenty-four hours before using. Add one cup to a tub of water.

### Moon Light Sky Perfume

2   cups distilled water

3   Tbl. vodka

10   drops rosewood essential oil

5   drops neroli essential oil

5   drops ylang-ylang essential oil

Same as above: Combine the ingredients in a glass jar, and allow to stand for twenty-four hours before using. Use one cup of perfume per each tub.

# For Further Study

Buchman, Dian Dincin. *The Herbal Way to Natural Health and Beauty*. New York: Gramercy, 2000.

Johnson, Ann Akers. *The Body Book: Recipes for Natural Body Care*. Palo Alto, Calif.: Klutz, Inc., 2001.

Kellar, Casey. *The Good Earth: Bath, Beauty and Health Book*. Iola, Wisc.: Krause Publications, 2001.

# Treating Acne and Cellulite the Herbal Way

### ❧ by Ruby Lavender ❧

We all want our skin to look good. It's the body's largest organ, and it is what people see foremost when they look at us. When our skin doesn't look its best, our confidence suffers. Fortunately, keeping the skin healthy is not hard to do—if we follow a few general rules for good health. We should always eat right, drink plenty of water, exercise, avoid stress, and get lots of rest. This is easier said than done in today's busy world.

This article will address two skin problems that most of us, especially women, deal with at some point in our lives—acne and cellulite—and the ways we can treat these problems with the natural healing power of herbs.

## We All Suffer Sometimes

Although most of us experience some degree of acne in our teenage years,

some adults experience mild acne into their adult years, well into their thirties and forties. Because the cause of these skin eruptions is not quite the same as it is for maturing adolescents, we need to treat it in different ways.

Some adults experience pimple outbreaks only occasionally, and for some it is a more chronic condition. There are many powerful antibiotics on the market for acne, but except in the most severe cases they are not necessary and can have undesirable side effects. Instead, by taking a holistic approach to skin care you can lessen the frequency and severity of skin outbreaks.

## What We Know about Skin

Back in the 1970s, some research studies were done to determine the effect of diet on teenage acne. It was discovered, surprisingly enough, that a diet of French fries, burgers, candy, and soda did not lead to more severe acne in teens. But, as with many scientific studies, results can often be misleading or hard to interpret. Because teens are susceptible to acne for many reasons directly connected to the rapidly maturing bodies and what we sometimes call "raging hormones," it may well be that diet was not a discernible cause in the studies.

Adults may have a different experience, however. Common knowledge tells us that our skin reflects what we take into our bodies—whether healthy or not. In fact, the skin is the body's largest organ of elimination. We literally excrete toxins from our pores via sweat. Acne is caused when our pores get clogged with excess oil and bacteria from this process. If our diets are full of chemicals or non-nutritious foods, we will have more toxic material to eliminate. This increase in activity makes our pores more likely to get clogged, which in turn leads to pimples. It's really that simple. So cleaning up our diets is an essential step in reducing adult acne.

Many of us notice that we can't do a lot of things "the way we used to." We need more regular sleep than when we were kids, and we need exercise to feel as healthy as we did in our teenage years. We can't pull all-nighters or go binge drinking on weekends like we did in college, because we find it makes us sick or we have a harder time functioning at our full capacity.

The same is true of our diets. To keep our skin healthy as adults, we need to avoid junk food and eat as much fresh, nutritious food as possible. Some nutrients are well-known for their healthy-skin properties. Vitamin A is necessary for healthy cell growth. Vitamin E helps the skin's elasticity and oil production. Vitamin C promotes healthy elimination, and the B vitamins are also important to the skin.

Eating plenty of fresh fruits and vegetables keep the skin looking healthy. Greens, rich in minerals and chlorophyll, will keep your skin looking vibrant—so eat plenty of salads and vegetables like broccoli, kale, spinach, and Swiss chard. The naturally occurring moisture in these foods is also good for the skin. Adequate protein intake is crucial, as is plenty of fiber to assist the body in the elimination of toxins.

For women who experience breakouts just before or during their menstrual periods, eating healthy is especially important. Try to resist the food cravings that come at this time. Not only will bad food increase skin eruptions, but it tends to worsen other PMS symptoms too—such as headaches or irritability. If you crave chocolate, resist, and eat a carob treat instead. If you want candy, instead have some fruit. If you need something salty and greasy, go for popcorn popped in canola oil, and go easy on the salt. It is important to stay hydrated when you're menstruating. Drinking several glasses of water a day is one of the best things you can do during menstruation, and also generally just to promote healthy skin.

## Herbal Skin Remedies

A number of herbs are useful for detoxification and as general overall tonics. Nettle tea is an excellent purifier and tone, as are fennel, anise, and celery. There are "detoxifying" teas available in health food stores. If you drink such teas, made from the various digestive herbs, this also helps detoxify the system and make digestion more efficient. In particular, try taking a cup or two of peppermint, chamomile, or ginger tea after meals.

You can also make herbal "rinses" from the same herbs used for these tea, and these are excellent for the skin. Steep the herbs in boiling water for ten minutes, and either soak a clean wash-cloth in the herbal infusion and apply to face, or splash the infusion directly on the face after it has cooled. You can wash your face with the teas alone, or use them after using your regular cleanser—though I suggest you try doing without your regular cleanser for a bit, as some commercial preparations aggravate acne by drying out the skin's surface oils. It is also possible that facial moisturizers can cause breakouts, so discontinue them for a bit and see if this makes a difference. Rinses can be made with teas from nettle, rosemary, peppermint, chamomile, yarrow, comfrey, lavender flowers, or fennel seeds.

If you feel you need an exfoliating cleanser to unclog your pores, try using oatmeal and water (or any of the above herbal rinses) mixed into a paste. Rub this paste gently on your face, and let it dry for five minutes. Then gently remove the paste with water. You can also make excellent facial masks from various fruits. The same ingredients that make commercial masks very expensive are found cheaply and abundantly in fresh fruit. Try a mix of crushed fresh strawberries or raspberries mixed with a bit of milk or cream. Leave this on your face for five minutes, then rinse off. Your skin will be soft and glowing. You can also rub a lemon or orange on your face as a natural astringent. Rinse off the juice and pulp immediately though, as it can cause irritation if left on too long. Don't apply any fruit to your skin if you know you get an allergic reaction from eating it.

Essential oils can also be used to make excellent anti-acne treatments. Tea tree oil and lavender oil are the most useful. You can dab these straight on to a pimple that is starting. These two antibacterial essential oils will help keep the pores free of the bacteria that aggravates pimples. You can add tea tree or lavender essential oil to rosewater for an excellent toner. This is especially nice to use while camping or if you have a job that exposes you to dust or dirt.

### A Natural Skin-Care Routine

Try this natural skin-care routine for a few weeks and see if your breakouts don't lessen.

**Mornings**

To wash your face in the morning, use a natural exfoliator such as oatmeal paste, or ground adzuki beans (said to be a beauty secret of Japanese women). Or using a clean washcloth, soak it in very hot (but not boiling) water (you should be able to comfortably place your hands on it). Squeeze the cloth out, and when it is cooled slightly hold it to your face. The washcloth's gentle abrasion will help exfoliate. The heat will open pores and help draw out impurities. Finish up with a toner made of rosewater with lavender or tea tree essential oil. Use three drops of essential oil to every half ounce of rosewater.

**Nightly**

At night, use the hot washcloth/rosewater toner. Every two or three days make an herbal rinse with nettle, rosemary, fennel, or one of the other herbs mentioned above. Do this before bed.

**Weekly**

Make a steam inhalation by boiling some water and letting your favorite herbs steep in the water for ten minutes. Pour the water and herbs into a bowl, and, using a towel to create a "tent" over your head, lean over the bowl so your face is a few inches away. Let the steam gently cleanse your skin. To avoid scalding your face, don't get too close. If the steam makes it hard to breathe take a break every minute or so. After steaming, make a facial mask from fresh fruits or oatmeal paste and an herbal infusion, and put this on your freshly steamed skin. You can also make masks from green clay or bentonite clay, and add crushed herbs (lavender, rosemary, and peppermint work well) to that. Clay draws out impurities and tightens pores, but can be drying so don't use clay more than once a week.

## The Problem of Cellulite

Cellulite is a different problem from acne, but some of the same principles are at work. Current theories on cellulite vary, but one of the most common ones suggests that cellulite forms when toxins are trapped in fat cells. Because cellulite responds well to detoxification methods such as a low-fat, low-carb diet, saunas, aerobic exercise, deep breathing, and yoga, it is believed that this theory is probably accurate.

For the most part, women have a greater problem with cellulite than men. We have a greater tendency to store fat on our bodies because it acts as a cushion for our reproductive organs, and aids in nutrient storage during breast feeding. The human body is remarkably efficient at storing fat cells. We can reverse this tendency by increasing our exercise level and eating better.

The same dietary tips for detoxification to treat acne (as described above) can also be used to treat cellulite. It has also been found that eliminating dairy products from the diet, at least temporarily, can be very helpful. So, eat plenty of fruits and vegetables, whole grains, and lots of fresh water to flush out the impurities from the body. Celery and grapefruit also seem to be especially beneficial in this effort. Exercise is also crucial, because the toxins trapped in our fat cells are more likely to stay there if we remain sedentary.

Aerobic exercise also improves the circulation and literally "burns" fat. Ask your doctor or a consultant at the local health club about what form of aerobic exercise is best for you. Simply walking for thirty minutes each day will help—especially if you are not currently active. Yoga or other forms of exercise that encourage deep breathing also help increase circulation and get oxygen moving through the body.

The purifying and digestive herbs discussed earlier will also help reduce cellulite. There are also some essential oils that, when used in the bath or applied to the skin, will help draw out toxins and give the skin a smoother appearance. There is no "magic potion" to cure cellulite, but if you combine an improved diet, an increased exercise regimen, and some detoxification efforts (including the essential oil treatments), you will see results in a few weeks.

## Bath Remedies for Cellulite

In the bath, the following essential oils have been found useful for cellulite, because they either increase circulation or help aid detoxification, or both. Try the recipes below or experiment to create your own combinations. It's helpful not to use the same combination all the time; switch off from week to week.

### Stimulating and Soothing

3   drops rosemary

2   drops lemon

1   drop geranium

### Citrusy

3   drops lemon

3   drops grapefruit

3   drops mandarin orange

### Herby

2   drops sweet fennel

2   drops cypress

2   drops rosemary

### Sweet and Soothing

2   drops geranium

2   drops grapefruit

2   drops sweet fennel

You can also use these essential oils to make preparations to apply directly to the problem areas. For most women, this means the backs of the thighs, the buttocks, and the hips. Just use the recipes above, but double the amount of oils. Add the essential oils to a base of some carrier oil, such as olive oil, almond oil, or apricot seed oil. In general, try to add about twelve to sixteen drops of essential oil to an ounce of carrier oil. Don't make up too much at once, so it won't go rancid. Apply the oil liberally to your problem spots after a bath or workout. Let the oil soak into your skin for a bit after applying. The oil may stain delicate fabrics, so wait a little while before getting dressed in anything other than casual wear.

After just a few weeks of using these preparations, you should have noticeably smoother skin, and the cellulite should be lessened. Here's to better skin and a healthier lifestyle!

# Herbs for the Bath

### ❧ by Ruby Lavender ❧

I s there anything more soothing and sensual than a nice hot bath? Well, it also turns out that baths are a time-honored method for improving health. Cultures around the world have relied upon various bathing therapies for centuries to help increase vigor, heal illness, preserve youthful beauty, and promote longevity.

For example, in Tom Robbins' popular novel *Jitterbug Perfume*, the two main characters were seeking a way to live forever, and they utilized different cures. One of the components of their daily regime is a hot bath. In Sweden, meanwhile, hot and cold baths are used for maintaining health, and of course Scandinavian-style spas use a variety of water therapies. If you're looking for good health, and healthy skin in particular, try some of these bath treatments.

# Bathing Our Skin

Our skin is one of our primary organs for eliminating toxins and wastes from the body. Baths help this process along very efficiently. Hot water opens pores, relaxes muscles, and allows medicinal herbal tonics to penetrate the skin. Cold water, when used carefully, closes pores, stimulates the skin, and increases resistance to infection.

It's generally recommended that you cool down with lukewarm or slightly cool water after a hot bath or shower, so as not to shock the system and to help regulate body temperature. If you are lucky enough to have access to both a pool and a sauna or hot tub, alternating between the two is an excellent health treatment. You will find you sleep much better and awaken refreshed.

Two ancient bath recipes from two famous beauties were collected by Paul Huson in his excellent book *Mastering Herbalism* (Madison Books, 2001). The French playwright Moliere's confidante, Madame de Lenclos, bathed with a sachet of equal parts lavender flowers, rosemary, spearmint, comfrey roots, and thyme. To try this yourself, mix the herbs and place them loosely in a muslin bag. Steep the bag in boiling water for ten minutes and then add to the water to your bath. Huson also mentions Marie Antoinette's bathing beauty secret: one part wild thyme, one part marjoram, and one part coarse salt.

There are many ways you can use the bath for relaxation and healing at home. This article offers suggestions for using herbs to treat a number of common complaints, and for general increased vitality. Before we get into actual recipes, let me help you make your bathtub into a "spa-like" environment!

First, be sure your bathroom is nice and clean. It's not exactly relaxing to lie back in the steaming water and look up at cobwebs on the ceiling, to rest your arms on the edge of the tub and have it knock over old bars of soap, half-empty shampoo bottles, or used razors. Clean the tub with a gentle cleanser (baking soda works fine), and wipe down all surfaces. You may want to put a lower wattage bulb in your light fixture, or a rose-colored one. You can also use candles for light, but place them carefully so you don't have to worry about possible fire mishaps while you are relaxing in your bath.

## Some Bathing Tips

Most people like their bath water at around 100 to 102 degrees Fahrenheit. Perhaps you like it a bit hotter. As the water sits and your body absorbs heat, the water will cool down a bit. You can add more hot water, but be aware that too much time in a hot bath can affect your blood pressure and make you feel light headed.

If you have any sort of chronic health condition, check with your doctor before using hot water therapy. Once you've been soaking a while, it's nice to finish off with a quick lukewarm shower, adjusting the temperature so it's cool just before you finish. Ironically, by finishing with cool water you will feel warmer because your body will adjust to the room's temperature more efficiently. In hot weather, a cooling bath is just the thing to help you relax and sleep through the night. These herbal cures can be used in hot or cool water.

In general, relaxing in the bath should be a total experience. Put on some calming music that you like, and try not to think about your job or any stressful events in your life. Clear your mind and breathe deeply the herbal aromas.

The best way to use herbs in the bath is in the form of bath salts. You can add crushed herbs to commercial bath salts or sea salt. To make bath salts that you will store for future use, try the following recipe.

      ½   cup baking soda

      ⅛   cup sea salt

      ½   cup powdered orris root

      Crushed herbs or essential oils

Keep the salts in a glass jar, and use them as needed. You can also put the herbs in a piece of cheesecloth, gauze, or muslin, and tie it up before dropping it in the bath or hanging it from the faucet while the water runs through it. It's also helpful to steep your sachet in boiling water for a few minutes, as mentioned in the French recipe above.

Lavender flowers are great for relaxation, but they can also serve as a pick-me-up if you're feeling sluggish. Skullcap and valerian are also relaxing, as are chamomile flowers or hops. The same goes for jasmine flowers, elder flowers, linden flowers, or catnip.

For a more stimulating bath experience, try the following herbs: fennel seeds, spearmint leaves, bay leaves, basil, rosemary, peppermint, or sage. These herbs can aid concentration and help keep you clearheaded and alert. Don't use these herbs just before bed, or it may interfere with your sleep. Some of these herbs are also good for sore muscles—particularly peppermint, rosemary, and lavender.

If you're feeling a bit under the weather, or it's cold and flu season at your office or school, an herbal bath makes an excellent preventive measure. You can also bathe while you have a cold, but try not to go to bed with your hair damp. The following herbs or essential oils are useful for upper respiratory infections: eucalyptus, tea tree, lemon, grapefruit, bergamot, rosemary, and yarrow. Bathe any time of day, and wrap yourself in soft and warm, loose-fitting clothing afterward. Be sure to keep your feet warm, eat light and nutritious foods, and drink plenty of clear fluids.

If you want an herbal bath without using actual herbs, essential oils are a convenient way to add healthful properties to your bath. Some materials that would be difficult to use in their solid or plant form—such as resins or barks—are in fact more easy to us in their essential oil form. Remember that essential oils are concentrated plant essences, and a little goes a long way. Also, the essential oils dissipate in steam, so you may want to add a bit more halfway through your bath. You can mix essential oil blends ahead of time, but it's best to add the drops fresh to your bath. Wait until the tub is full, and add the essential oils before you get in. Swirl the water a bit with your hand or a spoon to mix the oils into the water.

Try the following essential oil recipes for a relaxing, stimulating, or otherwise rejuvenating bath.

### End of a Long Day

3   drops frankincense

3   drops lavender

2   drops sandalwood

3   drops vetiver

### Sweet Dreams

2   drops lavender

3   drops clary sage

2   drops patchouli

2   drops chamomile

### Sore Muscles

2   drops rosemary

3   drops lavender

2   drops peppermint

### Relax (for Men)

2   drops patchouli

3   drops sandalwood

2   drops basil

### Relax (for Women)

3   drops lavender

2   drops rose

3   drops sweet orange

### Romantic Evening at Home

4   drops frankincense

3   drops sweet orange

4   drops vetiver

3   drops sandalwood

### *Cold and Flu Comfort*

2   drops eucalyptus

3   drops lemon

2   drops sweet orange

# Easy Herbal Wraps

## ❧ by Chandra Moira Beal ❧

B ody wraps work directly on the skin, producing therapeutic and cosmetic benefits by cleansing the body of toxins. The herbs and other ingredients in wraps are absorbed right into the body through the skin. Because wraps involve heat, they are great for soothing aches and pains and to soften and hydrate the skin. Wraps can be used for treating such diverse ailments as chronic back pain and tendonitis, poor energy flow or circulation, tight muscles, and over- or understimulated nerves.

Wraps are a popular spa service, but they are easy to do at home and require a minimal amount of equipment. Some recipes use herbs or essential oils alone. Others incorporate clay and seaweed, and require brushing on a paste and then wrapping up. Wraps are a great once-a-week beauty and health treatment, but they can also have surprising effects such as warding off a cold or aiding with sleep.

# Getting on with the Wrap

## *Equipment for Wraps*

Gather the following equipment to get started with your wrap treatments: several bath and hand-size towels; one cotton sheet, cut into strips of varying widths (three to six inches); a space heater; some plastic sheeting or an old plastic shower curtain; one or two winter-weight bed blankets or an electric blanket; some stainless-steel pots and bowls; one medium-sized, soft-bristle paint brush; rubber gloves.

## *The Wrap Method*

The method is essentially the same for all of the wrap treatments. You can do these on a bed, in a lounge chair, in the bathtub, or on a massage table. Involving a friend is also helpful—you can trade off pampering each other.

Before the treatment, remove all lotions, perfumes, dirt, and oils from your skin with a quick shower. Heat retention is an important part of this treatment, so warm all your tools, towels, sheets, and ingredients beforehand. Put a space heater nearby to prolong the heat during the treatment.

Place the plastic sheet nearby, so you can slip into it quickly. Turn on the space heater, and stack some blankets nearby. Set the herbs or other ingredients in a large pot, and fill it with water. For loose herbs, tie them in a piece of cheesecloth or muslin bag for easier clean-up. Bring the water to a boil, and simmer, covered, for five minutes. Turn off the heat and let the herbs steep for another five minutes. The ideal temperature of the water is about 180 degrees. Remove the herbs, and place the sheet strips in the pot to steep for five minutes.

Now you're ready to start applying the wrap. Remove one cotton strip at a time to retain maximum heat. Wearing rubber gloves, wring out the excess water, then start by wrapping the strips snugly around each leg, the arms, and then the torso. Use the narrow strips on the arms and the thicker strips around the trunk. Tuck in the ends, bandage-like, to ensure the strips won't fall away. Work quickly. Cover the body with blankets as you go.

When you are completely wrapped, lie down on the plastic sheet and wrap yourself up in it. Relax for ten minutes near the space heater and let your body build up heat. You will begin to absorb the elements in the wrap, and your body will sweat out what it doesn't need.

After ten minutes, unwrap yourself from the places and slowly remove the strips. Put on a warm bathrobe, and relax for twenty minutes before doing anything else. Don't shower right after the wrap (wait until the next day if possible to prolong the effects of the moist heat). Be sure to drink plenty of water or herbal tea after the treatment to replenish the body fluids lost during the process.

## *Easy Wrap Recipes*

### Chamomile, Lavender, Valerian Wrap

Valerian is a mild sedative used since ancient Roman times. It helps with sleep and anxiety. Chamomile is antispasmodic, so it will relax tight muscles. Lavender relaxes, soothes, restores, and balances the system. This wrap is perfect after a long stressful day.

1   cup fresh chamomile, chopped

1   cup freshly grated valerian root

1   cup fresh lavender petals, crushed

(You can also use one-quarter cup of each herb dried in place of the fresh.) Follow the wrap method instructions above.

### Ginger and Lemongrass Detoxification

This cleansing and invigorating wrap is a great way to start the morning. Ginger stimulates and cleanses the system and helps rid the body of flu-like symptoms. The warming quality of ginger also soothes and relaxes tense, sore, or overworked muscles.

Lemongrass, meanwhile, acts as a tonic and has antiseptic and invigorating qualities. This wrap is for stimulating the mind, body, and spirit.

1   cup fresh lemongrass, chopped (or ¼ cup dried)
1   inch-long piece of ginger root, grated or minced
    Camphor crystals
    Cinnamon sticks

Follow the basic instructions for steeping and wrapping.

## Citrus Cleansing Wrap

This wrap is great for cleansing the skin and opening the pores. The citrus oils have an antiseptic quality to them and an uplifting effect on one's mood.

½   cup galangal root, chopped
½   cup turmeric root, chopped
1   cup eucalyptus leaves (or 10 drops essential oil)
1   cup fresh orange rind, torn into pieces

Follow the basic instructions for steeping and wrapping.

## Cold Care Wrap

If a cold gets the best of you, this wrap is perfect for clearing out congestion in the lungs and sinus. Be sure to drink plenty of fluids afterward to thin the mucus and allow it to leave your body.

1   long piece of fresh ginger root, chopped
1   cup eucalyptus leaves or 10 drops essential oil
½   cup lime leaves
1   Tbl. whole cloves

## Aromatherapy Wrap

Here's an ultrasimple wrap that anyone can do. This blend of herbal essential oils has a relaxing mental effect. And it's a good all-purpose wrap for relieving stress, worry, and headaches.

10   drops each of the following essential oils: basil,
     peppermint, ylang-ylang, jasmine

For this wrap, there's no need to steep anything. Just boil the water and turn off the heat. Add the essential oils, followed immediately by the cotton strips. Dip the strips in the liquid and wrap yourself up as usual.

## *Wraps with Paste*

The following wraps require a little more effort because you paint your body with a paste, then wrap yourself in cotton strips. They are best done in the bathtub where you can easily clean up.

### Herbal Clay Body Wrap

This wrap can be messy, but its cleansing effects are worth the effort. French green clay can be found in natural health food stores. It draws out toxins and impurities from the skin. Mix your own herbs according to your needs.

- 1   cup powdered French green clay
- ½   cup mixed dried herbs (chamomile, lavender, and rose petals to relax; peppermint and rosemary to invigorate)
- 10   drops of essential oil (lavender for relaxing blend, rosemary for invigorating blend)
- 1   Tbl. sweet almond oil
- 1   cup distilled or spring water

Boil the water. Add the herbs and steep for fifteen minutes. Combine almond oil and essential oils. Place the clay in a medium-sized bowl and add the oil mixture, then add the herbal water. This will form a nice paste.

Boil two cups plain water and put it in a larger bowl. Sit in the bath tub, and brush on the clay mixture starting with the feet and legs. Dip the cotton strips in the hot water and wrap them over the paste. Continue with the arms, then the torso. You can also use this paste on your face, but do not wrap it; just let it dry.

After you are all wrapped, place a large, warm towel over yourself and relax for twenty minutes in the empty tub. Rinse yourself of with tepid water, and dry off.

## Seaweed Mineral Wrap

Seaweed is perfect for body wraps because the molecular formation of the human blood cell is similar to that of seawater. Nutrients from seaweed easily pass through the pores of the skin and into the bloodstream, making a seaweed wrap perfect for replacing minerals, nutrients, and elements in the body. Seaweed's antioxidants and amino acids to help lessen the effects of aging on the skin.

When used in a body wrap, seaweed builds up heat and activates the nutritional action of the plant. Seaweed works well for detoxification from excess drinking or smoking, improves the life force after surgery or stress, and helps chronic conditions such as arthritis and rheumatism. Seaweed wraps are a popular weight loss tool because they help eliminate cellulite, improve circulation, break down fat deposits, and balance metabolism.

There are more than 20,000 kinds of seaweed in the oceans of the world. Use kelp, the large, leafy brown algae that grows in cold coastal waters, for your body wraps.

8   ounces dried or powdered seaweed

Enough water to make a mayonnaise-like paste

(Use three ounces of fresh seaweed if you're lucky enough to live near the ocean.) Do this wrap in the bathtub. Lay a blanket down in the dry tub first, then the plastic sheet. Turn on the space heater. Sit down on the plastic, and cover yourself with the seaweed paste (or fresh seaweed). Use a brush to apply the paste. Wrap up in the sheet and blanket, and relax for twenty minutes. Unwrap and remove everything from the tub. Fill the tub with warm water, and relax for ten minutes. Afterward, pat dry and moisturize.

# How to Grow Your Own Loofahs

≫ by Chandra Moira Beal ≪

The loofah is a fast-growing annual vine that produces pretty yellow flowers and strange looking fruits that are edible when immature and used as back scrubbers or sponges when fully mature and dried. Contrary to popular belief, loofahs are not a member of the sea sponge family. They are in fact the only known vegetable plant that can be raised and used as a sponge. Loofahs—which are also known as luffas, sponge gourds, washrag gourds, and dishrag gourds—are actually part of the *Cucurbitaceae* family, which also includes pumpkins, cucumbers, squash, and melons.

The "smooth loofah" variety is native to tropical Africa and Asia. It is grown throughout most of Asia for food and for use as pot scrubbers, and it is cultivated commercially for export in Japan. In Japan, the ridged, or "vine," loofah *(Luffa acutangula)* is used for making slippers, table mats, and pillow stuffing. The young fruit of this plant is cooked like squash. Vine okra is harder to peel, so it is more popular as a food crop. The Chinese also eat the young shoots, leaves, and flower buds of the vine loofah. In fact, fried gourd flowers are quite a delicacy, and the raw flowers are a nice addition to tossed salads.

The large bright-yellow flowers of the smooth loofah are a visual treat for gardens. They resemble squash or hibiscus flowers and grow rampantly. The vine can grow more than thirty feet in length, and scrambles over anything in its path. The large leaves are lobed and have silvery patches on the topsides. The five-petaled flowers are showy and conspicuous, about two or three inches across. The green fruit can grow up to twenty-four inches in length and three inches in diameter. They are cylindrical and smooth, and shaped like a club, slighter wider on one end. Smaller fruits look like okra or small cucumbers.

Plan your loofah garden ahead of time, because loofah is an annual that needs a long growing season to produce mature fruit. You can expect to harvest the gourds, or fully mature fruit, around four months after planting. Immature gourds, for food, can be harvested within three months.

If your climate doesn't have at least four months of warm weather, start your loofah seeds indoors to give them a head start. Loofah seeds are large, flat, and black, resembling watermelon seeds. They can be ordered from nursery and garden supply stores, especially those specializing in exotics. You can speed up germination by soaking the seeds in water overnight before planting. Like other members of the squash family, loofahs resent transplanting, so start your seeds in peat pots so you can later move them outdoors without disturbing the root system. They can also be grown in containers with tomato cages or trellises.

Plant the loofah plants or seeds in the ground when all danger of frost is gone, and position them in full Sun. Also plan your location ahead of time, because the vine will take off in all directions. Loofah is a great choice to grow on a back fence or wall. The seedlings should be planted about one-half to three-quarter inches deep in good, rich soil. Loofah likes lots of water and fertilizer at the beginning of the season, and regular waterings as the plant continues to grow through the summer. It may grow slowly at first, but as the weather gets warmer you will notice some flowers appearing. The female flowers are solitary, while the males bloom in clusters.

As the vine gets bigger and more mature, more and more flowers will appear. The big leaves, with their splashes of silver, are showy and attractive to people and insects. The female flowers need to be pollinated for the fruit to set, which will likely be taken care of by bees. You'll know when you have pollination when you see the enlarged ovary at the base of the petals on the female plant. The ovary will develop into the fruit. The loofah fruit will continue to grow through summer—up to twenty-eight inches—and may weigh up to five pounds each. One vine may produce up to twenty-five individual fruits.

The immature green fruit, resembling cucumbers three to six inches in length, can be stir-fried whole or sliced, or they can be grated and used in soups and omelets. Larger fruits (beyond six inches) will need to be peeled first because the skin becomes rather bitter.

It will take several months for the fruit to set, grow, and dry out on the vine. If you plant your seeds around the Spring Equinox, the actual loofahs may not be ready to pick until October or November. Typically you will need to take them off the vine when it starts getting cold, around the first frost.

The skin of the loofah will turn papery and yellow, brown, or black when they are ready to pick. Clip the fruit from the vine and shake out the seeds into a container, saving them for next year's crop. The outer covering can be crumpled up and peeled off, much like a hard-boiled egg. Once you peel the outer husk from the loofahs you can start using them immediately. Some people soak the dry loofahs in water for a few hours to make it easier to peel off the skin.

After the loofah is peeled, there are a couple of ways to clean them. One simple method is to put several at a time in the washing machine with a little bleach and detergent. You can also wash them in the kitchen sink with soap and bleach, but be sure to rinse them thoroughly. Then they can be placed in the sun for additional bleaching and a final drying. Larger sponges can be cut to size, depending on their intended use.

A loofah holds water like a sponge, but is soft and pliable yet durable. Even with regular use, loofah sponges last for months if allowed to dry after each use. The sponges are versatile in that they can be used for bathing, washing dishes, or scrubbing pots and pans. Loofahs are great for washing vegetables such as carrots and potatoes.

The loofah is widely used for bathing to invigorate the skin and increase circulation. You can also grind the loofahs in a coffee grinder or food processor and add it to soaps and lotions or anything you want to have an exfoliating effect. Sponges can be fastened to a wooden handle for a back scrubber, or flattened and sewn to terrycloth for a wash mitt.

Loofahs are easy to grow and have so many useful household applications. Let your imagination grow wild—just like the vine.

# Herbal Skin Care

### ➢ by Vivian Ashcraft ➣

Y ou may be surprised to learn that it is easy and fun to make your own skin-care products. Many of them can be blended from normal household ingredients. The addition of homegrown herbs makes them unique, allowing you to create customized concoctions for a particular purpose.

Homemade products have no preservatives or chemicals. You know every ingredient personally. You can infuse them not only with your own chosen herbs, but also with energy.

## Where to Start with Home Skin Care

If you have the room and time, it's fun and economical to grow your own herbs, then dry and process them. Walking into the garden shed in the

winter and finding herbs hanging upside down can bring a little bit of summer to the cold, gray days. Growing your own herbs isn't always feasible for everyone, though, so check your local natural foods or bulk store for dried herbs.

The herbs that you use in these skin-care recipes are activated by infusing them in oil or water, then using the oil or water in your products. A method for creating these infusions is explained below.

Once you have basic recipes for creams, toners, masks, or scrubs, you can choose the herb or essential oil that you need. This list is not complete, but gives the most common herbs used for the named condition.

**Acne:** dandelion, elder, garlic, goldenrod, mullein, red clover, walnut

**Age spots:** black mustard, gotu kola, red clover, Siberian ginseng, Solomon's seal, white pond lily

**Aging skin:** alfalfa, carrot seed, echinacea, geranium, lavender, nettle, rose, rosemary, sage, tea tree

**Chapped skin:** beech, black mustard, comfrey, hops, olive oil, peanut oil, peppermint, plantain

**Cracked lips:** beech, comfrey, myrrh, olive oil, plantain

**Dry skin:** burdock root, calendula, chamomile, comfrey leaf or root, jasmine, lavender, lemongrass leaf, licorice root, orange blossom, rose, rosemary leaf, rosewood, sandalwood

**Hives and itching skin:** aloe, aspen, beech, bitterroot, cattail, chamomile, chicory, comfrey, dandelion, elecampane, goldenseal, hops, sassafras, walnut, yarrow, yucca

**Oily skin:** anise, calendula, chamomile, cypress, juniper, lemon, lovage, mallow root, rosemary, rosewood, thyme leaf, willow bark, witch hazel bark or leaf, yarrow leaf, ylang-ylang

**Scars:** carrot seed, chamomile, geranium, lavender, lemon, olive oil, patchouli, peanut oil, rosewood

**Sensitive skin:** chamomile, jasmine, rose

**Wrinkles:** carrot seed, frankincense, lavender, patchouli, rose, rosemary, rosewood, tea tree

# Making Infused Oils

Place dried or fresh but gently bruised herbs in a sterilized jar, then fill the jar with a slightly warmed carrier oil to about two inches above the level of the herbs. (A carrier oil is any oil you use in your recipes to "carry" the other ingredients.) If the herbs aren't completely covered they may tend to mold. You need to leave as little air space in the jar as possible, also to prevent mold. Seal tightly and place in a sunny, warm spot for about a week, shaking daily.

If you want a stronger aroma or more potent properties, strain the oil, and infuse it again with new herbs. Repeat this process until you have the strength you want. (Be sure to add the strained herbs to your compost pile.) The most popular carrier oils are grapeseed, sweet almond, sunflower, sesame, canola, and light olive oil.

Use the same method with sterilized or distilled water to make floral or herbal waters for your recipes.

Once you have made your infused oils, you will now turn around an use them as the carrier oils in the following recipes. You can use any combinations of oils you have on hand for most skin-care recipes, unless it is specifically stated. You can also use plain oil, with no infusion.

*Note:* It is important to sterilize every tool and container you use. Because these are homemade recipes that do make use of preservatives, it is best to use small jars and refrigerate the portions you are not currently using. Also, always please practice safety. Oils and waxes can cause serious burns when improperly or carelessly heated.

When a double boiler is called for, use a skillet with about an inch of water and place your ingredients in a glass container in the skillet.

Always keep a set of tools separate from food preparation tools as well. These include all measuring implements; a separate funnel for measuring oils, both infused and carrier; spatulas; eye-droppers, for measuring essential oils; chopsticks for stirring; a small kitchen scale; a hand mixer; a grater, for grating beeswax and some herbs.

# Recipes

### *Moisture Cream*

| | |
|---|---|
| 1 | cup aloe vera gel |
| 1 | tsp. lanolin |
| 1 | tsp. vitamin E oil |
| ⅓ | cup carrier oil |
| ½ | oz. beeswax |

Optional essential oils of your choice

Blend the aloe vera gel, lanolin, and vitamin E oil together, and set aside. In a water bath or double boiler, melt the beeswax and carrier oil. Add this mixture in a slow stream to the aloe mixture, while blending on slow or medium speed. (Add optional essential oil at this time.) Once all the oil is added, blend for two more seconds. Pot the mixture up in wide-mouth jars. The resulting cream will have beads in it, which will flatten and disperse when you blend it into your skin.

### *Cold Cream*

| | |
|---|---|
| 3 | oz. carrier oil |
| ½ | oz. beeswax |
| 2 | oz. rose water |
| 1 | large pinch borax |

Melt the oil and wax together in a double boiler. In another double boiler, put the rose water and borax, gently warming and stirring until the borax is completely dissolved. Add the rose water solution to the oil and wax mixture, then remove from heat and beat while it cools until the mixture is thick and creamy. Spoon into wide-mouth jars and seal.

### *Toner*

1   cup apple cider vinegar

5   Tbl. rose petals

4   Tbl. sage leaves

3   Tbl. lavender blossoms

2   Tbl. rosemary leaves

½   cup rose water

Heat the vinegar just to boiling and pour it over the herbs. Place the mixture in a jar, capping it with a non-metal lid. Shake it daily for ten days. Strain and add the rose water. This can be bottled or put in jar. To use, after cleansing blot the toner on your skin with a cotton ball.

### *Oat Grain Scrub*

1   cup rolled oats

½   oz. lavender buds or rose petals

1   tsp. ground almonds

1   tsp. powdered white or red clay

Blend all ingredients in a blender or crush with a mortar and pestle until the oats are completely ground. To use, place a small amount in your palm and add a bit of water, then rub the resulting paste on your face. Rinse with lukewarm water.

## Good Luck

Most of the ingredients in these recipes are readily available in local markets or health stores. If you can't find them locally, there are resources on the Internet that you can locate through any search engine.

Don't be afraid to try your hand at making home-blended skin-care products. You will love the way they feel and how good your skin looks. And when your friends ask you your secret, you can smile and tell them all about it.

Herb
Crafts

# Kodo: The Art of Japanese Incense

### ≈ by Stephanie Rose Bird ≈

Our cultural passion for incense was sparked when the earliest humans placed wood on an open fire. The fragrant smoke that numerous types of trees and plants send upward to the heavens has been the inspiration for folktales, myths, herbal remedies, and holistic remedies for thousands of years. As societies grew more sophisticated, so did our relationship to the fragrant smoke emitted from burning wood and leaves.

Today, all around the world, traditions, rituals, ceremonies, and even games gradually evolved around smoldering incense. This article focuses on some Asian incense traditions, especially those of Japan, for it was there that incense developed into a high art form—the art of kodo.

# A Brief History of an Ancient Art

Kodo is a *geido*, or, in Japanese, an artistic path. Kodo is ranked along with other classical arts such as *sado* (way of tea, or tea ceremony), *kado* (way of flowers), and *budo*, a variety of martial arts. Kodo is the art and philosophy of incense. The rewards of kodo are complex, as the art salutes the individual spirit, the community and culture, all of nature, and poetry and other arts. A timeline of kodo will help to explain its history, influences, and uses.

Sixth century, AD: Legend has it that a huge piece of dried aloeswood was floating off Awaji island, Japan. It was dried and used as firewood. The delightful aroma enchanted those around it. Eventually a piece of the wood was presented to the Empress of Japan as a gift and from there its reputation took off.

538: Buddhism was introduced to Japan. During the Asuka, Nara, and Heian eras there was fluent trade between T'ang China and Japan. Buddhism, herbal medicine, art, and incense were brought to Japan from China.

688–763: Buddhist master Jian Zhen brought the *soradaki* (see explanation below) practice to Japan. Around 753 he began teaching the process of making incense balls, and this practice grew in popularity. Today this tradition still exists; the balls are called *nerikoh*.

759: Chinese Buddhist master Ganjin established Toshadai-ji Temple in Nara. Master Ganjin, like most Buddhist leaders of the time, was a skilled herbalist.

Circa 1008: Lady Murasaki Shikibu wrote the highly influential text, "The Tale of the Genji." Most of the kodo games, rituals, systems, and even some incense recipes are derived from various chapters in this text.

1185–1333: In the Kamakura period, Japanese used raw woods as incense.

1490–1573: *Sengoku jidai* (joss sticks) were invented for convenience and practicality.

1603–1867: The fifty-four crests called *genji-mon* began to be used in *ukiyo-e* (woodblocks prints). People began to associate the crests with art rather than with kodo.

1657: The Baiedo corporation was founded by Jinkoya Sakubei. Sakubei specialized in creating unique blends of incense sold as sticks *(jinkoya)*.

1705: Rokubei Moritsume Hata began using the court's secret herbal traditions to create proprietary blends for the Shoyeido Corporation.

1869–1912: During the later Meiji period, kodo was banned because the games were thought to inspire gambling.

Present day: Kodo is once again being enjoyed internationally, albeit by a small circle of aficionados.

# The Herbs of Kodo

Buddha's words are believed to be scented, indicating that fragrance is central to the Buddhist faith. There are many beautiful scents associated with Buddhism, but five are most important.

### *The Buddha Family of Herbs*

Buddha family—aloeswood *(vairocana):* (Represents the) Transmutation of Ignorance

Vajra family—clove *(akshobhya):* Transmutation of Aversion

Ratna family—borneol *(Ratnasambhava):* Transmutation of Pride

Padma family—lotus/sandalwood *(Amitabha)*: Transmutation of Desire

Karma family—turmeric *(Amitabha):* Transmutation of Envy

## The Baieido Blends

The Baieido corporation creates traditional Japanese incense from the five families of scent listed above. Established in 1657, Baieido is the oldest incense company still in existence. Baieido blends are renowned, and they were one of the earliest suppliers to the head temple of each Buddhist sect. Here are some age-old Japanese incense blends.

*Zuikun jirushi* chips: Sandalwood, clove, cassia and Chinese herbs; used for ceremony and meditation.

*Tokko jirushi* chips: Sandalwood and star anise; used to invigorate the mind, lead to clarity, and calm body and spirit.

*Sutoko jirushi* chips: Aloeswood and sandalwood; a gentle, calming blend that restores the mind after hectic activity and stress.

*Byakudan* or *mysore* chips: A high grade of sandalwood used in initiation and to aid meditation.

Plum blossom: (A whole chapter in the "Tale of the Genji" is dedicated to the plum blossom.) Plum blossoms are known in China and Japan as the flower of peace. The incense called *baika* is created by kneading aloeswood with plum meat, lotus nectar, and other botanicals. Baika is widely available internationally, today.

## Aloeswood

While in-depth appreciation for the healing qualities of aromatic herbs inspired kodo, aloeswood, or *jinko* as it is known in Japan, is the single most important ingredient. The word "jinko" is derived from *jin*, "heavy wood," and *koh*, "incense." Jinko enjoys an important role also in African and Middle Eastern aromatic tradition, where it is called *oud*.

Today, jinko is gaining a following in the West as well as a medicine. Jinko is actually sold and used in a variety of forms around the world.

Jinko chips: Renowned for stress and anxiety relief; used to treat mental illnesses, healing the mind while also deepening faith.

Grades of jinko: *Kyara*, the aristocrat-connoisseur grade; *rakaku*, the samurai-pungent grade—bitter, rough, originates in Thailand; *sasora*, the monk-complex—delicate, cool, and sour, probably from India originally; *sumotara*, servant-disguised-as-a-noble—like kyara but without the depth, considered sour, originally from Sumatra; *manaka*, fickle one/moods-ever-changing—sweet, sour, bitter, hot, salty, or fleeting, originates in Indonesia and Malayasia; *manabank*, the lower coarse peasant-grade, sweet, unrefined, gritty, originally from South India. The finest types of jinko come from Vietnam, but it is also exported from Indonesia. Some sought-after types are: *kokonoekumo; tsukigase; ogurayama* and *hakusui*.

## Incense Resins

Benzoin *(Styrax tonkinensis craeb)* mixes well with other ingredients and imparts a warm, chocolately scent. As a fragrance in incense blends it imparts a sense of the body.

Camphor, also called borneol *(Dryobalanops camphoraor; Cinnamomum camphora)* and *hon-sho*, has a medicinal scent. Camphor is used in some incense bases and is considered a holy herb in Japan

Frankincense *(Boswellia carterii; B. thurifera)* is associated with high spirituality. It has a bright, somewhat astringent scent.

Oleoresin *(Commiphora erythrea;* var. *C. glabrescens)* is also called sweet myrrh or false myrrh.

Myrrh *(Commiphora myrrha)* is associated with strength, protection, and suffering. It has a earthy base scent, and also provides healthful antibacterial and preservative qualities.

## Herbs and Trees

Cassia *(Cinnamomum cassia)* is spicy and warm, and has an uplifting scent that was considered five times more valuable than frankincense during the Roman era. Cassia burns readily and acts as a scent fixative when included in incense blends.

Clove *(Eugenia caryophyllata)* is a sacred aroma to Buddhists. It has a spicy, warm, somewhat sharp aroma when used in incense

Galbanum *(Ferula galbaniferum; F. rubricaulis; F. galbaniflua)* is used, as a root, as the primary ingredient in many fine incense blends.

Nutmeg *(Myristica fragans)* is used as a relaxant, aphrodisiac, and scent preservative.

Patchouli *(Pogostemon patchouli; P. cablin)* is intense, sweet, earthy, moist, spicy, preservative, and complex.

Sandalwood *(Santalum album; Santalum rurum)* is the chief Japanese incense wood along with aloeswood. It is sacred in Hindu faith and very important in Japanese Shinto beliefs.

Spikenard *(Nardostachys jatamansi)* is also called nard or *jatamansi* in Japanese. It has a light scent that is revered in many incense formulas. Nard is imbued with mystical and spiritual associations. It is a symbol of love, and lent an air of preciousness in Christianity as an anointing ingredient used on the feet of Christ.

Star anise *(Illicium verum)* adds a complex, much-sought-after, and unique aroma as an incense.

Vetiver *(Vetiveria zizanioides)* is earthy, deep, damp, heavy, woodsy, sweet, rich, and preservative. It provides a good base note in many incense blends.

# Kumiko: Japanese Incense Games

Ceremonies and incense games are referred to generally as *kumiko*. Kumiko centers around the enjoyment of jinko. In fact, this is the only incense used for "official" kodo.

Many games are built around recognition of the subtle differences in aroma of jinko from various places. The following are a few ceremonies and games, ranging from the mundane to the esoteric.

## Sora Daki

*Sora daki* translates as "empty burning" in English. Sora daki is a unique aspect of Buddhist spirituality with distinct Zen overtones. It is burning incense for pleasure, something that comes natural to all of us. Sora daki encourages us to enjoy the fragrance of aromatic herbs; it is one of the simplest, purest forms of kumiko. Simply light and then extinguish the flame of your favorite incense; set it in a censer and delight in the aroma.

## Sonae Kho

*Sonae kho* translates roughly as "offering incense" and is a meaningful way of incorporating incense into the spiritual practice of remembering a departed friend, loved one, or ancestor. Though a Buddhist tradition, people from various faiths also practice Sonae kho, though they may not call it by the same name. Sonae Kho is also the name of incense burned on altars, at shrines, and in temples.

## Makko

*Makko* is a traditional Chinese trail-style incense burning technique that can be a component of incense games or meditation. Makko, or "incense seals," was also used to measure time in ancient Asia. Makko also means "incense powder," as it refers to *tabu no ki,* the bark of a tree grown in southeast Asia. Makko herb is graded. The higher grades have the lightest scent, and burns slowly and evenly as an incense base.

## Sankei-koh (The Three Beauty Spots Game)

This game unites the evocative scents of aloeswood with the beauty of some of Japan's most spectacular landmarks, including: Itukushima, an island whose gateway is a beautiful red Shinto shrine; Amanohashidate, a narrow spit of land, near Kyoto, covered with evergreens; and Matsushima, hundreds of small evergreen-covered islands near Sendai.

The game is one of togetherness, camaraderie, and sharing rather than one where there are winners and losers. The *ko-moto* (incense master) gives out four rounds of jinko. The first three represent each of the locations, and the fourth is the boat. Participants smell each type of jinko once, and then try to remember the order each was given when presented a second time.

The scoring of sankei-koh is poetic. If all three locations are guessed correctly and the boat, this is called "the Three Beauty Spots." When two locations are guessed correctly, this is called "Evening Mist." If only one spot is guessed correctly, it is called "Morning Mist." When the boat is the only correct guess, it is called, "the View."

If nothing is guessed correctly, the term is "Clouds and Mist," as the view has been obscured.

## Sanshu-Koh (Game of Three)

For this game, three pieces of koh are wrapped, usually in some beautiful handmade paper. Then the packets are discreetly marked, and the envelopes of koh are shuffled carefully. The object of the game is for the guests to identify each of the different types of koh. In the end, the record-keeper keeps a tally of the order.

## Ko-awase (Incense Contests)

Hundreds of years ago, it was quite common for nobles and common folk alike to compete with one another to create the most evocative incense blends. *Ko-awase*, or "incense contests," remain a wonderful activity today for those who enjoy natural fragrances.

For your own version of ko-awase, invite a few friends over and have each of them bring a unique blend of handmade incense. Each packet of incense should be discreetly marked. The guests give their assessment of the incense blends. The host should act as the ko-moto, making final decisions on which is the best blend.

## Koh o kiku, or Mon-koh (Listening to Incense)

*Koh o kiku*, or "listening to incense," is a pleasurable pastime. Koh o kiku involves smelling various botanical blends, though the emphasis is on the pure senses—as it is called "listening" rather than smelling.

The smoke is sniffed in a specially prepared kodo cup, wherein koh is smoldering. The object is to listen to the incense to hear its color, to stir memories, to remember places, or to recall experiences sparked by smell.

Anyone can listen to incense, using a simple store-bought cone or joss stick. But to hear incense clearly, proper tools and equipment is required, and traditional Japanese incense blends are recommended. Tools include the following:

*Gin-you*—A mica leaf on which incense is placed

*Habouki*—A feather tool used to clean vent and rim of the cup

*Haioshi*—Ash tamper (see *kouro-bai*)

*Hitori gouro*—A special heat-proof censer used to hold bamboo charcoal while it is heating

*Kiko-gouro*—A kodo censer, usually a handmade raku-fired cup or a porcelain cup

*Kou boku*—Used to place incense woods on mica plate

*Kouro-bai*—Rice chaff ash; a light fluffy botanical used to hold hot charcoal

### *Preparing the Kodo Cup*

To prepare the kodo cup, follow these fourteen steps.

1. Fill the kiko-gouro (cup) loosely with kouro-bai (rice ash).

2. Stir the kouro-bai with chop sticks to aerate and loosen the ash.

3. Create a vent hole in the center of the kouro-bai.

4. Heat bamboo charcoal.

5. Place the charcoal in the hitori gouro (heat-proof censer) using metal chop sticks or tweezers.

6. Place the heated charcoal in the kiko-gouro.

7. Make a mound over the charcoal, using a clockwise upwards motion.

8. Keep the ash loose using the haioshi.

9. Make a desirable pattern.

10. Set the gin-you over the listening hole.

11. Place your chosen incense (can be fine grade of aloes-wood, sandalwood, or a traditional Japanese blend) on top of the gin-you.

12. Hold the cup in one hand from the bottom; put your other hand over the top.

13. Lift your top hand slightly to allow the aroma and smoke to escape.

14. Listen to its messages and enjoy.

# An Incense Meditation

For a good incense meditation, follow these eight steps.

1. Light your incense and extinguish the flame.

2. Take on a comfortable yoga *asana* (position) or lie down on your back in the *savasana* (corpse position).

3. Regulate your breathing, so that it is slow, comfortable, rhythmic, and deep.

4. Inhale and exhale at even intervals.

5. Focus on an object near the incense (this is called *trataka*).

6. Listen to the incense, and appreciate the complexity of its smell.

7. Gaze, with eyes softly focused; do not stare at the object.

8. Do this until you are relaxed, comfortable, and filled with messages carried by the incense smoke.

## A Smoke Bath

In ancient Japan people bathed their bodies, hair, and kimonos in fragrant smoke. You can enjoy this pleasurable pastime. Try one of these ways of smoke bathing.

1. Choose your favorite incense blend. Light the incense, and set it in a censer outdoors or in a well-ventilated room. Immerse your body and hair in the aroma.

2. For an alternative idea, hang your freshly washed clothing on a clothesline. Light the incense and set it in a censer placed below your clothing. The smoke will travel upward, imparting its scent to your clothing.

## A Kodo Aficionado in His Own Words

Mark Ambrose, of Scent of Earth catalog and virtual store, is smitten with the great incense-burning traditions of Asia, and especially of Japan (though also of the Middle East and the Americas). Most likely you will also become enamored by the mood-altering power of superior-grade incense once you experience them. Ambrose regularly shares recipes, research, and poetic musings about incense, and he makes very choice products—some of which are Scent of Earth proprietary blends.

The website (www.scents-of-earth.com) is as useful for those who formulate their own blends, as it is for those who prefer to buy their incense ready-made. There are safety tips and tools that enable you to conduct authentic traditional incense rituals at home.

The following is a transcript of an interview with Mark Ambrose.

**Question:** What is kodo?

**Ambrose:** Kodo is actually a number of things: theater, a social gathering, a game, a mindfulness practice, and a celebration of and inquiry into one of the world's most treasured aromatics—aloeswood. Kodo is a Japanese incense ceremony probably created around the thirteenth or fourteenth century AD and was greatly influenced by the tea ceremony. In fact, the first game of Kodo was called "the game of ten," which is nearly identical to the early tea ceremony of the same name. Kodo translated as "the way of incense" or "incense appreciation." *Koh* means "incense," and *dou* means "the way of" or "the appreciation of." It is also written as kodo or koh do. Kumiko are the incense games played during a kodo ceremony. There are over 1,000 different games played in Japan and one's imagination can easily create many more.

**Question:** When did you become involved with incense, and why?

**Ambrose:** My interest in kodo grew out of my great love for natural aromatics and the study of their historical cultural uses around the world. The Japanese are arguably the world's foremost experts at incense making, and it is through reading more about Japanese incense customs that I discovered the kodo ceremony.

**Question:** Who have you studied with and where?

**Ambrose:** More recently I have been studying an informal American version of Japanese kodo with a U.S. organization called Kodo Kai, for which I am now a presenter of the ceremony on a national basis. The organization is headed by Mr. David Oller of Esoterics, LLC, who is the North American distributor for Baieido Japanese incense, and who has personally studied kodo in Japan.

**Question:** What does the ceremony have to offer contemporary Westerners?

**Ambrose:** I would say it offers westerners the same things it does to the Japanese—a form of theater, a social gathering, the enjoyment of playing a game with others, a mindfulness to help wash away the troubles of the day, and an opportunity to discover the many facet of one of the world's most treasured aromatics, aloeswood.

**Question:** How long does it take to become proficient, on the average?

**Ambrose:** Kodo is enjoyable immediately to anyone who participates in a ceremony. I suppose proficiency can be looked at in two ways; first would be training the nose or olfactory system in the brain to recognize and identify the scents of the different aloeswoods. Some people are immediately very good at this. For many others, kodo is an excellent way of training the nose to recognize aromas. Secondly, proficiency can be used in developmental stages, with hopes of eventually hosting a ceremony. One can usually begin hosting an informal kodo ceremony with friends and family shortly after reading the books suggested. To refine this further, one could attend a kodo kai ceremony to learn more of the presentation details and various host positions involved simply by participating and watching the ceremony unfold. Of course, kodo is a lifelong endeavor in which one continuously learns each time they practice and play. In Japan, a person trains and studies for over thirty years before they can become a certified kodo master; even then, if you asked one, most likely they'd tell you they are still in training and will be for the rest of their life.

**Question:** Is kodo expensive? Are there ways to defray the expenses or improvise?

**Ambrose:** Kodo can be as expensive as you want it to be. One can start with minimal tools such as a cup, ash, charcoal, mica plate, and aloeswood. All of the utensils used in kodo can be substituted with common household utensils. Most kodo books are very inexpensive, and Kodo Kai events, depending on location, are usually very reasonable or even offered in exchange for free will donations. As with all things in Japan, if one wishes to take kodo ceremony very seriously there is no ceiling to what one can spend on the activity. There is a wide variety of very beautiful and elegant kodo equipment. You can even create a specialized kodo room in your home. Kodo can be a form of artistic expression or a simple, inexpensive, pleasurable game.

**Question:** Where does the novice go to learn more?

**Ambrose:** For further education, there is authentic information on the website (www.japanese-incense.com) and a wealth of information on historical kodo lineages and such on Alice's Restaurant (a Yahoo Internet group). If someone wishes to study kodo more seriously in the U.S., you can contact the Kodo Kai organization and ask for an instructor in your area that may be willing to take you under his or her wing, so to speak. This is very common and because it takes three to five personnel to put on a ceremony, many local Kodo Kai instructors are eager to teach others—especially if the students are willing to help with events.

**Question:** What is your advice for a novice who would like to get started?

**Ambrose:** One can begin to learn more about kodo with easily obtained books from your local bookstore or library. Two I highly recommend, in order of complexity, are: *Kodo: The Way of Incense* by David Pybus (Tuttle, 2001), and, for the more advanced, *The Book of Incense: Enjoying the Traditional Art of Japanese Scents* by Kiyoko Morita (Kodansha International, 1992). Anyone can begin playing the incense games of kodo, called kumiko, right after reading these books and immediately have fun playing incense games with friends and family. To participate in a kodo ceremony I would recommend being a guest at a Kodo Kai event. Contact Kodo Kai toll-free at (877) 552-1328 for an event in your area. Contact me directly for a list of upcoming public events or to arrange for a private demonstration at my e-mail: info@scentsofearth.com, or call: 1-800-323-8159.

# Conclusion

*ki mi ga tame*
*haru mo no ni idete*
*wakena tsumu*
*wa ga koromode ni*
*yuki wa furitsutsu*

English translation:

*As I gather herbs*
*From this field in early spring,*
*Intending them for you,*
*The falling snow starts to gather*
*On the sleeve of my outstretched hand*

This poem by Emperor Koko illustrates the subtle relationship between herbalism, human experience, and the acute powers of observation that inspired kodo. There are hundreds of kumiko, designed as aromatic journeys to be shared between friends. The appeal of kodo is that it delights our senses, helps us relax, connects us to others, builds collective memories, and enriches our understanding of nature and of the arts.

Genji-ko is one of the most complex yet rewarding of the kumiko. If you want to learn more, read *The Tale of the Genji* and other books recommended below. Begin with the simple meditations, rituals and games included in this article. Relax and have fun on the aromatic journey, contemplating some of the Japans most treasured scents.

## For Further Study

Shikibu, Marasaki. *The Tale of the Genji*. New York: Penguin, 2002.

Hearn, Lafcadio. *In Ghostly Japan*. Rutland, Vt.: Tuttle, 1971.

Furuya, Kensho. *Kodo Ancient Ways: Lessons in the Spiritual Life of the Warrior*. Santa Clarita, Calif.: Black Belt Communications, 1996.

# Herbal Bouquets for Weddings and Handfastings

≫ by Ellen Dugan ≪

*I have here only made a nosegay of
culled flowers, and have brought
nothing of my own but the thread
that ties them together.*

–Michel Eyquem de
Montaigne 1533–92

The tradition of carrying brical flowers is not new. This idea goes back centuries. During medieval times it was believed that bad luck and malicious spirits were common. It was also whispered that using strong smelling herbs and enchanted flowers would drive these creatures away.

Some popular herbs in medieval times included rosemary for love and protection, thyme for courage, and sage for wisdom. Meadowsweet was very popular for weddings too. Its creamy-white, delicate flowers have an almond scent. It was so favored for weddings that it became known as "bridal wort." *Wort* is an old English word for "herb."

## Weddings through Time

Historically, both the bride and groom wore garlands of flowers to represent new life and fertility. The bride's bouquet symbolized the maiden in bloom. Flowers carried by the wedding party symbolized possibilities, love, and joy. The bride's bouquet was both fragrant and charming, traditionally signifying happiness and abundant possibilities.

In early times, brides gathered blooming herbs and native flowers that they fashioned into small hand-held bouquets for themselves and their attendants. Herbal foliage or blossoms were also worn by the groom and his men to drive off bad spirits or just general bad luck, and to promote fertility.

Do you know how the tradition of the bridesmaid and the groomsmen started? Traditionally, the bride was attended by several friends, her maidens, who would dress in a similar fashion as the bride and travel together with her to the ceremony site. It was believed that this practice confused the more spiteful fairies, or malicious spirits, into not being sure who was the bride. The men did the same thing, keeping the groom safe. As the spirits couldn't be sure just who was who, they could create no mischief for the couple.

Medieval weddings had earthy and seasonal floral displays. They incorporated whatever was abundant at the time. This could include foliage, twigs, wheat, fruit, and berries. Instead of veils, the medieval bride often wore a crown of flowers, greenery, or flowering herbs in her long and unbound hair.

At the beginning of the twentieth century, extravagant bouquets might measure up to two feet across. Sophisticated brides in their twenties carried sheaves of callalilies, or a simple posy of bright colors. Early in the 1930s, brides carried armloads full of large presentation-style bouquets. By the end of this decade, simpler flowers became in style once again, and the Victorian style tussie-mussie of bright mixed flowers, such as azaleas, violets, and pansies, became popular.

During World War II, when flowers were scarce, brides carried simple and fragrant lilies-of-the-valley and garden roses. In the 1950s and early 1960s, bridal flowers became larger and more elaborate and were often triangular in shape. My mother-in-law's bouquet, from 1957, actually had three white orchids in the center of the arrangement. These orchids could be removed and worn as a going-away corsage. In the 1950s, popular choices for bridal bouquets included trailing arrangements of white orchids, orange blossoms, carnations, stephanotis, and roses.

The flower children of the 1960s and 1970s were looking for natural bouquets—such as a clutch of wildflowers or simple daisies. It wasn't unusual to see lots of foliage worked into those bouquets. Floppy hats, floral prints, and flowers arranged on silk fans were also a big hit. In the 1980s, opulence was the keyword—meaning large arrangements of mostly white or ivory flowers fashioned into triangular or crescent-shaped arrangements, or large adaptations of the old fashioned "nosegays." Typically, bridal bouquets were once again mostly white with baby's breath to soften them and with perhaps some subtle color—pale pinks, peach, and maybe a soft yellow. The more daring bride added touches of brighter pink, red, or purple.

Today though, anything goes. Brides can feel free to choose from any style they like. If you'd prefer to go more with more old-fashioned and herbal-oriented arrangements, then work in a bit of plant folklore using herbs and referring to the language of flowers. Consider creating a traditional nosegay or tussie-mussie style bouquet.

### Tussie-Mussies

The term "tussie-mussie" is derived from the Old English word *tuzzy*, which means "a cluster, posy, or knot of flowers or leaves."

The botanicals chosen for the tussie-mussie are traditionally based on the language of flowers. Since the Middle Ages, particular blossoms have held magical meanings based on symbolism and folklore of plants. The posy, or little floral arrangement, was tied up into a small cluster, typically surrounded by ruffled foliage or lace and tied off with a beautiful ribbon. Traditionally, this type of bouquet was a fragrant, hand-held clutch of flowers, foliage, and herbs in which specific botanicals were chosen to convey special sentiment. In other words the recipient was given a scented, colorful, and "secret" message.

During the Victorian era, the language of flowers had its greatest popularity. The Victorians developed this art of communicating with flowers into a pastime so popular it was actually considered a essential part of a lady's education. There are dozens of lists and many variations on the theme. Everything from the placement of the bow on the arrangement to the direction the flowers were arranged had a subtle and secret meaning. Leaves in the arrangement signified hope. Thorns warned the recipient of the danger, perhaps of discovery. Touching your lips to the bouquet was a signal to let the giver know that you accepted the message and all of the sentiment behind it.

Do you want to incorporate the romantic language of flowers into your bridal bouquet and wedding flowers? Here is a primer to help you learn how to speak the lingo.

## The Language of Flowers and Fragrant Herbs

**Angelica:** Inspiration

**Apple blossoms:** Reference

**Asters:** Romantic memories

**Astilbe:** Love at first sight

**Azalea:** Love and romance

**Baby's breath:** A pure heart

**Basil:** Love, fidelity, good luck, and "best wishes"

**Bluebells:** Constancy

**Borage:** Courage

**Buddleia (butterfly bush):** Wantonness

**Carnation:** An enthusiastic and energetic lover

**Chamomile:** Comfort and patience

**Chrysanthemum:** Cheer and optimism

**Clover:** Good luck

**Comfrey:** Happy homes

**Coreopsis:** Cheer

**Daffodil:** Gracefulness

**Daisy:** Innocence, spring, and the maiden goddess

**Daylily:** Flirtatiousness and beauty

**Dill:** Irresistible

**Dusty-miller:** Happiness and industriousness

**Echinacea (coneflower):** Strength and health

**Elderberry (blossoms and foliage):** Enchantment, good luck, and the mother goddess

**Fennel:** "Worthy of all praise"

**Fern:** Sincerity, fascination, and fairy magic

**Feverfew:** Protection and health

**Forget-me-not:** True love and remembrance

**Gardenia:** Ecstasy and love

**Geranium:** In general, marital love. Colors: red—protection, health; pink—romance; white—fertility; wild—constancy

**Goldenrod:** Good fortune

**Holly:** Good wishes and protection

**Honeysuckle:** Prosperity and devoted affection

**Hosta (leaves):** Devotion

**Hydrangea:** Commitment, celebration, true-blue friendship

**Iris:** Message, passion, and promise

**Ivy:** Wedded love and fidelity

**Jasmine:** Joy

**Lady's mantle (foliage and blooms):** Love and attraction

**Lamb's ears:** Gentleness, a sense of playfulness

**Larkspur:** A devoted connection between bride and groom

**Lavender:** Devotion, success, and luck

**Lemon balm:** Freshness

**Lilac:** First love, beauty

**Lily of the valley:** Return of happiness, cheer

**Lovage:** Strength

**Magnolia:** Sweetness, old fashioned beauty

**Mint:** Prosperity and freshness

**Monarda:** Irresistible

**Myrtle:** Married love

**Nigella (love-in-a-mist):** "Kiss me twice"

**Oak (leaves):** Strength, longevity, steadfastness

**Orange blossoms:** Marriage and fertility

**Orchid:** Luxury, beauty, and lust

**Pansy:** Loving thoughts, heart's-ease

**Peony:** Beauty

**Phlox:** "We are united"

**Poppy:** Comfort

**Queen Anne's lace:** "I'll return home," faithfulness

**Ranunculus:** Glowing with charm

**Rose:** In general, love. Colors: red—romance; white—new beginnings; yellow—happiness; orange—vitality; coral—admiration; peach—charmed; pink—innocent love; purple—passion; ivory—romance; pale green—fertility; bicolored (red and white)—unity

**Rosemary:** Remembrance, devotion, and fidelity

**Rue:** Grace and virtue

**Sage:** Wisdom and domestic virtue

**Sedum (stonecrop):** "Welcome home husband"

**Snapdragon:** Dazzling and dangerous

**Snowdrop:** Hope and early spring

**St. John's wort:** Protection from fairy mischief

**Stephanotis:** A wedding and "let's take a trip"

**Sunflower:** Constancy and respect

**Tansy:** A safe pregnancy

**Thistle:** "I will never forget you"

**Thyme:** Courage and strength

**Tiger lily:** Erotic love

**Tuberose:** Voluptuousness

**Tulip:** In general, love. Colors: red—a permanent love; pink—dream lover; pale green—a jealous lover; yellow—"I am hopelessly in love with you"; white—"return to me, my love"; variegated—"you have beautiful eyes"; maroon-black—a loving enchantment

**Verbena:** Faithfulness in marriage

**Violet:** Sweetness and modesty

**Vervain:** Enchantment

**Wheat:** Prosperity and riches

**Willow:** Serenity, love, and patience

**Windflower:** Hope and anticipation

**Weigela (bloom):** "A heart that's true"

**Woodruff, sweet:** Long life

**Yarrow:** Health, love, and comfort

**Zinnia:** Thinking of faraway friends

## Tussie-Mussie Styles

Tussie-mussies characteristically feature bouquet designs that are rounded and compact. They are hand-tied or bound together with floral tape, and feature dainty and natural garden materials. Flower placement can be formal or ordered, or the flower placement may be casual and random. The inclusion of fragrant herbs and flowers is very important. Herbs are chosen for their folklore and their symbolism.

**The Beidermeier Tussie-Mussie:** This style of bouquet is dome-shaped and features larger flowers arranged tightly in concentric rings. This style of flower arranging was popular during the 1800s. Each ring featured a different type of flower—for instance, a large rose in the center, marigolds in the next ring, and carnations after that.

**Hand-tied Tussie-Mussies:** Hand tying is a European method for creating bouquets. Hand tied bouquets are very much the style at the moment. Typically these types of bouquets are rounded-mass arrangements with little to no greenery. Materials are held in one hand while the stems are placed in diagonally, in a spiral fashion, with the other hand. The stems are usually bound at the point where they all cross. The tie is covered with a decorative ribbon and most of the stems show.

**Monochromatic Hand-tied Tussie-Mussies:** These bouquets are very popular currently. They are bold and stylish, especially for a bridal bouquet. They are arranged as the hand-tied bouquets above, but use only one or several complementary colors—various shades of pinks and deep mauve, or deep burgundy and brownish red roses. If you choose to try a monochromatic bouquet for your special day, consider the symbolism of the enchanting colors of the blossoms.

# The Magic of Color

White bouquets are a symbol of tradition, elegance, and style. Still, the truth is that if you don't add a bit of color to an all-white arrangement, it often blends right into the bride's dress. Try adding a bit of soft or even bright color to break up the white. Even adding a touch of celadon green would help. Bottom line: Don't be afraid of color!

**Celadon Green:** Celadon is often called "the new white" in bridal magazines these days. An elegant and chic color, it is a fabulous neutral tone for florals and is stunning against white or ivory dresses. look for the pale green "limone" roses to add to a celadon-colored bouquet. Green encourages prosperity and good luck

**Orange:** This color is passionate, bold, and vivid, and perfect for fall ceremonies. Orange encourages vibrancy and lots of energy.

**Purple:** A dramatic and royal color. Purple bridal flowers announce that the bride is both mystical and confident.

**Periwinkle:** This is a very popular color for attendants these days. Its purple-blue hue brings peace and serenity on this hectic day. Try working with blue hydrangeas for a natural coordinating flower to go with periwinkle dresses.

**Coral:** This is another "hot" color for attendants. Coral is a siren's shade. It is a bold and confident color.

**Hot Pink:** Hot pink roses announce passion and are a cutting-edge color. Hot pink became popular recently as a few celebrities have been adding hot pink trim to their bridal gowns and carrying bright pink flowers.

**Bridal Pink:** Softer pink roses are old fashioned and declare a romantic heart and a dreamy first love. This is the ultimate "warm fuzzy" in rose colors.

**Burgundy:** This color symbolizes a deeper, darker more tempestuous love. Deep burgundy flowers add punch and drama. Add some colorful fall foliage and shake things up! (Deep burgundy is gorgeous with black attendants dresses.)

**Silver:** Try lamb's ears or dusty miller to add a soft silvery sheen to a bouquet. Silver evokes a touch of magic into your day.

## Helpful Hints for the Bridal Party Flowers

Overall, bridesmaids' bouquets should have shorter stems than the bridal bouquet. They should be a bit smaller in design as well. However, the attendants' flowers should echo the color and shape of the bride's.

Flower girls can carry natural baskets full of petals to scatter or miniature arrangements inside of satin baskets that echo the flowers that are in the bridesmaid's bouquets. Keep the floral arrangement simple and sweet. Don't overpower the flower girls. Whatever the girls carry, make sure that the flowers are tough enough to hold up to abuse, but light enough to be comfortable and secure enough that no water can spill out of the basket and onto the girls' dresses.

Try to choose flowers that are in season. White daisies look out of place in a fall wedding, while brilliant fall foliage, berries, and brambles looks absolutely magical during the autumn months. What about shiny holly leaves and bright berries in the winter? Or snowdrops in the early spring?

Looking to go medieval? Try working with ivy, lots and lots of ivy. Traditional Renaissance wedding dresses were predominately deep scarlet-red, purple, burgundy, green, gold, or cream—in other words, heavy velvety fabrics and rich jewel-toned colors. Also, the bride should wear a garland of flowers in her hair—again heavy on the ivy.

Work in items such as wheat for fertility (a popular accessory in medieval times we are told), berries, and small twigs. Adding berries and brambles to your arrangements gives them a real fifteenth-century feel. Look for pepper berries, rosehips, or bright orange bittersweet if you don't have to worry about small children getting hold of the berries. (While I adore bittersweet in fall arrangements, it is poisonous. So use good judgment.)

Create simple and elegant boutonnières for the men, and work in a sprig of rosemary for remembrance, or ivy for protection and fidelity for the groom. Use roses for love and carnations for energy and enthusiasm. Add a touch of fern and encourage the benevolence of the fairies on your big day.

## Creating Your Own Herbal Tussie-Mussie Bouquet

Now that I've filled your head with tons of ideas let's get down to the creation of the bouquet.

Supplies you will need include:

A wire cutter

Scissors

Green floral tape (to bind the stems together)

Floral wire or a pipe cleaner to tie the bow

Leather-leaf fern, or other gardeny foliage

Foliage from the garden, such as ivy, hosta leaves, lady's mantle, or coral bell leaves

Roses: your choice of color and style. *Note:* If roses are your main flower, go with an odd number, which is always more pleasing in an arrangement. Try to arrange your main flowers—be they lilies, gardenias, or roses—in a triangular pattern within the bouquet

Three or four stems of mini-carnations; in a pinch they fill out a bouquet, and they smell great

Two or three stems of Queen Anne's lace, feverfew, or baby's breath for filler

Three to seven stems of yarrow (fresh or dried)

Assorted herbs and garden flowers chosen for their symbolism or color

A floral foam bouquet holder (use only if you do not want to make a tussie-mussie style wrapped bouquet). *Note:* Soak the green foam for fifteen minutes before arranging the fresh flowers into the foam. You will have to clip the stems fairly short; practice a few times before the big day

Satin or sheer ribbon in coordinating colors to tie around the stem and to make a bow around the base of the bouquet.

One or two corsage pins.

Start the arrangement with a large central bloom—such as a rose, or lily—as your focal point. Then encircle it with contrasting foliage and flowers, wrapping the stems together with green floral tape as you go. Work out from the center in a circular pattern, and keep taping the flowers and foliage in each time you d on the type of materials) also adapt to making bouquets, ...ets, swags, and other decorations. You can make these sim-... or elaborate depending on your taste. Once you learn the ...cs, just modify as needed.

## Working with Fresh Flowers

...eneral, plants have rich associations. There are special flow-... herbs, and trees linked with the sabbats and other holy days. ...st gods and goddesses also have their own sacred plants. In ...king your garlands, choose flowers that send a congruent ...ssage. You might want to select the type of arrangement—...sh, dried, or silk—depending on the availability and proper-... of the plants you wish to incorporate.

Fresh-cut plants hold the greatest magical energy, especially ...hey come from your own garden. They are somewhat fragile, ...t they boast beautiful colors and fragrance. Many herbs and ...e clippings stand up well even if not placed in water. Flowers ...ually require more care, but some survive long enough for a ...ual or other activity without water. No matter what you do, the ...e of a fresh-cut garland is measured in hours or days; they don't ...eserve well and part of their appeal lies in their ephemeral ...ture. Cherish beauty while it lasts!

In working with fresh flowers, you can make them last longer ... using a base ring of florist's foam, sphagnum moss, or paper ...wels dampened in water. This makes for a somewhat heavier ...d more rigid wreath, though you need to cover it thoroughly ...) the base doesn't show through. Alternatively, you can twine or ...raid the stems themselves into a circle and do without the base, ...r make a very simple base of longer twigs or vines into which ...ou can weave flowers with shorter stems. This creates a light, ...exible wreath with an informal mood.

The boldest flowers should either be spaced out equally ...round the garland, or clustered in one place as an accent. ...oliage and smaller flowers fill in the gaps. Be careful not to

add a new stem. (This keeps the arrangement tight, and things won't be shifting around.) Build up the layers, and emphasize the outer rim with large-leafed herbs, ferns, or hosta leaves. The fuzzy leaves of lady's mantle are excellent for this purpose, as are variegated ivy, coral bells, and violet leaves. Trim the ends of the stems to an even length and cover with the tape. Make sure that the handle is smooth and the stems are completely covered in the green floral tape.

Now wrap the stems in a satin ribbon to create a handle. Start at the bottom, fold the ribbon over the edge, and wrap it up to the top of the stems, right under the flowers. Fold over a bit and secure with a corsage pin. Push the pin carefully down (at an angle) deep within the stems, or if you prefer secure the ribbon with hot glue as you wrap the stems. Tie a loose bow and attach or tie this right under the flowers. Secure the bow in place with a corsage pin. Turn the arrangement over and trim up the ribbon if necessary.

Store the bouquet in a cool place (i.e., a refrigerator) in an empty glass or vase until you're ready to use it.

If you have to make the bouquet ahead of time, leave the bottom of the flower stems uncovered by the floral tape, and set the flowers into a vase of water. Store the bouquet in the fridge no more than twenty-four hours.(You don't want the flowers to wilt.) Then pat the stems dry and trim out the ends to one even length. Tape up the bottom and make sure the sides of your stems are smooth. A few hours before the wedding, finish up the stems with the ribbon and bow.

## Take a Little Inspiration from the Garden

While planning out your flowers and reception decorations for the big day, don't forget to take a little inspiration from your own garden. What flowers do you enjoy? What scents make you comfortable, and what style do you prefer? How could you work with natural supplies and flowers and create your own practical bit of garden witchery? Your wedding day is one of the most memorable days of your life, so do your own thing and be creative with your floral accessories.

Maybe you could have little terra-cotta pots of herbs or ivy at your reception tables as decorations. Tie a tiny handmade tag on to the plant with a bit of satin ribbon, and list what the traditional meaning of the herb is. Do something different!

Try decorating your reception tables with pots of spicy mums in the fall, or containers of colorful bulbs in the spring. How about a simple clutch of bright sunflowers in a pail for the summer months? In the winter, trail ivy and holly down the center of the head table and add some sparkling lights. Incorporate the seasons and look to nature for a bit of inspiration and you can't go wrong.

A wedding is a joyous occasion filled with love, happiness, and hopes for the future. Here's hoping that your special day will be a merry one, a day filled with romance, flowers, enchantment, and many wonderful memories, and hopefully a bit of basil.

Basil? You betcha. In the language of flowers the herb basil expresses "best wishes."

*Beyond Daisy Ch...*
*Weaving H...*
*Flower Cr...*

≈ by Elizabeth Bar...

As children, many of us made garlands and bouquets of seasonal flowers. Today, we enjoy similar decorations in our rituals and celebrations and on our altars.

In fact, most sabbats involve plants that are associated with the holiday. A classic image of many a goddess is a beautiful woman bedecked with leaves and flowers. The god often appears crowned with foliage too. And what handfasting would be complete without flowers?

One of the most common Pagan uses of plants is a garland or crown worn on the head. The basic circular shape serves us well for wrist or ankle bracelets, necklaces, wreaths, candle garlands, and so forth. Just measure the ring to whatever it needs to fit. The same techniques (which differ slightly

overdo it! You typically get a better effect choosing just a few varieties than trying to cram in a dozen different kinds. Make the pieces work together instead of competing with each other.

Choose colors based on associations, if you like. You can also make a garland in shades of one color—such as a crown of yellow flowers for the Sun god. You can also use contrasts, such as red and green for the Holly King. Use restful colors like green and white to balance vivid red, orange, or purple hues.

It's best to cut your own flowers right before you use them. Harvest them with a sharp pair of garden scissors or pruning shears, and cut the stems at an angle. If you choose store-bought flowers, trim the stem ends before you start weaving them. Always make sure you have enough flowers and foliage to complete your entire project.

Make the base first, or a beginning circle if you're building the crown entirely of flower stems. If starting with loose stems or twigs, bend the longest one into a loop and fasten the ends together. Then wrap other stems around in a spiral, tucking the ends under until the garland is as thick as you want.

Next, lay out the flowers around the base. That way you can see how they look in different positions. Move them around and add or subtract some if necessary.

Develop the garland by adding more flowers and foliage. For pieces with longer, flexible stems—such as ivy—you can wrap them around and through the base. For objects like lilies with shorter or brittle stems, cut them short. Then tuck them through the existing stems. You can secure loose pieces with florist's tape, wire, or string; these come in green or brown so they don't show. If you're working with a moistened base, make sure all the cut ends of the stems poke well into the base material. If you're working with a simple ring, just see that they don't stick out. Trim any dangling ends.

Fresh garlands look best with little or no other embellishments. However, you can dress them up with streamers or bows of soft ribbon. For a handfasting, you might attach a veil to the crown.

Good choices for a live wreath include: apple, bachelor's button, carnation, chrysanthemum, daisy, hawthorn, holly, iris, ivy, lavender, lily, marigold, orchid, pansy, poppy, rose, rosemary, sage, snapdragon, tulip, wheat.

## Working with Dried Flowers

Dried arrangements have a subtler magical aura than fresh ones. However, if you grow and dry your own materials, they can still pack a fair punch. Here you have a softer, more earthy palette of colors to choose from, but a richer range of textures. These garlands easily incorporate many other items besides leaves, twigs, and flowers. Dried plants are very fragile and pieces easily break off. However, if you handle them with care, they last indefinitely. That is, you can put your Beltane wreath or handfasting crown under glass and keep it.

Because the stems are brittle, dried flowers need a base. It's usually best to make your own from a few grapevines or twigs of willow. Florist's wire can also make a nice base. Again, gather all your materials and lay out the flowers and other decorations around the base so you can see how they look.

You have several options for attaching dried flowers. A hot glue gun (found in a craft store) works very well. You can also wind a spiral of florist's tape or wire over the stems. Ribbon works, but not as well as tape. It's better to secure the pieces firmly and save ribbon for a finishing touch.

Begin fastening flowers to one end of the garland base and slowly work your way around the circle. Layer buds and leaves to cover the preceding stems. When you get all the way around the ring, tuck the last stems under the first flowers so that they do not show.

Now you can add embellishments. In this category you get to use the big craft ribbons—especially the kind with wire rolled into the edges. This helps you shape the bows or streamers exactly as you want. Small and soft ribbons don't stand up as well; save them for fresh flowers.

Most types of robust plant matter look great in a dried garland. This includes seed pods, nuts, pine cones, and so on. You can even include artificial antlers! Be creative. Artificial fruits also suit this format. Feathers make a nice, airy accent. For a rustic touch, add tiny birds sculpted from feathers—with or without a nest and eggs.

Good plant choices for dried arrangements include: amaranth, carnation, cinnamon, corn, grape (vines), lavender, marigold, mistletoe, oak (acorns), oats, pine (cones), poppy (seed pods), rose, sage, statice, tansy, yarrow.

## Working with Silk Flowers

Silk arrangements don't have an innate magical aura; instead, they rely on their strong symbolism. (In floral crafts, "silk" covers all artificial flowers, not just those made from actual silk. Plastic is the least desirable, silk the most.)

However, you can get artificial versions of exotic flowers that you can't find fresh or dried, or that are super fragile and don't work well for cutting or drying. Plus, you get to choose from absolutely every color imaginable. These craft materials stand up to quite a lot of handling and they last forever. This is your most durable and versatile option.

The key to mastering silk arrangements lies in understanding the modular nature of the materials. Almost all artificial plants consist of individual pieces that come apart pretty easily. Take a close look—you'll see that the leaves and blooms slide off the plastic-coated wire stems, attached only with tiny loops or cups. This means that you can take them apart and reassemble them into your own designs.

The quickest, easiest way to make a silk garland is to take one long piece of ivy or other greenery and twist it into a circle, then overlapping the ends and wrapping them around. Take a sprig of flowers and pull off the flower heads from their wires. Now part the leaves on the garland and look for the little stubs or side-spurs where the leaves fit on. Press the cups of the flower heads on to these. You may need to remove a few leaves to make room. Use four to eight flowers spaced around the garland.

For a more elaborate crown incorporating more types of plants, start by making the same base. Cut apart the sprigs of flowers so that you have just one flower and its leaves on each stem (they usually come in bunches). Thread the stem through a gap in the base, and pull it through until you have the flowers and leaves where you want them. Then tuck in the bottom end of the stem, twisting it around the base.

Continue adding flowers in this manner until you work your away around to where you started. If the pieces don't want to stay together neatly, you can use florist's wire or tape to secure them. For best results, choose vines and flowers with wire-cored plastic stems. They hold their shape much better than the floppier solid-plastic ones. With a wire crown, you can squeeze it gently into shape if it doesn't fit your head exactly on the first try.

Silk garlands don't need a great deal of embellishment. You might try some of the same things as for fresh or dried flowers: ribbons, pine cones, or feathers. Handmade items such as artificial fruits or strings of beads work especially well with silk flowers. To add fragrance, dab essential oil on a tiny piece of cloth and hide it inside the wreath.

Good choices for silk arrangements include: aster, camellia, carnation, fern, gardenia, grape, holly, ivy, jasmine, lily, magnolia, morning glory, oak, orchid, pansy, poppy, rose, sunflower, violet.

## The Flower Language

Many cultures assign a set of meanings to different plants. In most places, of course, flowers represent feelings of love and romance, but the interpretations can get a great deal more precise than that. The Victorian "flower language" is the most famous and detailed of these correspondences.

By drawing on this tradition, you can create garlands that "say" something. For example, a Pagan bard might wear a crown of chrysanthemum and oats to say: "I love bewitching music." This would also be suited for autumn events.

Here are just a few of the meanings behind some of the plants you might use in your garlands—listed by categories of meanings.

**Affection:** Amaranth (unfading love); carnation (encouragement); chrysanthemum (I love); fern (fascination); jasmine (amiability); lilac (beginning of love); linden (conjugal love); magnolia (love of nature); myrtle (love); pansy (you occupy my thoughts); rose (love); sunflower (adoration); tulip (declaration of love)

**Magic:** Dandelion (oracle); holly (enchantment); oats (bewitching music); witch hazel (a spell); yarrow (witchcraft)

**Marriage:** Honeysuckle (bonds of love); ivy (matrimony), linden (matrimony); meadowsweet (lovely bride)

**Success:** Apple (beauty, goodness); ash (grandeur); bachelor's button (hope in misery); bay (loyalty, victory); camellia (excellence); chamomile (energy in adversity); cherry (education); clover (industry); corn (riches); mistletoe (I surmount difficulties); tansy (safe pregnancy); wheat (riches)

**Virtues:** Broomstraw (humility); daisy (innocence); grape (charity); hawthorn (hope); holly (foresight); honesty (sincerity); iris (courage; faith); lavender (silence); lily (purity, sweetness); oak (bravery); olive (peace); poppy (compassion); rosemary (remembrance); sage (domestic virtue); violet (modesty); willow (freedom)

# Magical Correspondences

Pagan traditions make great use of symbolism. You can make flower crowns to match any aspect of your ritual activity. For instance, you might crown a priestess with apple and a priest with oak. Or you might surround candleholders in crocus for Brigid or bachelor's button for Robin Goodfellow.

You might honor the Moon and the Sun with bouquets of gardenia and marigold. Your quarter-callers could wear elemental garlands: white clover and meadowsweet for air; green fern or brown wheat for earth; red snapdragons and cinnamon for fire; and blue violets and heather for water. Casting a spell for protection? Try a fragrant crown of rosemary and sage. Whatever your needs, you can find materials to match.

**Feminine plants:** Amaranth, apple, bachelor's buttons, cherry, daffodil, daisy, gardenia, grape, heather, hibiscus, iris, ivy, lilac, lily, magnolia, morning glory, myrtle, oats, orchid, pansy, passion flower, poppy, rose, strawberry, tansy, tulip, violet, wheat, willow, yarrow

**Masculine plants:** Alder, bay, broomstraw, carnation, chamomile, cinnamon, clover, dandelion, fern, holly, honeysuckle, lavender, lemongrass, linden, maple, marigold, meadowsweet, mistletoe, oak, olive, pine, rosemary, sage, snapdragon, sunflower, sweet woodruff, witch hazel

**Goddess plants:** Amaranth (Artemis); apple (Aradia, Athena, Diana, Hera, Iduna, Olwen, Venus); crocus (Brigid); daisy (Artemis, Freya); dandelion (Brigid, Hecate); fern (Freya); gardenia (Artemis, all Moon goddesses); grape (Hathor); hawthorn (Cardea, Flora); heather (Isis); iris (Hera, Iris, Isis); lily (Juno, Kwan Yin, Lilith, Nephthys, Venus); myrtle (Aphrodite, Artemis, Astarte, Hathor); olive (Minerva, Irene); poppy (Demeter); rose (Diana, Freya, Hathor, Holda, Isis, Lilith, Selene, Venus);

strawberry (Freya); violet (Venus); wheat (Demeter, Ishtar); willow (Artemis, Ceres, Hecate, Hera, Lilith, Persephone)

**God plants:** Apple (Apollo, Dionysus, Zeus); ash (Gwydion, Mars, Odin, Poseidon, Thor, Uranus); bachelor's button (Robin Goodfellow); bay (Apollo, Eros, Faunus); carnation (Jupiter); daisy (Thor); fern (Puck); grape (Bacchus, Dionysus); holly (Holly King); ivy (Bacchus, Dionysus, Osiris); jasmine (Vishnu); mistletoe (Apollo, Odin); oak (Dagda, Dianus, Herne, Janus, Jupiter, Oak King, Pan, Thor, Zeus); olive (Apollo, Ra); pine (Attis, Dionysus, Pan, Sylvanus); poppy (Hypnos); sage (Wakan Tanka); sunflower (Apollo, Ra, all Sun gods); willow (Belinus, Mercury); yarrow (Diancecht)

**Moon plants:** Camellia, eucalyptus, gardenia, grape, jasmine, lemon balm, lily, poppy, willow

**Sun plants:** Ash, bay, carnation, chrysanthemum, cinnamon, juniper, marigold, mistletoe, oak, olive, rosemary, sunflower, witch hazel

**Air plants:** Aspen, broomstraw, clover, dandelion, lavender, lemongrass, linden, maple, meadowsweet, mistletoe, pine, sage

**Earth plants:** Corn, fern, honesty, honeysuckle, magnolia, oats, tulip, wheat

**Fire plants:** Alder, bay, carnation, chrysanthemum, cinnamon, hawthorn, holly, marigold, oak, olive, rosemary, snapdragon, sunflower, sweet woodruff, witch hazel

**Water plants:** Apple, aster, bachelor's buttons, camellia, chamomile, daffodil, daisy, eucalyptus, gardenia, grape, heather, iris, lilac, lily, orchid, pansy, passion flower, poppy, rose, strawberry, tansy, violet, willow, yarrow

**Cleansing plants:** Bay, broomstraw, chamomile, iris, lavender, lily, rosemary, sage, willow

**Fertility plants:** Daffodil, grape, hawthorn, mistletoe, myrtle, oak, olive, pine, poppy, sunflower, wheat

**Healing plants:** Amaranth, apple, bay, carnation, cinnamon, fern, gardenia, ivy, oak, olive, pine, rose, rosemary, sage, tansy, violet, willow

**Love plants:** Apple, cinnamon, daffodil, daisy, gardenia, jasmine, linden, maple, meadowsweet, mistletoe, myrtle, orchid, pansy, poppy, rose, rosemary, strawberry, tulip, violet, willow, yarrow

**Luck plants:** Daffodil, fern, heather, holly, linden, oak, poppy, rose, strawberry, violet

**Magical enhancement:** Bay, carnation, grape, honeysuckle, marigold, rose, rosemary, yarrow

**Prosperity plants:** Ash, camellia, cinnamon, clover, fern, grape, honesty, maple, myrtle, oak, oats, pine, poppy, snapdragon, tulip, wheat

**Protection plants:** Amaranth, bay, broomstraw, carnation, chrysanthemum, eucalyptus, fern, heather, holly, ivy, lavender, lilac, lily, marigold, mistletoe, oak, olive, rose, rosemary, sage, snapdragon, tulip, violet, witch hazel

# Conclusion

Following a nature religion means incorporating nature into as much of our lives and ceremonies as possible. The use of flowers and other plants for decoration is so basic that people do it almost without thinking.

The custom of flower crowns has spanned millennia and continents. No matter what your tradition or experience level, this is something you can try.

Today we enjoy a much greater diversity of flowers than our ancestors did. We can get them in any season and from many different climates. We also have very convenient tools and supplies to make the work easier.

Still, if you find all of these associations and crafting too "detached," you can still go outside, sit in a sunny meadow, and weave yourself a garland of whatever fresh flowers are within reach.

Under a flower crown, every woman is a goddess, every man a god.

# For Further Study

Anonymous. *Creative Floral Arranging: How to Decorate with Fresh, Dried, and Silk flowers*. Minnetonka, Minn.: Creative Publishing International, 1997.
Covers basic tools and techniques, design and cover theory, and projects like baskets, wreaths, and accessories.

Bremness, Lesley. *The Complete Book of Herbs: A Practical Guide to Growing & Using Herbs*. New York: Viking Studio Books, 1988. Describes individual herbs and covers crafts like wreaths and hangings, and techniques for growing, harvesting, and preserving herbs.

Clements, Julia. *Flower Arranging for All Occasions*. London: Cassell; distributed in the United States by Sterling Publishing Co., Inc., 1993.

Cunningham, Scott. *Cunningham's Encyclopedia of Magical Herbs*. St. Paul, Minn.: Llewellyn Publications, 1991. Describes each herb in detail; includes tables of correspondence for the elements, planetary rulers, and other properties.

Dugan, Ellen. *Garden Witchery: Magick from the Ground Up*. St. Paul, Minn.: Llewellyn Publications, 2003.

A comprehensive guide to raising and using magical plants; see especially chapter 8 on garden Witch crafts for making tussie-mussies and wreaths.

Nelson, Teresa, ed. *Creative Wedding Decorations You Can Make*. Cincinnati, Ohio: Betterway Books, 1998.
Gives brief basic details on making headpieces, bouquets, and accessories.

Rankin, Chris. *The Complete Book of Wreaths: 200 Delightful & Creative Designs*. New York: Lark Books, 2001.
Features basic tools and techniques, bases and shapes, holidays, and unusual materials.

# Herb
# History,
# Myth, and
# Magic

# Nutmeg, It's Not Just for Eggnog

### ≈ by Edain McCoy ≈

The familiar scent of nutmeg is much more than a common household spice used for cooking or for inclusion in potpourris. The gentle smell of the mouth-watering spice evokes for many of us images of happy holidays past. It calls up visions of warm homey kitchens, winter days, time with family, festive cookies baking in the oven, rich vanilla ice cream, and the pleasant fragrance of the first eggnog of the winter season.

## The Story of Nutmeg

Some botanists believe nutmeg to be one of the earliest spices specifically cultivated by human beings as both a food flavor-enhancer and as a fragrance. The tree from which nutmeg is harvested is a member of the evergreen family (species *myristicaceae*). It is

native to, as far as we know, Indonesia, where nearly a hundred variant species of nutmeg trees, shrubs, and bushes are known and catalogued. The most common of the nutmeg trees (species *fragrans*) can grow forty to fifty feet in height and produce enough ground nutmeg in one year to give every person on the planet a quarter cup all their own.

Nutmeg is now actively cultivated in southern Asia, and is grown, in the western hemisphere, in Brazil, and the islands of the Caribbean—an enclave once known as "the Spice Islands." Common kitchen nutmeg (genus *Myristica*) grows on a tree, hidden inside yellow pods approximately two inches in diameter. The pods are often called "nutmeg apples." Though these "apples" cannot be eaten, when split in half the seeds can be seen beneath a thin, sticky membrane. These seeds are removed from the apple, then dried and grated to make the cooking herb. Mechanization has removed most of the tedious labor from the grating process, resulting in a finer powder and a cleaner final product.

The sticky membrane covering the nuts is also allowed to dry and, like the seed, is ground into a powder. This is the primary source of mace, another common food spice.

Some historians believe nutmeg first appeared in Europe in the thirteenth century when the explorer Marco Polo, and his family of merchants, returned to their native Venice from a long expedition into southeast Asia where nutmeg's use in household incenses was very popular. These incenses were used to mask unpleasant odors in the home the same way rushes were used as floor coverings in medieval western Europe.

Polo returned with many curiosities never before seen by Europeans, not only were there new spices, but from China he brought back the first pasta ever seen in Italy.

What most people do not know about nutmeg is that it is actually a deadly poison. As little as two full nuts can, and has, killed the average-sized adult. However, the ability to kill and the actual killing process are not always the same.

There are relatively few recorded deaths from nutmeg poisoning because the body can successfully purge small amounts of nutmeg from the body before its toxicity causes death. Still, an overdose of nutmeg will land you in the hospital, and you will have to be fed intravenous liquids or else dehydration will cause death. You'll spend about three days wishing the nutmeg had killed you—as convulsions, hallucinations, projectile vomiting, intense stomach and intestinal cramping, and an almost continual flow of diarrhea will attempt to flush the poison from your body while you wallow in a state of temporary psychosis.

However, it is not advisable to play games with nutmeg just to see how much you can tolerate. Those that survive the hellish purging episode are usually left with severe kidney damage and, on occasion, permanent brain damage from the repeated convulsions.

Another little-known fact about nutmeg is that it contains a naturally occurring chemical called myristicin, which is a mild but nonaddictive hallucinogenic. During the height of the youth counterculture of the 1960s and 1970s nutmeg was referred to for a time as "the poor hippie's LSD." This craze of trying to substitute the inexpensive kitchen herb for the conscious altering power of LSD didn't last long, since both the hallucinogenic and fatal doses for nutmeg were found to be about the same. The survivors of nutmeg poisoning spread the word about the "bad trip" inherent in the purging process.

Even within the confines of modern research hospitals, there is no known antidote for nutmeg poisoning. Remaining hydrated while the body vigorously expunges the overdose is all that can be done, and, as previously mentioned, survivors will likely be left with permanent damage to vital organs.

By the way, to the surprise of many in the counterculture, the expensive and illegal drug LSD, which is an abbreviation for a chemical known also as lysergic acid diethlamide-25, does have an antidote. An injection of 50 mg of chlorpromazine, administered quickly after ingestion, can reverse the worst of the psychotic episode or "trip." The drawback, of course, is that the antidote is not just lying around where anyone could get to it. It was and still is in the possession of hospital emergency rooms and in the ambulances of paramedics, neither one of which always reach the scene of a serious overdose in time to stabilize the patient.

A bit more on this sidetrack: LSD was discovered in 1938 by Dr. Albert Hofmann, a medical doctor and researcher who was seeking cures for addictive and obsessive-compulsive disorders. Unlike nutmeg, LSD was once legally used to treat alcoholism and psychiatric disorders during the 1940s and 1950s. It first appeared on the black market in the late 1960s as a dangerous "recreational drug" among those in the counterculture.

## Modern Nutmeg

Nutmeg has never been used in modern medicine, and practicing herbalists today discourage its medicinal use because there are safer herbs to treat the same symptoms nutmeg treats (lethargy and constipation, among others). On this point it appears the the healers of the old ways and those trained in the new ways agree. Nutmeg as a medicine is not worth the risk. As the famous Hippocratic Oath, taken by doctors and other healers, begins, "First, do no harm." So nutmeg is not good medicine, as it can be harmful.

As a popular kitchen spice, nutmeg has been included in a wide variety of foods, especially desserts, as a garnish or minor ingredient too small to be harmful. It gives French vanilla its rich smell, gives sugar cookies a holiday feel, tops rich cream pies, adds tang to carrot cakes, and gives a new twist to glazed carrots. The scent is often reproduced artificially to make fragrant atmospheric candles.

Following are recipes for two decadent confections that use nutmeg as a flavoring or a garnish. These dishes can be enjoyed by both the cholesterol counters and weight watchers, as well as by the rest of you. Simply put, the nutty and complex flavor of nutmeg makes these dishes remarkable.

### *Old Fashioned Cream Pudding Pie*

1½ cups granulated white sugar

1 cup whole milk or cream

3 Tbl. cornstarch

2 Tbl. real salted butter

1⅛ tsp. vanilla extract

Ground nutmeg

6 dessert cups or 1 nine-inch graham cracker pie crust

Melt the butter in a heavy cooking man. Keep stirring as you fold in the sugar, milk, and cornstarch. Reduce heat to allow for a slow thickening of the mixture. Continue stirring until the mixture has reached a pudding consistency. Remove from heat and stir in the vanilla extract. Pour this into the six dessert cups or the graham cracker crust and sprinkle a liberal amount of ground nutmeg on top.

### *Fried Apple and Spice Balls*

4 cups sifted flour

1 cup apple sauce

¼ cup white granulated sugar

¼ cup whole milk or cream

2 well-beaten eggs

2 tsp. baking powder

1 tsp. baking soda

1 tsp. ground cinnamon

1 tsp. ground nutmeg

¼ tsp. table salt

1 small bowl of confectioner's sugar and ice cream
    sprinkles, mixed
½ cup raisins

Blend all the ingredients except the flour in a large mixing bowl.
Fold in the flour slowly, so it does not leave lumps in the mixture.
Meanwhile heat a deep fryer or a skillet filled with oil. Roll the
mixture into round one-inch balls. Using a slotted spoon, place
the balls in the hot oil. Let them cook until the outer shell of the
balls is crisp and firm.

Test your first ball by placing it on a strainer to drain off the
excess oil, and cut the ball in half. If the ball inside resembles a
finished cake, then you have cooked the ball for the correct
amount of time. If it is still doughy inside, try increasing frying
time by thirty seconds until the balls look correct. Fry the rest of
the balls, draining the oil as you go. Before they are completely
dry, roll them in the confectioner's sugar and sprinkles.

# Red Bush Blessings

### ❧ by Dallas Jennifer Cobb ❧

Rooibos (*Aspalathus linearis*) is know as the "miracle tea" of South Africa. It has been used as a traditional drink of the indigenous inhabitants of the western cape of Africa for more than 300 years.

The word "rooibos" itself is an Afrikaners slang word, of Dutch origin, meaning "red bush." Pronounced *roy-bos*, it is said that a "cup a day keeps the doctor away." It is also known simply as red bush tea, or just red tea. As the plant ripens, fermentation turns the leaves from green to deep red, giving the tea its name, as well as a slightly sweet note.

## Rooibos Today

North Americans are now discovering the extraordinary qualities of rooibos. This tea is an elixir for mind, body, and spirit, and it promotes vast health benefits. Rooibos is versatile and delicious consumed as tea.

While rooibos is only now gaining popularity in North America, it has been one of the most highly consumed teas worldwide. Japan imports and consumes over 310 tons of rooibos annually, and has done extensive research on its healing properties. In Japan, rooibos is called the Long Life Tea because of its anti-aging properties.

Rooibos tea has no known negative side effects. It contains no caffeine and very little tannin—only about 1 to 4 percent. Rooibos has healing medicinal properties that aid in the treatment of a variety of disorders, and it relieves a great multitude of illnesses. Still, best of all rooibos tastes fantastic.

## Rooibos Facts

The following list details some of the most interesting facets of rooibos and red bush tea.

Rooibos is good for our health and free from any harmful stimulants.

Rooibos is sold in almost every health food store in the United Kingdom, and is becoming readily available in Canada and the United States.

The World Intellectual Property Organization (WIPO) awarded a gold medal to rooibos in 1997 for its anti-allergic properties.

Annekie Theron, attributed with discovering the first medical applications of rooibos, received the 1986 Woman Inventor of the Year award. She developed a rooibos extract that is used in cosmetic and health-care products worldwide.

The top ten importers of rooibos are (in order): Germany, Japan, the Netherlands, the U.K., Malaysia, South Korea, Poland, the United States, Colombia, and China.

Rooibos has a natural hint of sweetness, but also tastes great
with honey and lemon. Unlike many other herbal teas,
rooibos can be mixed with milk.

Children love rooibos tea.

Because it is harvested fresh from nature, rooibos is organic,
with no additives, preservatives, or colorants.

## The History of Rooibos

Rooibos is an indigenous herb that has traditionally grown in
only one location in the world—the area within an one-hun-
dred-mile radius around the village of Clanwilliam in the South
African western cape region of Cedarberg. Rooibos grows at alti-
tudes between 1,500–2,500 feet above sea level.

With the current recognition of its health benefits and large
scale marketability, there are now attempts to successfully cultivate rooibos in other regions.

Rooibos seeds are best planted during February and March.
The plants are tended for approximately eighteen months and
then harvested, bundled, and milled to a uniform length. The
plant material is then bruised between rollers, triggering the fermentation process that resulting in the development of rooibos'
characteristic flavor and sweet aroma.

Indigenous inhabitants have been using rooibos for over
three hundred years. The traditional drink was made by bruising
the wild plants with wooden hammers or mallets, then laying the
leaves and stems in the Sun to ferment. They found that the fine,
needle-like leaves of the plant made a tasty, aromatic tea.

In 1772, botanist Carl Humberg reported the "discovery" of
rooibos to the European market. At the time, the wide variety of
healing powers of the plant were unknown, and it became popular simply because of its delicious taste.

With the waves of European colonization of South Africa in
the early 1900s, rooibos' fame spread to the new immigrants.
When the health benefits were discovered, it became known as

the "miracle tea." In 1904, Benjamin Ginsberg, a Russian immigrant to South Africa, realized rooibos' marketing potential. He traded with the indigenous mountain people for rooibos, then marketed and sold it in Europe. Descended from a tea industry family, Ginsberg possessed the background and experience to market this new "Mountain tea."

After the Second World War, the rooibos market collapsed. Local producers, eager to reestablish the once vibrant market, established the Clanwilliam Tea Cooperative in 1948 and collectively requested the Minister of Agriculture to appoint a rooibos tea control board. The board was established in 1954 with the defined goals of regulating marketing, stabilizing prices, and improving and standardizing quality.

Today, rooibos is still processed in much the same way as it was originally, though of course the methods are more mechanized and refined. The tea control board's leadership has guided the industry toward stability and prosperity, and has focused on refining production methods, experimenting with packaging and storage, and expanding the distribution of rooibos around the world.

Rooibos has been widely available in British health food stores for many years, but international sanctions against the South African apartheid regime kept it from becoming more widely exported. Many North Americans have only recently discovered rooibos—since the collapse of the apartheid regime and the end of trade sanctions.

## The Health Benefits of Rooibos

With a broad spectrum of therapeutic uses, rooibos is a versatile tonic with many innate healing qualities. Here is a list of just a few of these qualities.

High levels of antioxidants give rooibos anti-aging properties.

With its soothing effect on the central nervous system, rooibos can help relieve irritability, headaches, sleep disturbances, insomnia, nervous tension, depression, and hypertension.

Rooibos has anti-spasmodic properties and can relieve stomach cramps, colic, constipation, and allergy symptoms. It can relieve nausea and vomiting, aid in the treatment of stomach ulcers, and relieve heartburn.

Rooibos also has a soothing effect on skin, relieving itching and irritations. Applied directly to the affected area, rooibos is a great treatment for diaper rash, acne, heat rash, poison ivy, bug bites, and eczema.

Rooibos' anti-allergenic qualities can aid in the management of hay fever, asthma, and eczema.

Because it is high in minerals, rooibos is an ideal sports drink, replenishing lost essential minerals like iron, zinc, and sodium.

Because rooibos replenishes iron levels, it is especially helpful to breast-feeding or pregnant women.

Rooibos is beneficial in the treatment of diabetes, atherosclerosis, liver disease, and cataracts, and it boosts the immune system.

Rooibos contains no oxalic acid, allowing those suffering from kidney stones to drink it freely.

Rooibos aids your body's natural schedule, relaxing you at night and stimulating you in the day.

# A Medical Wonder

In April 1986, a South African mother named Annique Theron accidentally added rooibos tea to her baby's milk. The allergy-prone infant had been struggling with severe and ongoing attacks of colic. After drinking the tea, however, the fourteen-month streak of constant crying and vomiting stopped, and the baby slept peacefully for more than three hours. Annique then decided to do more research on the properties of rooibos.

Eighteen other babies with similar problems were given the rooibos tea treatment, and the mothers quickly sent in news that the babies were doing better. Annique's findings were quickly published, and she was attributed with discovering the first medical applications of rooibos. And, as a result, she received the Woman Inventor of the Year award. In time, she developed a rooibos extract that is now used in cosmetic and health-care products worldwide.

## Beneficial Antioxidants

Antioxidants are substances that have the ability to neutralize free radicals, the highly reactive byproducts of cell metabolism. Free radicals are electrically charged molecules that steal electrons from other substances, causing damage to critical cellular elements. By bombarding cells, they break them down—causing everything from wrinkles to cancer. The number of damaging free radicals is increased by such common human activities as smoking, exposure to ultraviolet rays, air pollution, and a diet of highly saturated fats.

Antioxidants are substances that slow the rate of random free radical reactions. They help to slow the process of aging and prevent the decline of cell health. Studies have shown that the addition of antioxidants to a rodent's diet can increase its life span by up to 30 percent. Scientists hope that this is true for humans as well. Some of the sources of antioxidants include vitamins A, C, and E, and bioflavonoids. These are commonly found in fruits, vegetables, and herbs.

Rooibos has fifty times more antioxidants than found in green tea, and as such it provides superb anti-aging properties. Super oxide dismatase (SOD) is an enzyme, present in rooibos, that is a prime preventer of free radical damage. SOD also helps to prevent fats from changing into harmful lipid peroxide.

methods for consuming rooibos include preparing it as a tea,
e consumed hot or cold, making rooibos ice cubes to add to
r drinks, or simply prepared with a bit of honey and made
popsicles for children's consumption.

For hot rooibos tea, bring freshly drawn cold water to a
ng boil. Place one teaspoon of rooibos for each cup of tea
a teapot, and pour boiling water over it. Cover and let it
p for two to four minutes, then pour. Add milk and sugar to
e, if you prefer.

For iced tea, place five teaspoons of rooibos into a teapot.
r one and a quarter cups of freshly boiled water over the
ibos and steep for five minutes. Partially fill a pitcher
cold water, and pour the hot rooibos infusion into the
cher, straining the leaves out. Add lots of ice, and fill
pitcher with cold water. Pour the drink into tall glasses, and
nish and sweeten to taste. This recipe makes about one quart
ea.

# Rooibos Recipes

upply of cold rooibos tea can be kept in the fridge for up to
weeks and used in food preparation, mixed with fruit juices,
made into cocktails.

When making stewed fruit, add the nutritious qualities of
ibos. Soak dried fruit overnight in cold rooibos before
king. No additional sugar needs to be added during the cook-
process. The minerals in rooibos increase the nutritional
ue of any dish—such as stewed fruit, jams, or jellies—that you
pare.

### *Rooibos Fizzies*

1   quart strong, cold rooibos tea (see recipe above)
2   cups apple juice
1   cup cranberry juice

Quercetin is a flavanol, present in rooibos, that in
lary strength, aids in circulation, prevents hemo
protects against infections.

## The Nutrient Contents of Roo

The following list describes the amount of nutri
each 200 milliliters of rooibos, as well as the nutri
in the body (in parentheses).

Iron (transportation of oxygen in the blood)—0.07

Potassium (aids in metabolic function)—7.12 mg

Copper (aids in metabolic processes)—0.07 mg

Calcium (maintains strong teeth and bones)—1.09

Manganese (aids in metabolic processes and bone
    ment)—0.04 mg

Fluoride (maintains health of teeth and bones)—0.2

Zinc (facilitates normal growth and development
    motes healthy skin)—0.04 mg

Magnesium (maintains healthy nervous system and
    metabolic processes)—1.57 mg

Sodium (necessary for fluid and acid base balance)—

## Consuming Rooibos

Rooibos can be used in cosmetic, culinary, and heali
tions. The use of rooibos in cosmetics is curre
research, and there is hope that the herb's anti-aging
can lead to the development of new moisturizers, t
skin washes.

The most popular and accessible recipes involvi
currently are in teas, cold drinks, and desserts. Rooib
act as a natural food coloring and food flavoring. Pr

1   quart soda water or sparkling lemonade

½   cup strawberries, hulled and sliced

If you prefer, substitute banana slices or fresh pineapple cubes for the strawberries. Mix the rooibos tea and fruit juices in a punch bowl. Chill the soda water or sparkling lemonade and add to the bowl just before serving. Decorate the bowl with strawberry slices (or banana or pineapple), and add ice. Makes about twenty glasses.

### Rooibos Shakes

2    cups very strong rooibos tea

2¼   cups vanilla ice cream

4    tsp. lemon juice

1½   cups sparkling lemon juice

Combine the rooibos tea and ice cream and beat well. Stir in the lemon juice. Pour the mixture into glasses, and fill the glasses with sparkling lemon juice. Makes eight glasses.

### Non-alcoholic South African Punch

1¼   quarts of freshly brewed rooibos tea

⅔    cup sugar

1    quart orange juice

1    quart apple juice

3    cups spring water

1    quart ginger ale

While the tea is still hot, add the sugar and stir until it is dissolved. Combine the tea, juice, water, and ginger ale in a punch bowl filled with ice. Garnish the bowl with mint leaves and cherries, or apple and lemon slices.

### Classic Bubble Tea

½    cup cooked and chilled large Chinese tapioca pearls

1    cup crushed ice

1 cup very strong, chilled rooibos tea

1 cup milk

1 cup honey or sugar (or less to taste)

Place the pearls in a large parfait glass. Combine all the remaining ingredients in a cocktail shaker. Shake the drink vigorously until the mixture is frothy. Pour the mixture into the glass, and serve with extra-thick straws.

### South African Fruit Cooler

1 tsp. loose rooibos tea (or one tea bag)

1 glass of ice

    Juice from one half orange

1 tsp. sugar, if needed for sweetening

Boil enough water to fill a tea cup. Pour the water over the rooibos tea, and steep for three to five minutes. Pour the tea into the ice-filled glass. Add the orange juice. Add sugar if desired. Stir and enjoy

### Citrus Refresher

3 cups hot rooibos tea

¼ cup sugar

1 cup lemon or lime juice

1 cup orange juice

1 lemon or lime, sliced

1 orange, sliced

1 handful of fresh mint

In a pitcher, add the sugar to the rooibos tea, and stir until it is dissolved. Add the fruit juice and slices. Chill in the refrigerator, and serve cold over ice and decorated with fresh mint or candied cherries. Recipe makes about eight tall glasses.

# Alcoholic Beverages

### *Rooibos Rocket*

½  cup strong rooibos tea

1¼  cups cranberry juice

½  cup grapefruit juice

⅔  cup vodka

1  orange, sliced

Combine the tea and then fruit juices, then chill the mixture. Once it is cold, mix it with the vodka. Pour the drink into glasses over ice cubes and decorate with orange slices. Makes four glasses.

### *Glühwein*

1  cup strong rooibos tea

   Rind of 1 lemon, peeled in a single strip

5  Tbl. sugar

1  cinnamon stick

1  tsp. ground cloves

2  cups red wine

Boil rooibos, lemon rind, sugar, cinnamon, and cloves together until sugar dissolves. Add the red wine, and bring it to a boil. Remove the cinnamon stick and the lemon rind, taste for sweetness, and add more sugar if you prefer. Pour the mixture into glasses, and serve each with a slice of lemon. Makes five glasses.

### *Irish Tea*

2  cups strong, hot rooibos tea

3  Tbl. brown sugar

⅓   cup Irish whiskey

⅓   cup fresh cream, lightly whipped

     Grated chocolate

Place one tablespoon of the brown sugar and two tablespoons of whiskey into each of four glasses. Pour one-half cup of hot rooibos tea into each glass, and stir until the sugar is dissolved. Carefully float cream on top of each glass by pouring it over the back of a metal spoon. Do not stir the mixture or disturb the layers. Sprinkle grated chocolate on top of each and serve immediately. Makes four glasses.

## Rooibos Specialty Teas

Rooibos combines well with many other herbs to make a tasty tea-based beverage that can be consumed both hot and cold at all all times and during all seasons.

Rooibos is caffeine-free and makes a healthy alternative to black teas and coffee. Rooibos tea is a thirst quencher, and therefore makes an excellent beverage for active people.

This tea contains no oxalic acid, making it a good beverage for people prone to kidney stones. In South Africa, nursing and pregnant women drink rooibos because it contains no caffeine, no colors, and no artificial additives or preservatives.

The recipes for rooibos teas below include suggestions for herbs to mix with rooibos to create distinct tastes and for various health benefits.

Mix rooibos with cinnamon, cardamom, vanilla, and ginger to make a delicious decaf chai tea. Along with the previously stated health benefits of rooibos, chai tea is renowned for stimulating the lymph system and liver function, and for detoxifying the body.

For a quick pick-me-up, combine rooibos, dried orange peel, a squeeze of lemon juice, and thistle petals to make a fruity, fresh-tasting south Florida tea. The rooibos and orange peel combine to make subtle, but healthy, sweet notes.

Combine rooibos tea with lavender, rose petals, currants, and rose hips to give your tea the flavor of sunny Provence in France. The flavorful floral bouquet of this tea helps promote a tranquil sense of well-being and ease, and imparts a touch of the splendor and culture of one of the great cuisines of Europe.

Fighting a flu or fever? Combine rooibos with lemongrass (also known as fever grass), calendula petals, and chamomile flowers to make a very soothing and healing tea. A cup of this tea will help you get a bit of rest at long last.

When rooibos is combined with raspberry leaves, dried orange peel, sunflower blossoms, and cornflowers, the resulting tea is great for preventing and easing the blues. Have a sip of this stuff, and feel the Sun beaming into your soul—even on the darkest and coldest of deep winter days.

If you generally have trouble sleeping, at bedtime make yourself a calming, sleep-inducing tea by mixing rooibos with some chamomile and add a spoonful of honey. This tea has the ability to lay to rest even the most hyperactive and overwrought mind and body. Nighty-night, sleep tight.

If you're looking to tap into a bit of rooibos magic, you can stimulate your intuition by brewing a fragrant mix of rooibos, chamomile, and jasmine petals. The scent alone will stimulate hidden mysteries and make you long for more. (You'll have to try the tea yourself to find out what magic you may experience.)

# Conclusion

Experiment with teas made from subtle mixtures of rooibos and your favorite herbs. Let your taste buds guide you, and let health be your reward.

However you decide to use rooibos, make it a regular habit. Let the versatility and flavor seduce you, then settle down and marry the long-term effects of improved health.

Rooibos really is a red bush blessing.

# Working with Traditional Celtic Herbs

≈ by Sharynne MacLeod NicMhacha ≈

Many sacred plants and herbs were used in Scottish and Irish folk magic and healing rituals. Ancient practitioners used a range of plants—from the tiniest flowers to the enormous oak.

A wide variety of herbs were traditionally utilized in healing and protective magic, as well as love charms and spells. Certain plants and trees were associated with rituals which took place on the quarter days—Samhain, Beltane, Imbolc, and Lugnasadh. Herbal charms and spells were employed to invoke good fortune—health, friendship, joy, love, eloquence, bounty, victory, confidence, and safety—as well as to encourage magically the herds of cattle that were the source of sustenance and life to produce milk and young calves.

Herbal magic was a common method for overcoming or protecting against malice, envy, fear, falsehood, ill luck, fraud, oppression, scarcity, bad news, and the evil eye.

Sometimes there were special circumstances associated with finding or gathering sacred plants. In some instances, the plant had to appear in one's path "unbidden." That is, the plant's magic was effective only if you were not intentionally looking for it.

Some plants had to be gathered during the flow of the sea, rather than during ebb tide. Others had to be collected or prepared during certain phases of the Moon. St. John's wort had to be gathered with the right hand (associated with the earthly realm) and preserved with the left (associated with the otherworld).

In addition, many Scottish charms refer to traditional prophecies that specified how the plant could be used or what powers it contained. Magical charms were recited prior to and during the actual culling of the sacred plant. Often these charms included special phrases which were spoken at the exact moment the plant was taken: "Pluck will I mine honored plant," or "I cull thee now."

The wording of some herbal charms indicates that the gathering of magical plants was considered a prayer to a particular deity: "I will pluck my plant as a prayer to my god." Sometimes the plant was said to be gathered in the manner of holy persons of yore (although the method of gathering is not always described). Since many of these folk charms were recorded during the Christian era, saints from the new religion were included in (or grafted on to) the original verses.

The most common figures are Bridget, who was originally a Pagan goddess, and Mary, invoked as the "mother of the people" (perhaps replacing a mother goddess or goddess of the land). Bridget was associated with a number of herbs—including dandelion, bog-violet, figwort, red-stalk, and catkins. Mary is mentioned in connection with ivy, shamrock, fairy wort, figwort, bog violet, passion flower, catkins, and St. John's wort.

A Celtic deity may also have been associated with the figwort, which in Scottish Gaelic is sometimes referred to as *lus an tor-ranain*, or "the plant of the thunderer." Torannan was the name of a legendary missionary who traveled to Scotland after his Christian teachings were rejected in Ireland. It is noteworthy that the early Celts also worshiped a god called Taranis, whose name literally means "the Thunderer." It is possible that figwort and other plants were originally associated with this Celtic deity.

## Scottish Herbal Magic

The following are some of the plants and herbs commonly used in Scottish folk magic.

**St. John's wort:** This "noble yellow plant" was used to ward off the malicious use of second sight or enchantment, as well as death and the evil eye. It was believed to ensure victory in battle, grant wishes, bring good luck, encourage abundance and the growth of herds, fields, and people, and bring peace and prosperity. St. John's wort was effective only if found without seeking it. When encountered, the plant was secretly placed in the bodice or vest under the left armpit, and the happy recipient recited a charm of happiness and gratitude: "Happy are those who have thee . . . Whoever gets thee in the herd's fold shall never be without kine." This herb also bestowed spiritual power and was used in divination rites. Many charms reflect its attributes: "I will cull my plantlet as a prayer to my King that mine may be its power over all I see."

**Ivy:** Ivy was associated with an abundance of milk and the bringing forth of young calves. On the quarter days, young girls pinned three leaves of ivy onto their night-gowns to encourage dreams of their future partners. Wreaths of ivy, rowan, and woodbine or bramble (alone or together) were twisted into wreaths to protect the home and hearth.

**Figwort:** Figwort was called the plant of a thousand blessings or virtues. In addition to many medicinal uses (treating cuts, bruises, and sores, and ensuring a good supply of milk) it had a variety of magical applications. Figwort had to be gathered during the flowing tide (as opposed to ebb tide) for it was associated with the flowing or releasing of various substances (milk, water, produce of land and sea, calves, and general bounty). It was also believed to bring goodness, joy, love, peace, and power. In addition, figwort was associated with several divine figures, as well as "the nine joys which came with the nine waves."

**Shamrock:** Like St. John's wort, the *seamrag* had to be found without searching for it, and the four- or five-leaved clover was cherished as an invincible talisman. Often referred to as the "shamrock of blessings" or the "shamrock of power," it was associated with good omens and with "seven joys" of health, friends, cattle, sheep, sons, daughters, peace, and deity.

**Catkins:** The wool or fiber of the catkin was used in magical charms to increase milk and herds, to protect against the loss of animals or one's means of survival, to bring about success, and to protect against the loss of friends.

**Fairy wort:** The fairy wort was said to have the power to overcome every oppression, and this power was perceived as emanating from the fairy realm. It could repel scandal, hatred, falsehood, fraud, bad luck, ill love, or a bad life for the entire length of one's existence. It was said: "There is nothing that the Sun encircles but is to her a sure victory."

**Club moss:** This plant was considered sacred by the Druids, and in folk magic it protected against all harms or mishaps and ensured safety during travel (even in darkness). It was said that no harm could befall you if the club moss was in your path.

**Purple orchis:** The purple orchis has two roots, one larger than the other, and this is where its magical properties lie. The smaller root was said to represent a woman and the larger one a man. The plant had to be pulled up by the roots before sunrise, with the puller facing south. It was then placed in water, taking care that no part of the Sun was above the horizon while doing so. If the plant sank, the person whose love was sought would indeed become your partner. A charm could also be made from purple orchis by taking roots home, drying them, and the placing the powder underneath the pillow to invoke dreams of one's future partner.

**Yarrow:** In addition to being prized for medicinal uses, yarrow was utilized in love divination on the quarter days. It was believed to promote fairness of face, swiftness of foot, and eloquence. It also seems to have also been associated with personal power. Charms associated with yarrow include descriptive visualizations of the power of nature and the power of the individual (such as the one below).

*May I be an isle in the sea,*
*May I be a hill on the shore,*
*May I be a rock on land,*
*May I be a star in the waning of the Moon.*

**Bog-violet:** This lovely herb was used to promote knowledge, wisdom, and eloquence, as well as to overcome oppression and the evil eye. One traditional charm for gathering the *mòthan*, or bog-violet, went as follows.

*I will pluck the gracious mòthan,*
*Plant most precious in the field,*
*That mine be the holiness of the seven priests*
*and the eloquence that is within them . . .*
*That mine be their wisdom and their counsel,*
*While the mòthan is mine.*

The bog-violet was also used in love spells. The woman performing the spell would gather nine roots of the plant while resting on her left knee. These were knotted together to form a ring which was placed in the mouth of a young woman. If the young woman kissed a man while the ring was in her mouth (without him being aware), he would fall in love with her forever. Bog-violet was also used to promote safe childbirth and journeys.

**Mountain yew/juniper:** This plant is the ancestral plant badge of my Scottish clan (clan MacLeod). Juniper was used to protect against misfortune, fear, danger, or fatigue, and was traditionally burned in the house and barn on New Year's morning as a purifying incense for the coming year. The plant had to be pulled up by the roots, with the branches made into four bundles, which rested between the five fingers while a charm was recited to invoke its protective powers.

## Witch Herbs, Ancestors, and Sacred Trees

In addition to using ivy, rowan, and bramble or woodbine (honeysuckle) in protective wreaths, the Scotch-Irish also used other herbs. Small wreaths of milkwort, butterwort, dandelion, and marigold—each about three or four inches in diameter (and bound by a triple cord of flax)—were placed under milk vessels to prevent the fairy folk from stealing the essence of the milk.

Some herbs were said to deter Witches or fairies, although the origin of this belief is probably that the herbs provided general protection from harm, scarcity, or unwanted influences. A combination of trefoil, vervain, St. John's wort, and dill was said to "hinder Witches in their will" and protect against malicious or nonbeneficial influences.

Certain parts of the country traditionally used certain herbs, and those with Scottish ancestors may choose to work with the magical plants and herbs associated with their ancestral regions.

In the south of Scotland, Witches were said to ride on stalks of thorn, ragweed, or broom. They preferred foxglove, night-shade, and hemlock, and avoided ivy, bindweed, fern, yew, elder, witch-elm, and holly.

In Buchan, in the north, healers and magicians used vervain, fern seed, and orpin (stone crop). I traditionally work with plants sacred to the Isle of Skye, where my Scottish clan is from. These include: mistletoe, club moss, watercress, ivy, bramble, figwort, St. John's wort, and bog violet.

In addition to herbs, plants, and shrubs, a number of sacred trees were also used in folk magic. A traditional Scottish rhyme enumerates the trees which were to be sought out:

*Choose the willow of the stream*
*Choose the hazel of the rocks*
*Choose the alder of the marshes*
*Choose the birch of the waterfalls*
*Choose the (mountain) ash of the shade*
*Choose the yew of resilience*
*Choose the elm of the brae*
*Choose the oak of the Sun.*

**Oak:** The oak tree was used in Druidic rituals and was still considered sacred in later folk tradition. It was revered for its size, age, and longevity, and seems to have been associated with wisdom. When mistletoe was found in connection with the oak it was considered especially sacred, as this is quite a rare occurrence. Mistletoe was a myste-rious plant—neither an herb nor a tree, it grew neither in water nor in soil, and remained alive while other plants were lifeless during the winter. Therefore it seemed to exist betwixt and between the worlds.

**Rowan or mountain ash:** This tree is often found growing near cairns, stone circles, and other sites of Pagan wor-ship. It was considered a powerful protective charm and was therefore planted near houses and barns and used to make household and agricultural tools and implements. Sometimes rowan trees were trained to grow in an arch over the barn door or the farmyard gate to protect the animals. Highland women twisted red thread around their fingers or wore necklaces of rowan berries as a charm. On the quarter days, a wand of rowan was placed above the doorway and a rowan twig carried in pocket for protection. Sacred cakes were often baked over a fire of rowan or other sacred wood.

**Elder:** The elder was second only to rowan for protection and was used in a similar way. If the juice of the inner bark of the elder was applied to the eyelids it was said to give a person the ability to see through the veil on the quarter days. In addition, standing under an elder tree located near a fairy hill at Samhain enabled one to see the fairy train pass by.

**Hazel:** The hazel tree and its nuts were associated with divination, prophecy, and divine wisdom. Hazelnuts were commonly used in love divination rites at Samhain. Children born in the autumn were considered fortunate because they could have the "milk of the nut" as their first food. Hazel rods were used to detect water and underground minerals.

**Yew:** The yew tree was a symbol of longevity and immortality and may have been the world tree of the Irish. A sacred yew was associated with Tom na hIubhraich, "the knoll of the yew wood," a well-known fairy haunt in Scotland.

**Apple:** The apple tree was a symbol or token of passage to the otherworld. In Britain, the Isle of Avalon was associated with this sacred tree, as was the otherworld realm of Emain Ablach in Ireland. In the saga called *Voyage of Bran*, a fairy woman appears to Bran, inviting him to the otherworld: "I bring you a branch of Emain's apple tree, with silver twigs and crystal buds and blossoms."

# The Quarter Days in Ireland and Scotland

A number of sacred herbs and trees were associated with the quarter days and their divine rites. These plants were used in folk ceremonies, as offerings or in great rituals, and were associated with abundance, protection, healing, and power.

At Imbolc, "Bridget's crosses" were fashioned in a variety of shapes from straw, reeds, or rushes, and a doll representing Bridget was made from these plants or a sheaf of grain. The dandelion was also associated with Bridget, as it is the first flower to bloom after her festival. In Scotland, the image of Bridget was decorated with shells, stones, crystals, primroses, snowdrops, and any seasonal greenery which was available. Sometimes a small wand of birch, broom, bramble, or white willow (or other sacred wood) was placed alongside the doll in the basket, which was called "Bridget's bed."

At Beltane, rowan wands and boughs were used for protection around the house and barn. Vervain was also used for this purpose. In Ireland farmers and farm hands sometimes worked around the boundaries of the farm in a sunwise circle carrying tools or symbols of farming and herding, seed grain, and a spring of vervain. The procession started in the east and paused in each of the four directions. May Eve and May Day were some of the best days of year for gathering medicinal herbs, and those skilled in the craft of healing would be out searching for healing plants at this time. People often took purifying medicines on Beltane made from nettles or boiled white-thorn blossoms.

One of the most popular Beltane customs in Ireland was the bringing home of yellow flowers on May Eve or May Morn. These included primroses, cowslips, buttercups, marigolds, and furze blossoms. Small bouquets were hung in the house, over the doorway, or placed on doorsteps or windowsills. Loose flowers were strewn on thresholds, in the house or barn, and in or around wells or pathways. May boughs of rowan, hazel, elder, ash, or holly were also used in some areas. The May bush—a green bush covered with yellow flowers that was set up in front of the doorway—was believed to bring an abundance of milk. In some areas, a branch or bough of hawthorn decorated with flowers and ribbons were lit up at night with candles prior to the holiday.

In Scotland, rowan wands or crosses tied with red thread were used in the house and barn (as were ivy and bramble). Purification and protection rites took place and featured rowan, elder, and juniper. A "need fire" was made from nine kinds of sacred wood, and torches of dried heather were lit at the sacred flame and used to circle the herds to ensure fertility and protection. Yarrow was used in love divination rites. Young girls washed their face in May dew or picked sprigs of ivy with May dew on them to encourage health, beauty, and well-being.

In Christian times, this harvest festival Lugnasadh was renamed Lammas (from Anglo-Saxon *hlaf-mass*, meaning "loaf mass"). The original holiday was associated with cultivated plants like oats, barley, wheat and rye and was also a time to gather fresh fruits from the wild, such as blueberries, strawberries and raspberries. Offerings of fruit or garlands of flowers were placed at holy sites, including standing stones or stone circles. In Scottish folk tradition, sacred cakes were made from barley that had been dried in the Sun, and these were toasted over a fire made from rowan or other sacred wood. After each person took a bit of the cake, the group walked in a sunwise circle singing songs of blessing and thanks.

An age-old tradition maintained that the harvest had to be in by the holiday of Samhain, and that no wild plants or fruits were to be gathered after this day. There was a great bounty at this time of year, and apple cakes, blackberry pies, and nuts were served at feasts and gatherings. Apples and hazelnuts (the produce of sacred trees associated with the otherworld) were used in rites of divination, as were ivy leaves, flax seed, hemp seed, oats, and yarrow (in some cases, nine stalks of yarrow cut with a black-handled knife). In Scotland, after the Samhain bonfire was lit, torches made from heather or bog fir were carried in a sunwise direction around the farm and the fields. Lanterns were made from hollowed-out turnips, and hazelnuts were gathered for Samhain divination. A sacred cake made of oat flour was created by the women, their work beginning after sunset and proceeding in a sunwise direction as each women took part in creating the sacred cake.

## Personal Pathways and Ancient Lore

There are many ways to work with ancestral Celtic lore. In addition to learning about and carrying forward these ancient folk traditions, we can go into the wild and learn to identify sacred herbs, plants, and trees. When gathering plants for magical or medicinal use, many traditions suggest that it is fitting to ask the plant beforehand and give an offering of thanks (whether physical or spiritual). I typically place my hand over the branch where the plant was taken and infuse the area with a soothing and healing energy.

When you encounter plants in a natural setting, take some time to see where and how they grow. Do they grow near water? What other plants are nearby? Do any of these plants have a relationship with each other?

Keep a journal noting when the plants appear and how long they live. In many cases, young shoots are best gathered in spring and roots in the spring or fall. If possible, take time to meditate and connect with the living plant prior to gathering it for magical purposes. Many of the folk charms described above provide a wonderful basis for creating your own magical herbal charms or spells, and these can be recited when you find and gather plants in the wild.

In addition, there are many fine herbal outlets and farms throughout the country. It is best to use organic herbs whenever possible, as pesticides and other toxins may interfere with the plant's natural energies and vibrations. Whether you work with fresh or dried herbs, a great deal can be learned by meditating and connecting with the plant's wisdom and energies. Simply hold the plant in the right palm to learn about its worldly uses and wisdom, or in the left palm to learn its spiritual applications, esoteric lore, and teachings.

Sacred plants, herbs and trees can be accessed and utilized year-round for personal or group rituals and ceremonies, whether for healing, purification, power, protection, or other purposes. They can also be used in divine rites associated with deities, path workings, or seasonal festivals.

Irish and Scottish folk tradition provides us with a truly magical source of ancient wisdom from which we can create our own seasonal rituals as we honor, give thanks for, and make use of the sacred plants which the earth has provided for us.

# The Lore and Magic of Honeysuckle

### ➤ by Tammy Sullivan ➤

Honeysuckle, a perennial, is also known as goat's leaf and woodbine, and has long been a staple in the Witch's garden. There are over 180 species of honeysuckle in the Northern Hemisphere alone. The three most common are: *Lonicera japonica* (Japanese honeysuckle), *Lonicera sempervirens* (woodbine or trumpet honeysuckle), and *Lonicera periclymenum* (European honeysuckle).

The name *Lonicera* honors Adam Loncier, a German botanist from the sixteenth century. *Caprifoliaceae*, the plant family honeysuckle belongs to, relates to the goat and its agility in climbing. Elder also belongs to the plant family *Caprifoliaceae*, and so honeysuckle retains some of the spirit of the elder in its history and its protective character. *Periclymenum*

comes from Periclymunus, one of the Argonauts from Greek myth, who had the power to change shape at will. There is also a winter honeysuckle, *Lonicera purpush*, that blooms through the winter and early spring. The aroma of this plant is very concentrated.

Honeysuckle flower change shape and color daily to attract butterflies and night-flying moths for pollination. The name "woodbine," meanwhile, comes from the twisting habits of the plant's woody branches. The name "honeysuckle" itself stems from Middle English, and means, as you might expect, "from which honey can be sucked"—in reference to the sweet nectar produced by the plant.

Japanese honeysuckle was introduced to the United States in the mid- to early 1800s and was used by the wealthy primarily for ornamental purposes. Later it was used to control soil erosion.

The hardiness of honeysuckle makes it an excellent ground cover and safeguard to protect against erosion. It sprouts new growth directly from the roots. The root system is strong and deep-reaching with many fine offshoots. By the 1920s, honeysuckle had become so popular it had spread across the Atlantic region and into New England.

## Growing Honeysuckle

Honeysuckle prefers full sunlight, but tolerates some shade. It also prefers moderate to dry soil conditions. Honeysuckle has the unique ability to create its own ideal habitat—which it does by climbing smaller trees and bushes and felling them under the added weight, thus reaching to the top of the forest canopy even as it creates its own shaded bower underneath.

The honeysuckle leaf ranges in shape from ovate to oval. It is sometimes lobbed, semi-evergreen, light green in color, and somewhat pubescent. The plant's leaves are opposite and almost always linear.

Care should be used when planting honeysuckle in garden, as it grows at a very rapid rate. Planting it next to sm shrubs and trees is not recommended, as it will climb strangle them. While classified a shrub, honeysuckle is a a hardy climbing vine. Individual vines can grow from six ten feet in length, and the plant can grow up to thirty feet height overall.

Don't let the gentle beauty and fragrance of honeysuc delude you into thinking it is a gentle plant. This plant the strength of barbed wire coupled with an invasive nature. F will not destroy it, as honeysuckle has the ability to sprout v orously from the root crown following fire, gaining need nutrients from the ashes. Hard pruning in the winter months needed to control the growth of honeysuckle, and will al increase flowering the next year. A combination of fire ar herbicides seem to do the best at controlling honeysuckle. Or avoid overgrowth simply use careful selection to decide whi species you plant.

Several states have classified the Japanese honeysuckle as noxious weed. Japanese honeysuckle climbs and drapes ove native vegetation, strangling it. It is capable of extinguishin native plant life. Since it follows a growth pattern that continue prior to and after dormancy of other plants, it is quite easy fo honeysuckle to take over the garden and effectively smothe other plant life.

Using honeysuckle to cover an ugly chain-link fence can make for a stunningly beautiful and natural looking hedgerow. Honeysuckle can be trained to grow on a trellis or arbor. Maintenance is practically nonexistent. Honeysuckle prefers mild to moderate conditions and fine to medium textured soils.

To propagate the Japanese honeysuckle, you may use cuttings taken when the plant is not in bloom. The roots will strike within one to three months. You may propagate this and other honeysuckle varieties from seeds, but doing so differs from plant

to plant. Some will germinate in one week while others may take six months. Japanese honeysuckle is widely available in gallon pots in the early spring. After frost danger has passed, prepare the soil and set the plants three feet apart. Water thoroughly and repeat the watering every week until plant shows signs of growth. Mulch with a heavy cover of leaves to protect the root system and retain moisture. You may prune after the plant is two years old.

## The Uses of Honeysuckle

Japanese honeysuckle is an important food to the white-tailed deer in fall and winter. This is particularly important during times of snow, when food is scarce. Field observations show that the deer will stay and graze upon the honeysuckle for extended amounts of time, thus preserving their lives. Some species of honeysuckle produce a berry, a wonderful treat for songbirds, as well as providing nesting opportunities in the spiraling vines. Some berries are toxic, however, to humans. The berries from the bush varieties are perfectly safe and delicious. However, one should be very careful about which part of what honeysuckle they consume. There are reported cases of hunters using the berries to stupefy or kill fish.

Honeysuckle is also an important thermal barrier to small animals in winter months. The white tailed deer and wild game use it for bedding.

Native American tribes use the wood from honeysuckle in the weaving of baskets. The wood must be boiled to soften it before use. The wood is so hard that it takes up to four hours of boiling to soften it adequately.

Today, small slivers of honeysuckle wood are sold as cat toys. Washing or sanding the wood is said to bring out a natural quality that cats find relaxing and uplifting. Honeysuckle wood is reputed to be an alternative for cats that don't respond to catnip.

The wood of the fly honeysuckle is very hard, and the clear portions between the joints and stems, with pith removed, were

used in Sweden for making tobacco pipes. It is also used for walking sticks and the teeth of rakes.

Historically, honeysuckle vines were used to make rope. It is probable that the vines were split and fibers from other plants mixed in or that the vines were braided to make the ropes stronger.

Dwarf honeysuckle has been used for creating bonsai trees. It is an excellent tree to grow inside, as it tolerates a wide temperature range and roots easily.

Asian women use honeysuckle tea as a base for facials, due to its skin-cleansing properties. In Asia, honeysuckle is also made into beer, toothpaste, cigarettes, and many herbal medicines.

The honeysuckle flowers are known to attract butterflies and hummingbirds. The white admiral butterfly uses honeysuckle as its sole source of food.

Honeysuckle flowers range from lipstick red in the trumpet honeysuckle to yellow and white in the Japanese honeysuckle. The flowers of this plant grow in pairs—one yellow and one white—and each can reach one and a half inches in length. They are tubular shaped.

The white and yellow flowers of the Japanese honeysuckle are edible and delicious. The nectar the flowers produce is sweet and light and is excellent as a base for wine, jellies, syrups, and puddings. To candy the flowers, simply rinse them and boil one and a half cups of sugar with one and a half cups of rosewater. Stir in the flowers, reducing the heat to a gentle boil. Allow it to cook for fifteen minutes or until the mixture begins to caramelize. Remove the flowers, and drain them on waxed paper. Keep the flowers cool until you eat them.

Other recipes include using the whole flower as a candy in and of itself. Just wash and toss on a cake to add instant excitement. It's no surprise that there is a sweet rum cocktail named after the honeysuckle.

Some honeysuckle leaves may be boiled and eaten as a vegetable and are high in calcium, magnesium, and potassium.

However, due to the content of toxic saponins, they should be washed thoroughly; the water changed several times.

Honeysuckle tea is simple to make and has health properties as a detoxifier and a sore throat treatment. To prepare the tea take a half-cup of honeysuckle flowers (white or yellow), a half cup of chrysanthemum flowers, and one quart of boiling water. Add the flowers to the water, and steep for fifteen minutes, strain, and drink. For use in topical applications, it is best to make this tea stronger. For a sore throat syrup, you may gather two cups of yellow and white blossoms, and add them to one quart of boiling water. Simmer for ten minutes, and strain. Add one cup of sugar or honey, and boil for one minute. You may take one ounce of this liquid every two hours. It will keep in the refrigerator for one month.

If you are experienced in wine making you may want to try your hand at honeysuckle wine. Be sure to use only the flowers for this, as some of the berries are poisonous. The best time to gather the flowers for the wine is shortly after they open and when they are dry. You will need four cups of honeysuckle blossoms (yellow and white), five and a half cups of granulated sugar, the juice and rind of two oranges, a half pound of raisins, two teaspoons of acid blend, one teaspoon of pectic enzyme, one campden tablet, one teaspoon of nutrients, one teaspoon of tannin, one package of wine yeast, and enough water to fill a one-gallon container. Gently rinse the flowers in cold water. Place them in your primary fermentor. Add water and all other ingredients with the exception of the yeast. Stir until the sugar is dissolved. Let the mixture sit overnight. The next day, add the yeast. Stir the mixture daily until frothing stops—normally about three to five days. Strain out the flowers and siphon into a secondary fermentor. Attach an air lock. Rack the wine after six weeks by adding a half cup of sugar dissolved in one cup of wine. Stir and repeat every six weeks. Bottle the wine when it is six to twelve months old. The wine is ready to drink one year from the day the batch was started. Honeysuckle flowers also are a wonderful addition to mead.

Because of the delicious aroma of honeysuckle, it has been used to scent bath products and toiletries for over a hundred years. Many people like to dry the flowers whole for later use in potpourri. Its use in aromatherapy as a relaxant, a psychic booster, and a weight-loss aid has been well noted.

Adding fresh honeysuckle flowers to the bath can make for a wonderful cleansing experience. You may want to use honey-suckle powder and Epsom salts to make a shower scrub type of cleanser. A wonderful elixir can be made by taking two cups of fresh honeysuckle flowers and drying them thoroughly. Grind the flowers into a powder. Add a splash of water, a pinch of blessed salt, and a quartz crystal. Let it sit for thirty days, and then pour a drop or two in your next bath. Ideally, you should charge it under the Full Moon.

Medicinally, Japanese honeysuckle has been used for hundreds of years as a drastic purgative. Known for its antimicrobial properties, honeysuckle has been said to cure salmonella, staphylococcus, and streptococcus. It works as an antibiotic on colds, flu, fever, sore throat, conjunctivitis, and urinary tract problems. Honeysuckle is hailed as a laxative, expectorant, diuretic, diaphoretic, and emetic. The leaves are used in an infusion (1 part to 100 parts of boiling water) as a laxative. The flowers, used in the same proportion, are taken for coughs and asthma. (Note: Taken in too large doses, this plant can be toxic.)

The oil made by a honeysuckle infusion is said to have a calming effect. Bach Remedies recommends honeysuckle as a mood booster, to aid in releasing the past and a cure for homesickness. Historically, fly woodbine, a certain species of honeysuckle, has been used to treat asthma, hysterics, and syphilis. Honeysuckle, in general, is reputed to have a healing effect on breathing difficulties.

Native Americans used to chew the leaves and place the ground flowers on bee stings for relief. Chewing the leaves and using the ground flower mixture on afflictions eases itching. You can use a strong honeysuckle tea on rashes such as from poison oak.

Bush honeysuckle has been used in an infusion for an eye wash to treat sore eyes, and also in a poultice to increase milk flow in nursing mothers.

Overall, honeysuckle is ranked as one of the ten most valuable medical materials in Asian medicine. (The traditional Chinese medicine properties of honeysuckle are sweet and cold.) In fact, a full one-third of all prescriptions in China have some form of honeysuckle in them. It is even included in breath fresheners. In a study of 425 Chinese students with strep throat, a powdered compound of dried honeysuckle flowers, a small amount of borneol (found in honeysuckle flowers), and blackberry lily roots were blown into the backs of their throats. The results were excellent and honeysuckle is now used extensively for strep throat, colds, flu, and tonsillitis.

In similar medical testing with honeysuckle, there have been encouraging reports of lowered blood pressure and blood cholesterol. It has also shown to be effective against tuberculosis and as a cure for food poisoning.

Honeysuckle contains tannins, which are currently being tested for use as an inhibitor against the HIV virus.

## Honeysuckle Lore

Honeysuckle is known as a visionary herb, an herb of immortality, and a religious herb. In 1988, a team from the University of Arizona excavated Poggio Gramignano, a hilltop in Italy known for containing the ruins of a first-century AD villa. Artifacts associated with burials suggested that honeysuckle wood was burned at the site. Scientists are not sure if it was intended as an offering or a hoped-for cure, but it helped to identify a timeline as to the deaths.

Incorporating honeysuckle into magical use is amazingly easy. You can shape its flexible vine part into protective balls or wreaths. It is very popular to fashion yourself a circlet of honeysuckle to wear in your hair. The flowers air-dry well and may be crushed into a powder if you like. Honeysuckle can be burned whole and green—though I don't recommend it. The stench of burning honeysuckle flowers is not very pleasant, and there are other ways to use this plant and enjoy the pleasing fragrance. Grinding the bark into an incense is more common. Honeysuckle wands and staffs are another magical use.

Honeysuckle is normally used as decoration for the altar and temple to celebrate Ostara, and fresh new beginnings. It is used again, on the opposite of the solar wheel, at Mabon. Honeysuckle is seen as a representation of the rebirth and survival of life through the long winter's death. It is also thought to be the flower of unity.

In spellwork, honeysuckle is used for weight loss, flu relief, protection, money matters, psychic aid, cleansing, and purifying, Among other things, the plants represents secrets and hidden knowledge. Here are some common associations for honeysuckle.

Ogham—Unillean

Rune—Daeg (ᛞ)

Color—Pale yellow

Animal—Mouse

Element—Earth

Affinity—Masculine

Month—June

Tarot—Suit of wands and the Magician

Zodiac—Aries

Plane—Jupiter

Magical properties—These include wisdom, good judgment, confidence, protection, psychic abilities, prosperity, healing, calm, cleansing, luck, beauty, generosity, attraction, affection, health, peace, and marriage. Honeysuckle is also thought to be a good additive to enchantments, due to it intoxicating fragrance. Honeysuckle also has an association as a necromancer's herb and is connected to the lapwing in Celtic folklore. Being that the honeysuckle is such an aggressive plant, it is thought that it encourages us to reach for our desires and ignore any and all distractions.

Honeysuckle flowers are said to attract fairies. Indeed, the aroma of these flowers is so intoxicating that Shakespeare wrote of it in *A Midsummer Night's Dream*. Honeysuckle is also thought to be a preferred living space for fairies.

Honeysuckle flowers are said to increase psychic vision if crushed and rubbed on the forehead. They are also said to encourage erotic dreams in females. In the language of flowers, honeysuckle meant devoted affection. In Victorian times, teenage girls were not allowed to bring honeysuckle inside the home—because of the risqué dreams.

Still other lore says that honeysuckle will help you increase your understanding of images and impressions collected on the astral plane. A true occult herb, honeysuckle represents hidden secrets and knowledge. This makes it a wonderful addition to dream pillows and the like. It is said that if you wear honeysuckle to bed, you will dream of your true love.

Another legend says that bringing a honeysuckle plant inside the home will result in a wedding. Placing honeysuckle in the home is also thought to draw prosperity. The Chinese believed that honeysuckle increased your longevity.

If a honeysuckle grows on your property it is said to bring good luck. If it grows over the door, it is thought to keep fevers at bay. Growing honeysuckle in a pot in your garden is said to protect Witches from the evil eye.

# Harvesting Honeysuckle

Harvesting honeysuckle during particular Moon phases can increase its power. Harvesting under a Full Moon is best for protection and cleansing, under a waning Moon for calming effects, and under a waxing Moon for prosperity. Again, it is best to harvest when the flowers are open and dry. Don't forget to ask permission before harvesting.

Whatever use you choose for honeysuckle, you are sure to be thrilled with the aggressiveness, beauty, and aroma of one of nature's strongest plants.

# Allium Family Lore

≫ by Magenta Griffith ≪

The *Allium* family are not some obscure tribe of Gypsies or hereditary Witches, but it is the Latin classification for a botanical family that includes onions, garlic, leeks, shallots, scallions (also called green onions), and chives. All of the alliums are related to lilies. Various parts of different alliums are eaten. The roots of onions, garlic, and shallots are eaten, but only the leaves of chives. Most of the scallion, or green onion, is edible. With the leek, all but the tougher parts of its green tops are eaten.

Some of the oldest references to food are to onions. The Sumerians of Mesopotamia, were the first to establish a written language—in the form of cuneiform inscriptions. Archeologists found inscriptions dating back to 2400 BC that read: "The oxen of the gods plowed the city governor's onion patches. The onion and cucumber patches of the city governor were located in the gods' best fields." Meanwhile, the Code of Hammurabi states that the needy should be given a monthly ration of bread and onions.

## Earliest Onions

The earliest onions were found in tombs created about 3,500 years ago. They were buried to provide food for the afterlife. When King Tut's tomb was excavated, bulbs of garlic were found scattered throughout the rooms. Garlic was so prized that during the reign of King Tut fifteen pounds of garlic would buy a healthy male slave. Egyptian slave masters fed garlic to laborers who built the Great Pyramid of Giza because they believed garlic gave workers superhuman strength and motivated them to work harder. An inscription on one of the pyramids states how much silver was used to purchase garlic and onions for the slaves who built that structure.

Onions were worn in garlands for certain festivals in ancient Egypt. Onions are depicted in murals on the walls in some of the Egyptian tombs. That's appropriate, because one of the earliest dyes known were made from onion skins. The color was probably used in the paintings on the tombs. The skins of two yellow onions can dye up to a dozen eggs, and the dye was also used to color cloth.

The ancient Greeks believed garlic had supernatural powers. Greek athletes would eat garlic before competition, and Greek soldiers would eat garlic before going into battle. Greek midwives used to hang garlic cloves in birthing rooms to keep evil spirits away.

In India, texts from the sixth century BC note the onion is a diuretic, and is good for the heart, the eyes, and the joints. Because of the onion's odor, it was not considered fit to be eaten, except for medicinal purposes.

The Roman writer Pliny the Elder listed Roman beliefs about the onion. For instance, onions were considered a cure for feeble vision; they were used to induce sleep and chewed with bread to heal sores in the mouth. Boiled onions were given to people affected by dysentery and used as a suppository to cure hemorrhoids.

## Onion Legends

An old Turkish legend tells that when Satan was thrown out of heaven, garlic sprouted where he first placed his left foot, and onions grew where he placed his right foot.

In 1772, four grave-robbers raiding plague victims' corpses in Marseilles were amazingly immune to the plague. Their secret was garlic-infused vinegar, which became known as the Vinegar of the Four Thieves. They ate it, bathed in it, put in on their clothes, and rubbed in into the rags that covered their mouths. The custom of covering one's nose and mouth with garlic and vinegar-soaked rags caught on during the plague, as did wearing strings of garlic around one's neck.

Onions were known everywhere in Africa, Asia, and Europe, but were unknown in the Americas and Australia until they were introduced by Europeans. In colonial America, garlic cloves were bound to the feet of smallpox victims and placed in the shoes of whooping cough sufferers.

Culpeper, author of the first modern herbal, attributes garlic to Mars, because of its "heat." Recipes using onions, garlic, and other alliums abound in herbals. An early recipe to prevent hair loss recommended a mixture of onion juice and honey be rubbed into the scalp twice a day.

Onion juice and vinegar has been used to treat pimples. Eating onions has long been considered a remedy for a cold. Recipes call for placing a slice of onion in your shoe for the same result. Other sources call for a poultice containing onions to be placed on the chest of a child with croup, a cough, or a fever.

The stronger the onion, the better the cure. The juice of raw onions or scallions is an old remedy for applying to bee stings and insect bites.

According to Richard Folkard, the nineteenth-century English writer, in his book *Plant Lore, Legends and Lyrics*, country lasses used a method of divination employing an onion named for St. Thomas. They peeled the onion and wrapped it in a clean kerchief, then placed it under their heads (presumably before they went to sleep), and repeated the following lines:

> *Good St. Thomas, do me right,*
> *And let my true-love come to-night,*
> *That I may see him in the face,*
> *And him in my fond arms embrace.*

In Chinese medicine, onions are said to calm the liver, moisten the intestines, and benefit the lungs. Raw onions are prescribed for constipation, for lowering high blood pressure, and for healing wounds or ulcers of the skin. Spring onions are used to induce sweating. One cure for the common cold is to take twenty spring onions and simmer them with rice to make porridge. Add a little vinegar, and eat the dish while it is warm. Then wrap yourself up in heavy blankets to induce sweating.

Donar, the Dutch name for Thor, played a big part in Dutch folklore. *Donderdag*, or "Thor's day," is the Dutch name for Thursday. *Donderbaard* ("thunderbeard") in popular speech was a term for *huislook*, a form of leek which was dedicated to Donar. The flowers from the plant are what form the "beard." These leeks were grown on roofs to protect houses from lightning. The leek was also used to treat numerous ills—including toothaches, hemorrhoids, rashes, warts, sores, corns, bee stings, throat afflictions, and burns.

Leeks are the national symbol of Wales. From the time of Shakespeare, the leek was the recognized emblem of the Welsh, and there is written evidence that it became their emblem considerably earlier.

Entries in the household accounts of the Tudor kings include payments for leeks worn by the household guards on St. David's Day. According to one legend, the leek is linked to St. David because he ordered his soldiers to wear them on their helmets when they fought a victorious battle against the Saxons in a field full of leeks. It was more likely, however, that the leek was linked with St. David and adopted as a national symbol because of its importance to the diet in Wales, especially during the time of Lent.

The full version of the fairy tale *Rapunzel* begins with a pregnant woman who is craving *ramps*, or *rampion*, that only grow in the old Witch's garden. "Ramps" is an old word for leeks.

There isn't much folklore about chives, even though they may be the toughest plant of the whole family. Chives are known to survive winter temperature of -40° to -50° F. They are found in Alaska, Siberia, and Newfoundland.

## Onions Today

In modern times, onions are known to be a good source of vitamins A and C, as well as some of the B vitamins. They are also very low in calories.

Onions have no fat and no cholesterol. In fact, recent research suggests onions help reduce the build-up of cholesterol and inhibit the blood from clotting. Garlic and onions have been found to have antiseptic and antibiotic properties. A few scientists have found cancer-fighting compounds in onions, and there is speculation that onions may produce enzymes that fight free radicals.

If you eat onions and garlic, you or your friends may be bothered by bad breath afterward. Some of the cures for onion breath include rinsing your mouth with equal amounts of lemon juice and water, eating a sprig of parsley, or eating an apple. Other cures include chewing any of the following: citrus peel, dill seeds, a whole clove, anise seeds, coffee beans, or coriander seeds.

Alas, there is no definitive cure for the crying that accompanies chopping onions and other alliums. The two best suggestions seem to be, chill the vegetable before you chop it—or get someone else to chop it for you.

# The
# Quarters and
# Signs of the
# Moon and
# Moon
# Tables

# The Quarters and Signs
of the Moon

Everyone has seen the Moon wax and wane through a period of approximately twenty-nine and a half days. This circuit from New Moon to Full Moon and back again is called the lunation cycle. The cycle is divided into parts, called quarters or phases. There are several methods by which this can be done, and the system used in the *Herbal Almanac* may not correspond to those used in other almanacs.

## The Quarters

### First Quarter

The first quarter begins at the New Moon, when the Sun and Moon are in the same place, or conjunct. (This means that the Sun and Moon are in the same degree of the same sign.) The Moon is not visible at first, since it rises at the same time as the Sun. The New Moon is the time of new beginnings, beginnings of projects that favor growth, externalization of activities, and the growth of ideas. The first quarter is the time of germination, emergence, beginnings, and outwardly directed activity.

### Second Quarter

The second quarter begins halfway between the New Moon and the Full Moon, when the Sun and Moon are at right angles, or a ninety-degree square to each other. This half Moon rises around noon and sets around midnight, so it can be seen in the western sky during the first half of the night. The second quarter is the time of growth and articulation of things that already exist.

### Third Quarter

The third quarter begins at the Full Moon, when the Sun and Moon are opposite one another and the full light of the Sun can shine on the full sphere of the Moon. The round Moon can be seen rising in the east at sunset, and then rising a little later each evening. The Full Moon stands for illumination, fulfillment, culmination, completion, drawing inward, unrest, emotional expressions, and hasty actions leading to failure. The third quarter is a time of maturity, fruition, and the assumption of the full form of expression.

### Fourth Quarter

The fourth quarter begins about halfway between the Full Moon and New Moon, when the Sun and Moon are again at ninety degrees, or square. This decreasing Moon rises at midnight, and can be seen in the east during the last half of the night, reaching the overhead position just about as the Sun rises. The fourth quarter is a time of disintegration, drawing back for reorganization and reflection.

## The Signs

### Moon in Aries

Moon in Aries is good for starting things, but lacking in staying power. Things occur rapidly, but also quickly pass.

### Moon in Taurus

With Moon in Taurus, things begun during this sign last the longest and tend to increase in value. Things begun now become habitual and hard to alter.

### Moon in Gemini

Moon in Gemini is an inconsistent position for the Moon, characterized by a lot of talk. Things begun now are easily changed by outside influences.

### Moon in Cancer

Moon in Cancer stimulates emotional rapport between people. It pinpoints need, and supports growth and nurturance.

### Moon in Leo

Moon in Leo accents showmanship, being seen, drama, recreation, and happy pursuits. It may be concerned with praise and subject to flattery.

### Moon in Virgo

Moon in Virgo favors accomplishment of details and commands from higher up while discouraging independent thinking.

### Moon in Libra

Moon in Libra increases self-awareness. It favors self-examination and interaction with others, but discourages spontaneous initiative.

### Moon in Scorpio

Moon in Scorpio increases awareness of psychic power. It precipitates psychic crises and ends connections thoroughly.

### Moon in Sagittarius

Moon in Sagittarius encourages expansionary flights of imagination and confidence in the flow of life.

### Moon in Capricorn

Moon in Capricorn increases awareness of the need for structure, discipline, and organization. Institutional activities are favored.

## Moon in Aquarius

Moon in Aquarius favors activities that are unique and individualistic, concern for humanitarian needs, society as a whole, and improvements that can be made.

## Moon in Pisces

During Moon in Pisces, energy withdraws from the surface of life, hibernates within, secretly reorganizing and realigning.

# January Moon Table

| Date | Sign | Element | Nature | Phase |
|------|------|---------|--------|-------|
| 1 Sat. | Virgo | Earth | Barren | 3rd |
| 2 Sun. 11:19 am | Libra | Air | Semi-fruitful | 3rd |
| 3 Mon. | Libra | Air | Semi-fruitful | 4th 12:46 pm |
| 4 Tue. 7:00 pm | Scorpio | Water | Fruitful | 4th |
| 5 Wed. | Scorpio | Water | Fruitful | 4th |
| 6 Thu. 10:44 pm | Sagittarius | Fire | Barren | 4th |
| 7 Fri. | Sagittarius | Fire | Barren | 4th |
| 8 Sat. 11:11 pm | Capricorn | Earth | Semi-fruitful | 4th |
| 9 Sun. | Capricorn | Earth | Semi-fruitful | 4th |
| 10 Mon. 10:07 pm | Aquarius | Air | Barren | New 7:03 am |
| 11 Tue. | Aquarius | Air | Barren | 1st |
| 12 Wed. 9:50 pm | Pisces | Water | Fruitful | 1st |
| 13 Thu. | Pisces | Water | Fruitful | 1st |
| 14 Fri. | Pisces | Water | Fruitful | 1st |
| 15 Sat. 12:27 am | Aries | Fire | Barren | 1st |
| 16 Sun. | Aries | Fire | Barren | 1st |
| 17 Mon. 7:06 am | Taurus | Earth | Semi-fruitful | 2nd 1:57 am |
| 18 Tue. | Taurus | Earth | Semi-fruitful | 2nd |
| 19 Wed. 5:24 pm | Gemini | Air | Barren | 2nd |
| 20 Thu. | Gemini | Air | Barren | 2nd |
| 21 Fri. | Gemini | Air | Barren | 2nd |
| 22 Sat. 5:42 am | Cancer | Water | Fruitful | 2nd |
| 23 Sun. | Cancer | Water | Fruitful | 2nd |
| 24 Mon. 6:21 pm | Leo | Fire | Barren | 2nd |
| 25 Tue. | Leo | Fire | Barren | Full 5:32 am |
| 26 Wed. | Leo | Fire | Barren | 3rd |
| 27 Thu. 6:24 am | Virgo | Earth | Barren | 3rd |
| 28 Fri. | Virgo | Earth | Barren | 3rd |
| 29 Sat. 5:13 pm | Libra | Air | Semi-fruitful | 3rd |
| 30 Sun. | Libra | Air | Semi-fruitful | 3rd |
| 31 Mon. | Libra | Air | Semi-fruitful | 3rd |

# February Moon Table

| Date | Sign | Element | Nature | Phase |
|------|------|---------|--------|-------|
| 1 Tue. 1:51 am | Scorpio | Water | Fruitful | 3rd |
| 2 Wed. | Scorpio | Water | Fruitful | 4th 2:27 am |
| 3 Thu. 7:21 am | Sagittarius | Fire | Barren | 4th |
| 4 Fri. | Sagittarius | Fire | Barren | 4th |
| 5 Sat. 9:32 am | Capricorn | Earth | Semi-fruitful | 4th |
| 6 Sun. | Capricorn | Earth | Semi-fruitful | 4th |
| 7 Mon. 9:26 am | Aquarius | Air | Barren | 4th |
| 8 Tue. | Aquarius | Air | Barren | New 5:28 pm |
| 9 Wed. 8:59 am | Pisces | Water | Fruitful | 1st |
| 10 Thu. | Pisces | Water | Fruitful | 1st |
| 11 Fri. 10:21 am | Aries | Fire | Barren | 1st |
| 12 Sat. | Aries | Fire | Barren | 1st |
| 13 Sun. 3:18 pm | Taurus | Earth | Semi-fruitful | 1st |
| 14 Mon. | Taurus | Earth | Semi-fruitful | 1st |
| 15 Tue. | Taurus | Earth | Semi-fruitful | 2nd 7:16 pm |
| 16 Wed. 12:18 am | Gemini | Air | Barren | 2nd |
| 17 Thu. | Gemini | Air | Barren | 2nd |
| 18 Fri. 12:13 pm | Cancer | Water | Fruitful | 2nd |
| 19 Sat. | Cancer | Water | Fruitful | 2nd |
| 20 Sun. | Cancer | Water | Fruitful | 2nd |
| 21 Mon. 12:54 am | Leo | Fire | Barren | 2nd |
| 22 Tue. | Leo | Fire | Barren | 2nd |
| 23 Wed. 12:44 pm | Virgo | Earth | Barren | Full 11:54 pm |
| 24 Thu. | Virgo | Earth | Barren | 3rd |
| 25 Fri. 10:59 pm | Libra | Air | Semi-fruitful | 3rd |
| 26 Sat. | Libra | Air | Semi-fruitful | 3rd |
| 27 Sun. | Libra | Air | Semi-fruitful | 3rd |
| 28 Mon. 7:21 am | Scorpio | Water | Fruitful | 3rd |

# March Moon Table

| Date | Sign | Element | Nature | Phase |
|------|------|---------|--------|-------|
| 1 Tue. | Scorpio | Water | Fruitful | 3rd |
| 2 Wed. 1:29 pm | Sagittarius | Fire | Barren | 3rd |
| 3 Thu. | Sagittarius | Fire | Barren | 4th 12:36 pm |
| 4 Fri. 5:12 pm | Capricorn | Earth | Semi-fruitful | 4th |
| 5 Sat. | Capricorn | Earth | Semi-fruitful | 4th |
| 6 Sun. 6:49 pm | Aquarius | Air | Barren | 4th |
| 7 Mon. | Aquarius | Air | Barren | 4th |
| 8 Tue. 7:32 pm | Pisces | Water | Fruitful | 4th |
| 9 Wed. | Pisces | Water | Fruitful | 4th |
| 10 Thu. 9:03 pm | Aries | Fire | Barren | New 4:10 am |
| 11 Fri. | Aries | Fire | Barren | 1st |
| 12 Sat. | Aries | Fire | Barren | 1st |
| 13 Sun. 1:05 am | Taurus | Earth | Semi-fruitful | 1st |
| 14 Mon. | Taurus | Earth | Semi-fruitful | 1st |
| 15 Tue. 8:44 am | Gemini | Air | Barren | 1st |
| 16 Wed. | Gemini | Air | Barren | 1st |
| 17 Thu. 7:44 pm | Cancer | Water | Fruitful | 2nd 2:19 pm |
| 18 Fri. | Cancer | Water | Fruitful | 2nd |
| 19 Sat. | Cancer | Water | Fruitful | 2nd |
| 20 Sun. 8:17 am | Leo | Fire | Barren | 2nd |
| 21 Mon. | Leo | Fire | Barren | 2nd |
| 22 Tue. 8:10 pm | Virgo | Earth | Barren | 2nd |
| 23 Wed. | Virgo | Earth | Barren | 2nd |
| 24 Thu. | Virgo | Earth | Barren | 2nd |
| 25 Fri. 6:00 am | Libra | Air | Semi-fruitful | Full 3:58 pm |
| 26 Sat. | Libra | Air | Semi-fruitful | 3rd |
| 27 Sun. 1:29 pm | Scorpio | Water | Fruitful | 3rd |
| 28 Mon. | Scorpio | Water | Fruitful | 3rd |
| 29 Tue. 6:56 pm | Sagittarius | Fire | Barren | 3rd |
| 30 Wed. | Sagittarius | Fire | Barren | 3rd |
| 31 Thu. 10:48 pm | Capricorn | Earth | Semi-fruitful | 3rd |

# April Moon Table

| Date | Sign | Element | Nature | Phase |
|------|------|---------|--------|-------|
| 1 Fri. | Capricorn | Earth | Semi-fruitful | 4th 7:50 pm |
| 2 Sat. | Capricorn | Earth | Semi-fruitful | 4th |
| 3 Sun. 1:31 am | Aquarius | Air | Barren | 4th |
| 4 Mon. | Aquarius | Air | Barren | 4th |
| 5 Tue. 4:45 am | Pisces | Water | Fruitful | 4th |
| 6 Wed. | Pisces | Water | Fruitful | 4th |
| 7 Thu. 7:28 am | Aries | Fire | Barren | 4th |
| 8 Fri. | Aries | Fire | Barren | New 4:32 pm |
| 9 Sat. 11:50 am | Taurus | Earth | Semi-fruitful | 1st |
| 10 Sun. | Taurus | Earth | Semi-fruitful | 1st |
| 11 Mon. 6:55 pm | Gemini | Air | Barren | 1st |
| 12 Tue. | Gemini | Air | Barren | 1st |
| 13 Wed. | Gemini | Air | Barren | 1st |
| 14 Thu. 5:03 am | Cancer | Water | Fruitful | 1st |
| 15 Fri. | Cancer | Water | Fruitful | 1st |
| 16 Sat. 5:17 pm | Leo | Fire | Barren | 2nd 10:37 am |
| 17 Sun. | Leo | Fire | Barren | 2nd |
| 18 Mon. | Leo | Fire | Barren | 2nd |
| 19 Tue. 5:27 am | Virgo | Earth | Barren | 2nd |
| 20 Wed. | Virgo | Earth | Barren | 2nd |
| 21 Thu. 3:27 pm | Libra | Air | Semi-fruitful | 2nd |
| 22 Fri. | Libra | Air | Semi-fruitful | 2nd |
| 23 Sat. 10:25 pm | Scorpio | Water | Fruitful | 2nd |
| 24 Sun. | Scorpio | Water | Fruitful | Full 6:06 am |
| 25 Mon. | Scorpio | Water | Fruitful | 3rd |
| 26 Tue. 2:46 am | Sagittarius | Fire | Barren | 3rd |
| 27 Wed. | Sagittarius | Fire | Barren | 3rd |
| 28 Thu. 5:33 am | Capricorn | Earth | Semi-fruitful | 3rd |
| 29 Fri. | Capricorn | Earth | Semi-fruitful | 3rd |
| 30 Sat. 7:54 am | Aquarius | Air | Barren | 3rd |

# May Moon Table

| Date | Sign | Element | Nature | Phase |
|------|------|---------|--------|-------|
| 1 Sun. | Aquarius | Air | Barren | 4th 2:24 am |
| 2 Mon. 10:43 am | Pisces | Water | Fruitful | 4th |
| 3 Tue. | Pisces | Water | Fruitful | 4th |
| 4 Wed. 2:36 pm | Aries | Fire | Barren | 4th |
| 5 Thu. | Aries | Fire | Barren | 4th |
| 6 Fri. 8:01 pm | Taurus | Earth | Semi-fruitful | 4th |
| 7 Sat. | Taurus | Earth | Semi-fruitful | 4th |
| 8 Sun. | Taurus | Earth | Semi-fruitful | New 4:45 am |
| 9 Mon. 3:29 am | Gemini | Air | Barren | 1st |
| 10 Tue. | Gemini | Air | Barren | 1st |
| 11 Wed. 1:20 pm | Cancer | Water | Fruitful | 1st |
| 12 Thu. | Cancer | Water | Fruitful | 1st |
| 13 Fri. | Cancer | Water | Fruitful | 1st |
| 14 Sat. 1:17 am | Leo | Fire | Barren | 1st |
| 15 Sun. | Leo | Fire | Barren | 1st |
| 16 Mon. 1:46 pm | Virgo | Earth | Barren | 2nd 4:57 am |
| 17 Tue. | Virgo | Earth | Barren | 2nd |
| 18 Wed. | Libra | Air | Semi-fruitful | 2nd |
| 19 Thu. 12:30 am | Libra | Air | Semi-fruitful | 2nd |
| 20 Fri. | Libra | Air | Semi-fruitful | 2nd |
| 21 Sat. 7:49 am | Scorpio | Water | Fruitful | 2nd |
| 22 Sun. | Scorpio | Water | Fruitful | 2nd |
| 23 Mon. 11:38 am | Sagittarius | Fire | Barren | Full 4:18 pm |
| 24 Tue. | Sagittarius | Fire | Barren | 3rd |
| 25 Wed. 1:11 pm | Capricorn | Earth | Semi-fruitful | 3rd |
| 26 Thu. | Capricorn | Earth | Semi-fruitful | 3rd |
| 27 Fri. 2:10 pm | Aquarius | Air | Barren | 3rd |
| 28 Sat. | Aquarius | Air | Barren | 3rd |
| 29 Sun. 4:09 pm | Pisces | Water | Fruitful | 3rd |
| 30 Mon. | Pisces | Water | Fruitful | 4th 7:47 am |
| 31 Tue. 8:07 pm | Aries | Fire | Barren | 4th |

# June Moon Table

| Date | Sign | Element | Nature | Phase |
|------|------|---------|--------|-------|
| 1 Wed. | Aries | Fire | Barren | 4th |
| 2 Thu. | Aries | Fire | Barren | 4th |
| 3 Fri. 2:20 am | Taurus | Earth | Semi-fruitful | 4th |
| 4 Sat. | Taurus | Earth | Semi-fruitful | 4th |
| 5 Sun. 10:36 am | Gemini | Air | Barren | 4th |
| 6 Mon. | Gemini | Air | Barren | New 5:55 pm |
| 7 Tue. 8:46 pm | Cancer | Water | Fruitful | 1st |
| 8 Wed. | Cancer | Water | Fruitful | 1st |
| 9 Thu. | Cancer | Water | Fruitful | 1st |
| 10 Fri. 8:39 am | Leo | Fire | Barren | 1st |
| 11 Sat. | Leo | Fire | Barren | 1st |
| 12 Sun. 9:22 pm | Virgo | Earth | Barren | 1st |
| 13 Mon. | Virgo | Earth | Barren | 1st |
| 14 Tue. | Virgo | Earth | Barren | 2nd 9:22 pm |
| 15 Wed. 8:59 am | Libra | Air | Semi-fruitful | 2nd |
| 16 Thu. | Libra | Air | Semi-fruitful | 2nd |
| 17 Fri. 5:23 pm | Scorpio | Water | Fruitful | 2nd |
| 18 Sat. | Scorpio | Water | Fruitful | 2nd |
| 19 Sun. 9:45 pm | Sagittarius | Fire | Barren | 2nd |
| 20 Mon. | Sagittarius | Fire | Barren | 2nd |
| 21 Tue. 10:52 pm | Capricorn | Earth | Semi-fruitful | 3rd |
| 22 Wed. | Capricorn | Earth | Semi-fruitful | Full 12:14 am |
| 23 Thu. 10:36 pm | Aquarius | Air | Barren | 3rd |
| 24 Fri. | Aquarius | Air | Barren | 3rd |
| 25 Sat. 11:03 pm | Pisces | Water | Fruitful | 3rd |
| 26 Sun. | Pisces | Water | Fruitful | 3rd |
| 27 Mon. | Pisces | Water | Fruitful | 3rd |
| 28 Tue. 1:51 am | Aries | Fire | Barren | 4th 2:23 pm |
| 29 Wed. | Aries | Fire | Barren | 4th |
| 30 Thu. 7:45 am | Taurus | Earth | Semi-fruitful | 4th |

# July Moon Table

| Date | Sign | Element | Nature | Phase |
|------|------|---------|--------|-------|
| 1 Fri. | Taurus | Earth | Semi-fruitful | 4th |
| 2 Sat. 4:26 pm | Gemini | Air | Barren | 4th |
| 3 Sun. | Gemini | Air | Barren | 4th |
| 4 Mon. | Gemini | Air | Barren | 4th |
| 5 Tue. 3:07 am | Cancer | Water | Fruitful | 4th |
| 6 Wed. | Cancer | Water | Fruitful | New 8:02 am |
| 7 Thu. 3:11 pm | Leo | Fire | Barren | 1st |
| 8 Fri. | Leo | Fire | Barren | 1st |
| 9 Sat. | Leo | Fire | Barren | 1st |
| 10 Sun. 3:57 am | Virgo | Earth | Barren | 1st |
| 11 Mon. | Virgo | Earth | Barren | 1st |
| 12 Tue. 4:09 pm | Libra | Air | Semi-fruitful | 1st |
| 13 Wed. | Libra | Air | Semi-fruitful | 1st |
| 14 Thu. | Libra | Air | Semi-fruitful | 2nd 11:20 am |
| 15 Fri. 1:51 am | Scorpio | Water | Fruitful | 2nd |
| 16 Sat. | Scorpio | Water | Fruitful | 2nd |
| 17 Sun. 7:35 am | Sagittarius | Fire | Barren | 2nd |
| 18 Mon. | Sagittarius | Fire | Barren | 2nd |
| 19 Tue. 9:26 am | Capricorn | Earth | Semi-fruitful | 2nd |
| 20 Wed. | Capricorn | Earth | Semi-fruitful | 2nd |
| 21 Thu. 8:55 am | Aquarius | Air | Barren | Full 7:00 am |
| 22 Fri. | Aquarius | Air | Barren | 3rd |
| 23 Sat. 8:12 am | Pisces | Water | Fruitful | 3rd |
| 24 Sun. | Pisces | Water | Fruitful | 3rd |
| 25 Mon. 9:23 am | Aries | Fire | Barren | 3rd |
| 26 Tue. | Aries | Fire | Barren | 3rd |
| 27 Wed. 1:54 pm | Taurus | Earth | Semi-fruitful | 4th 11:19 pm |
| 28 Thu. | Taurus | Earth | Semi-fruitful | 4th |
| 29 Fri. 10:02 pm | Gemini | Air | Barren | 4th |
| 30 Sat. | Gemini | Air | Barren | 4th |
| 31 Sun. | Gemini | Air | Barren | 4th |

# August Moon Table

| Date | Sign | Element | Nature | Phase |
|------|------|---------|--------|-------|
| 1 Mon. 8:52 am | Cancer | Water | Fruitful | 4th |
| 2 Tue. | Cancer | Water | Fruitful | 4th |
| 3 Wed. 9:10 pm | Leo | Fire | Barren | 4th |
| 4 Thu. | Leo | Fire | Barren | New 11:05 pm |
| 5 Fri. | Leo | Fire | Barren | 1st |
| 6 Sat. 9:54 am | Virgo | Earth | Barren | 1st |
| 7 Sun. | Virgo | Earth | Barren | 1st |
| 8 Mon.10:08 pm | Libra | Air | Semi-fruitful | 1st |
| 9 Tue. | Libra | Air | Semi-fruitful | 1st |
| 10 Wed. | Libra | Air | Semi-fruitful | 1st |
| 11 Thu. 8:35 am | Scorpio | Water | Fruitful | 1st |
| 12 Fri. | Scorpio | Water | Fruitful | 2nd 10:38 pm |
| 13 Sat. 3:47 pm | Sagittarius | Fire | Barren | 2nd |
| 14 Sun. | Sagittarius | Fire | Barren | 2nd |
| 15 Mon. 7:13 pm | Capricorn | Earth | Semi-fruitful | 2nd |
| 16 Tue. | Capricorn | Earth | Semi-fruitful | 2nd |
| 17 Wed. 7:39 pm | Aquarius | Air | Barren | 2nd |
| 18 Thu. | Aquarius | Air | Barren | 2nd |
| 19 Fri. 6:52 pm | Pisces | Water | Fruitful | Full 1:53 pm |
| 20 Sat. | Pisces | Water | Fruitful | 3rd |
| 21 Sun. 7:01 pm | Aries | Fire | Barren | 3rd |
| 22 Mon. | Aries | Fire | Barren | 3rd |
| 23 Tue. 9:58 pm | Taurus | Earth | Semi-fruitful | 3rd |
| 24 Wed. | Taurus | Earth | Semi-fruitful | 3rd |
| 25 Thu. | Taurus | Earth | Semi-fruitful | 3rd |
| 26 Fri. 4:43 am | Gemini | Air | Barren | 4th 11:18 am |
| 27 Sat. | Gemini | Air | Barren | 4th |
| 28 Sun. 2:57 pm | Cancer | Water | Fruitful | 4th |
| 29 Mon. | Cancer | Water | Fruitful | 4th |
| 30 Tue. | Cancer | Water | Fruitful | 4th |
| 31 Wed. 3:14 am | Leo | Fire | Barren | 4th |

# September Moon Table

| Date | Sign | Element | Nature | Phase |
|------|------|---------|--------|-------|
| 1 Thu. | Leo | Fire | Barren | 4th |
| 2 Fri. 3:56 pm | Virgo | Earth | Barren | 4th |
| 3 Sat. | Virgo | Earth | Barren | New 2:45 pm |
| 4 Sun. | Virgo | Earth | Barren | 1st |
| 5 Mon. 3:52 am | Libra | Air | Semi-fruitful | 1st |
| 6 Tue. | Libra | Air | Semi-fruitful | 1st |
| 7 Wed. 2:10 pm | Scorpio | Water | Fruitful | 1st |
| 8 Thu. | Scorpio | Water | Fruitful | 1st |
| 9 Fri. 10:03 pm | Sagittarus | Fire | Barren | 1st |
| 10 Sat. | Sagittarus | Fire | Barren | 1st |
| 11 Sun. | Sagittarus | Fire | Barren | 2nd 7:37 am |
| 12 Mon. 2:56 am | Capricorn | Earth | Semi-fruitful | 2nd |
| 13 Tue. | Capricorn | Earth | Semi-fruitful | 2nd |
| 14 Wed. 5:02 am | Aquarius | Air | Barren | 2nd |
| 15 Thu. | Aquarius | Air | Barren | 2nd |
| 16 Fri. 5:24 am | Pisces | Water | Fruitful | 2nd |
| 17 Sat. | Pisces | Water | Fruitful | Full 10:01 pm |
| 18 Sun. 5:43 am | Aries | Fire | Barren | 3rd |
| 19 Mon. | Aries | Fire | Barren | 3rd |
| 20 Tue. 7:47 am | Taurus | Earth | Semi-fruitful | 3rd |
| 21 Wed. | Taurus | Earth | Semi-fruitful | 3rd |
| 22 Thu. 1:07 pm | Gemini | Air | Barren | 3rd |
| 23 Fri. | Gemini | Air | Barren | 3rd |
| 24 Sat. 10:10 pm | Cancer | Water | Fruitful | 3rd |
| 25 Sun. | Cancer | Water | Fruitful | 4th 2:41 am |
| 26 Mon. | Cancer | Water | Fruitful | 4th |
| 27 Tue. 10:03 am | Leo | Fire | Barren | 4th |
| 28 Wed. | Leo | Fire | Barren | 4th |
| 29 Thu. 10:44 pm | Virgo | Earth | Barren | 4th |
| 30 Fri. | Virgo | Earth | Barren | 4th |

# October Moon Table

| Date | Sign | Element | Nature | Phase |
|------|------|---------|--------|-------|
| 1 Sat. | Virgo | Earth | Barren | 4th |
| 2 Sun. 10:24 am | Libra | Air | Semi-fruitful | 4th |
| 3 Mon. | Libra | Air | Semi-fruitful | New 6:28 am |
| 4 Tue. 8:03 pm | Scorpio | Water | Fruitful | 1st |
| 5 Wed. | Scorpio | Water | Fruitful | 1st |
| 6 Thu. | Scorpio | Water | Fruitful | 1st |
| 7 Fri. 3:28 am | Sagittarius | Fire | Barren | 1st |
| 8 Sat. | Sagittarius | Fire | Barren | 1st |
| 9 Sun. 8:43 am | Capricorn | Earth | Semi-fruitful | 1st |
| 10 Mon. | Capricorn | Earth | Semi-fruitful | 2nd 3:01 pm |
| 11 Tue. 12:05 pm | Aquarius | Air | Barren | 2nd |
| 12 Wed. | Aquarius | Air | Barren | 2nd |
| 13 Thu. 2:05 pm | Pisces | Water | Fruitful | 2nd |
| 14 Fri. | Pisces | Water | Fruitful | 2nd |
| 15 Sat. 3:39 pm | Aries | Fire | Barren | 2nd |
| 16 Sun. | Aries | Fire | Barren | 2nd |
| 17 Mon. 6:04 pm | Taurus | Earth | Semi-fruitful | Full 8:14 am |
| 18 Tue. | Taurus | Earth | Semi-fruitful | 3rd |
| 19 Wed. 10:44 pm | Gemini | Air | Barren | 3rd |
| 20 Thu. | Gemini | Air | Barren | 3rd |
| 21 Fri. | Gemini | Air | Barren | 3rd |
| 22 Sat. 6:41 am | Cancer | Water | Fruitful | 3rd |
| 23 Sun. | Cancer | Water | Fruitful | 3rd |
| 24 Mon. 5:48 pm | Leo | Fire | Barren | 4th 9:17 pm |
| 25 Tue. | Leo | Fire | Barren | 4th |
| 26 Wed. | Leo | Fire | Barren | 4th |
| 27 Thu. 6:28 am | Virgo | Earth | Barren | 4th |
| 28 Fri. | Virgo | Earth | Barren | 4th |
| 29 Sat. 6:15 pm | Libra | Air | Semi-fruitful | 4th |
| 30 Sun. | Libra | Air | Semi-fruitful | 4th |
| 31 Mon. | Libra | Air | Semi-fruitful | 4th |

# November Moon Table

| Date | Sign | Element | Nature | Phase |
|------|------|---------|--------|-------|
| 1 Tue. 2:29 am | Scorpio | Water | Fruitful | New 8:25 pm |
| 2 Wed. | Scorpio | Water | Fruitful | 1st |
| 3 Thu. 8:55 am | Sagittarius | Fire | Barren | 1st |
| 4 Fri. | Sagittarius | Fire | Barren | 1st |
| 5 Sat. 1:17 pm | Capricorn | Earth | Semi-fruitful | 1st |
| 6 Sun. | Capricorn | Earth | Semi-fruitful | 1st |
| 7 Mon. 4:31 pm | Aquarius | Air | Barren | 1st |
| 8 Tue. | Aquarius | Air | Barren | 2nd 8:57 pm |
| 9 Wed. 7:22 pm | Pisces | Water | Fruitful | 2nd |
| 10 Thu. | Pisces | Water | Fruitful | 2nd |
| 11 Fri. 10:22 pm | Aries | Fire | Barren | 2nd |
| 12 Sat. | Aries | Fire | Barren | 2nd |
| 13 Sun. | Aries | Fire | Barren | 2nd |
| 14 Mon. 2:02 am | Taurus | Earth | Semi-fruitful | 2nd |
| 15 Tue. | Taurus | Earth | Semi-fruitful | Full 7:58 pm |
| 16 Wed. 7:10 am | Gemini | Air | Barren | 3rd |
| 17 Thu. | Gemini | Air | Barren | 3rd |
| 18 Fri. 2:42 pm | Cancer | Water | Fruitful | 3rd |
| 19 Sat. | Cancer | Water | Fruitful | 3rd |
| 20 Sun. | Cancer | Water | Fruitful | 3rd |
| 21 Mon. 1:10 am | Leo | Fire | Barren | 3rd |
| 22 Tue. | Leo | Fire | Barren | 3rd |
| 23 Wed. 1:41 pm | Virgo | Earth | Barren | 4th 5:11 pm |
| 24 Thu. | Virgo | Earth | Barren | 4th |
| 25 Fri. | Virgo | Earth | Barren | 4th |
| 26 Sat. 1:58 am | Libra | Air | Semi-fruitful | 4th |
| 27 Sun. | Libra | Air | Semi-fruitful | 4th |
| 28 Mon. 11:33 am | Scorpio | Water | Fruitful | 4th |
| 29 Tue. | Scorpio | Water | Fruitful | 4th |
| 30 Wed. 5:32 pm | Sagittarius | Fire | Barren | 4th |

# December Moon Table

| Date | Sign | Element | Nature | Phase |
|------|------|---------|--------|-------|
| 1 Thu. | Sagittarius | Fire | Barren | New 10:01 am |
| 2 Fri. 8:42 pm | Capricorn | Earth | Semi-fruitful | 1st |
| 3 Sat. | Capricorn | Earth | Semi-fruitful | 1st |
| 4 Sun. 10:36 pm | Aquarius | Air | Barren | 1st |
| 5 Mon. | Aquarius | Air | Barren | 1st |
| 6 Tue. | Aquarius | Air | Barren | 1st |
| 7 Wed. 12:44 am | Pisces | Water | Fruitful | 1st |
| 8 Thu. | Pisces | Water | Fruitful | 2nd 4:36 am |
| 9 Fri. 4:02 am | Aries | Fire | Barren | 2nd |
| 10 Sat. | Aries | Fire | Barren | 2nd |
| 11 Sun. 8:46 am | Taurus | Earth | Semi-fruitful | 2nd |
| 12 Mon. | Taurus | Earth | Semi-fruitful | 2nd |
| 13 Tue. 2:59 pm | Gemini | Air | Barren | 2nd |
| 14 Wed. | Gemini | Air | Barren | 2nd |
| 15 Thu. 11:01 pm | Cancer | Water | Fruitful | Full 11:16 am |
| 16 Fri. | Cancer | Water | Fruitful | 3rd |
| 17 Sat. | Cancer | Water | Fruitful | 3rd |
| 18 Sun. 9:18 am | Leo | Fire | Barren | 3rd |
| 19 Mon. | Leo | Fire | Barren | 3rd |
| 20 Tue. 9:39 pm | Virgo | Earth | Barren | 3rd |
| 21 Wed. | Virgo | Earth | Barren | 3rd |
| 22 Thu. | Virgo | Earth | Barren | 3rd |
| 23 Fri.10:26 am | Libra | Air | Semi-fruitful | 4th 2:36 pm |
| 24 Sat. | Libra | Air | Semi-fruitful | 4th |
| 25 Sun. 9:04 pm | Scorpio | Water | Fruitful | 4th |
| 26 Mon. | Scorpio | Water | Fruitful | 4th |
| 27 Tue. | Scorpio | Water | Fruitful | 4th |
| 28 Wed. 3:43 am | Sagittarius | Fire | Barren | 4th |
| 29 Thu. | Sagittarius | Fire | Barren | 4th |
| 30 Fri. 6:35 am | Capricorn | Earth | Semi-fruitful | New 10:12 pm |
| 31 Sat. | Capricorn | Earth | Semi-fruitful | 1st |

# About the Authors

**VIVIAN ASHCRAFT** is a freelance writer living in rural Ohio. She has an extensive herb garden and uses the herbs she grows in healing, skin care, aromatherapy, and cooking.

**ELIZABETH BARRETTE** is the managing editor of *PanGaia* and assistant editor of *SageWoman*. She has been involved with the Pagan community for more than thirteen years and lives in central Illinois. Her other writing fields include speculative fiction and gender studies. Visit her website at: http://www.worth-link.net/~ysabet/index.html.

**CHANDRA MOIRA BEAL** is a writer living in Austin, Texas. She self-publishes books and has authored dozens of articles. In her day job, she is a massage therapist and reiki practitioner. She lives with a magical house rabbit named Maia. *Chandra* is Sanskrit for "the Moon."

**STEPHANIE ROSE BIRD** is an artist, writer, herbalist, healer, mother, and companion. She studied art at the Tyler School of Art and at the University of California at San Diego, and she researched Australian Aboriginal art, ritual, and ceremonial practices as a Fulbright senior scholar. Currently, she leads herbcraft workshops at the Chicago Botanic Gardens. Her column "Ase! from the Crossroads" is featured in *SageWoman*. Her book *Sticks, Stones, Roots & Bones*, was published by Llewellyn in 2004.

**DALLAS JENNIFER COBB** lives an enchanted life in a waterfront village with her partner and their daughter. Treating parenting as a top priority, she also writes, runs, dreams, and frequents the beaches in her spare time. She especially enjoys the harvests of rural life: more time, more quiet, a contented family, and lots of magical mamas to conspire with.

**ELLEN DUGAN,** also known as the Garden Witch, is a psychic-clairvoyant and a practicing Witch of more than seventeen years. Ellen is a master gardener, and she teaches classes on gardening and flower folklore at her local community college. Ellen is the author of *Garden Witchery* (Llewellyn, 2003). She and her husband raise their three magical teenagers and tend to their enchanted gardens in Missouri.

**MAGENTA GRIFFITH** has been a Witch for more than twenty-five years, and she is a founding member of the coven Prodea. She leads rituals and workshops across the Midwest, and is the librarian for the New Alexandria Library, a Pagan and magical resource center (http://www.magusbooks.com/newalexandria/).

**JAMES KAMBOS** is an herbalist, writer, and painter. He celebrates the changing seasons by tending his herb and flower gardens at his home in the beautiful Appalachian hills of southern Ohio. He is a regular contributor to Llewellyn's annuals.

**JONATHAN KEYES** lives in Portland, Oregon, where he likes to fiddle around in the garden and play with his cat. Jon works as an astrologer and herbalist and has written an astrological health book titled *Guide to Natural Health* (Llewellyn, 2002), as well as an herb book titled *A Traditional Herbal.* He is currently working on a book titled *Healers,* a series of interviews with various herbalists, *curanderos,* and medicine people from around the United States.

**RUBY LAVENDER** is a singer, herbalist, perfumer, poet and free-lance writer who teaches creative writing and film studies. She is also a Romano-Celtic Witch practicing with an Alexandrian-derived Hellenistic coven founded in 1974.

**EDAIN MCCOY** has practiced Witchcraft for more than twenty years, during which time has studied many magical traditions including Wiccan, Jewitchery, Celtic, Appalachian, and Curanderismo. When the economy began to slow in 2001, Edain made the difficult decision to leave her career as a stockbroker in order to write full time. She is listed in the reference books *Who's Who in America* and *Contemporary Authors*. She the author of seventeen books, including: *A Witch's Guide to Faery Folk* (Llewellyn, 1994), *Celtic Myth and Magick* (Llewellyn, 1995), *Inside a Witches' Coven* (Llewellyn, 1997), *Celtic Women's Spirituality* (Llewellyn, 1998), *Entering the Summerland* (Llewellyn, 1996), *Bewitchments* (Llewellyn, 2000), *Enchantments* (Llewellyn, 2001), *Spellworking for Covens* (Llewellyn, 2002), and *Advanced Witchcraft* (Llewellyn, 2004).

SHARYNNE MACLEOD NICMHACHA is a Celtic priestess and Witch, and a direct descendant of Clan MacLeod—long recorded in oral tradition as having connections with (and the blood of) the *sidhe*, or fairy folk. Sharynne has studied Old Irish, Scottish Gaelic, and Celtic mythology through Harvard University where she has published a number of research papers. She teaches workshops and sings and plays bodran, woodwinds, and stringed instruments with the group Devandaurae. She recently published her first book, *Queen of the Night: In Search of a Celtic Moon Goddess* (Red Wheel/Weiser, 2004).

LEEDA ALLEYN PACOTTI practices as a naturopathic physician, nutritional counselor, and master herbalist, specializing in dream language, health astrology, and mind-body communication.

PEARLMOON is a solitary Celtic Witch and a registered nurse. She has been growing and studying herbs and their uses since 1995. She loves gardening, listening to music, and being a mother, and belongs to several e-groups that discuss herb-related subjects. She lives in the western New York area with her son and her partner, and is a member of the Buffalo Pagan community.

SHERI RICHERSON has more than twenty years experience in newspaper, magazine, and creative writing. She is also a lifetime member of the International Thespian Society. Sheri is a longtime member of both the Garden Writers Association of America and the American Horticultural Society. She is also a member of the Tropical Flowering Tree Society, the North American Rock Garden Society, and the American Orchid Society. Her favorite pastimes are riding her motorcycle, visiting arboretums, traveling, horseback riding, and working in her huge garden. Sheri specializes in herb gardening and in growing tropical, subtropical, and exotic plants. She is a master gardener. For more information, please visit Sheri's website at: http://SheriAnnRicherson.exoticgardening.com.

LYNN SMYTHE is a freelance writer living in Delray Beach, Florida, with her husband and two children. She spends too much time playing outside in the dirt where her main gardening passions are attracting butterflies and growing organic herbs and vegetables. She is a member of the Evening Herb Society of the Palm Beaches, and she writes a monthly column for their newsletter *The Herbin' Times*. Additional information can be found on her website: http://users.adelphia.net/~lynnsmythe.

TAMMY SULLIVAN is a solitary Witch who writes from her home in the beautiful foothills of Tennessee's Great Smoky Mountains. The mother of four, Tammy is currently working on a spell book for teens.

S. Y. ZENITH is three-quarters Chinese, one tad bit Irish, and a lifelong solitary eclectic Pagan. She has lived and traveled extensively in Asia to such countries as India, Nepal, Thailand, Malaysia, Singapore, Borneo, and Japan for over two decades. She is now based in Australia where her time is divided between writing, experimenting with alternative remedies, and teaching the use of gems, holy beads, and religious objects from India and the Himalayas. She is also a member of the Australian Society of Authors.

# Notes

# *Notes*

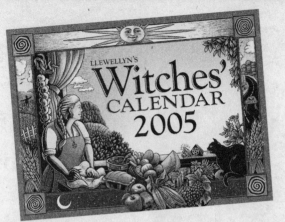

# Best-selling Guide to Successful Living Since 1905!

No other book on the market tops the *Moon Sign Book* in supplying tips for daily success, weather forecasts for eight U.S. zones year round, economic forecasts, tips on planting, best hunting and fishing dates, and timing tips for personal and financial decisions. Plus, there are special articles on topics that affect us all. This year's features include "Night Gardening" by Janice Sharkey, "Kitchen Concoctions for Pest Control" by Louise Riotte, "Cross-cultural Perspectives" by Robin Antepara, and "Adaptive Gardening for Seniors" by Maggie Anderson.

**LLEWELLYN'S 2005 MOON SIGN BOOK**
384 pp. • 5¼ x 8
0-7387-0136-X / J139 • $7.95 U.S.    $10.50 Can.
**To order call 1-877-NEW-WRLD**

# Read your Future in the Cards

Tarot enthusiasts rejoice! Look for an array of news, advice, and in-depth discussions on everything tarot in Llewellyn's new *Tarot Reader*. Renowned authors and tarot specialists deliver deck reviews and articles concerning card interpretation, spreads, magic, tarot history, and professional tarot reading. Each year's almanac will also feature a calendar with pertinent astrological information, such as Moon signs and times. This year's *Tarot Reader* includes articles by Ruth Ann and Wald Amberstone, Joan Cole, Mary K. Greer, and James Wells.